Beyond Barolo AND *Brunello*
Italy's Most Distinctive Wines

by **TOM HYLAND**

Text and Photos by Tom Hyland

Including essays from chefs
Maria Cristina Rinaudi, Roberto Rossi and Antonella Iandolo

ISBN: 1480117986
ISBN-13: 9781480117983

Wine menu on a street in the town of Barbaresco

To i *contadini*, the farmers who are the heart and soul of Italian wine

Contents

———

Introduction

———

This book is the result of a twelve-year odyssey, visiting wine zones across the width and breadth of Italy. But in reality, this journey is an endless one. Discovering the world of Italian wines is not just a look at work in the vineyards and cellars, but also at the history, tradition and heritage that is the foundation of each and every wine area across the country.

I began visiting Italy in the late 1990s and instantly fell in love with the land, the wines, the food and most of all, the people. I've always been one who took the road less traveled, so it was only a matter of time before Italian wines would become a big part of my life. After all, here was a wine industry where grapes such as Nebbiolo, Sangiovese, Vermentino and Fiano were incorporated into the finest wines; as for Cabernet Sauvignon, Merlot and Chardonnay, they were present, but represented a very small part of the overall wine industry.

Indigenous varieties – or autochonous, as the Italians refer to them – are at the heart and soul of Italian wines. Some varieties, such as Sangiovese (red) and Trebbiano (white) are planted in several regions, while some, such as Schiopettino (red) and Arneis (white) are found in only one region. Then you have certain varieties that are found in only one small zone. Take for example, the white varieties planted in the Costa d'Amalfi vineyards; these include Fenile, Ripoli and Ginestra, which thrive in this territory, yet are not among the plantings in Irpinia, some thirty miles away.

No one knows the exact number of grape varieties in Italy; estimates range from 500 to 800 to as many as 2000! Then take into effect that some varieties are produced in different fashions; Erbaluce from northern Piemonte is often vinified as a dry white, yet there are also lovely sparkling as well as *passito* versions of this type; the same is true for Garganega in the Soave zone, where styles range from mineral-driven dry whites to delicate *spumanti* to the luscious Recioto di Soave. Thus the possibilities for Italian wine types are endless!

I have organized this book geographically, from north to south; this is the typical manner for most guides dealing with Italian wines. I begin this journey with Piemonte and end with Sicilia and Sardgena. Along the way, I report on some of the finest examples of hundreds of Italian wines, be they famous or relatively unknown outside their home. Barolo, Brunello di Montalcino and Amarone may be the most celebrated wines of Italy, yet the producers of Greco di Tufo, Dolcetto d'Alba and Morellino di Scansano – to name only three wines – work just are hard to offer as excellent a product as do the vintners that craft the more notable releases. They deserve more credit and I'm out to see that they get it!

For the most part, I do not deal with the DOC, DOCG and IGT designations in this book. To me, this has become quite confusing; it's also become very temporary, as some wines that were DOC a year or so ago are now DOCG (as with Amarone). I'll let others deal with the so-called importance of this regulatory system; I'd rather discuss the merits of each wine.

The list of wines in this book is mine and mine alone. I am a true freelancer and do not work for any of these producers; I selected wines that impressed me. You may have favorites that you do not see listed; there are also some famous wines I did not include for various reasons. I couldn't include every Italian wine I like (if I did, the book would be several thousand pages long), so what I've set out to accomplish is an overview of the best examples, from the everyday to the rare and much in between. I suppose if come back to this book in a year or two, there will be another 50 or 100 wines

I'd like to add, but so be it. Researching a book like this is a bit like maturing - you learn something every day. As I wrote earlier, this is an endless journey!

Tom Hyland
2012

The chapters are generally organized according to wine types, with whites first followed by reds and then rosé; as for Basilicata, I have not included any whites. Regarding sparkling wines, they are listed in each chapter according to importance in that particular region. Thus for Lombardia, that chapter leads off with Franciacorta, while for Trentino, the Trento sparkling wines are listed first as is the case with Lambrusco for the chapter on Emilia Romagna. Dessert wines are generally included at the end of a chapter, although the examples of a dessert wine such as Recioto di Soave appear immediately after the listings of Soave.

After the description for certain wines, you will note the letters, **BRV**, which stands for "best recent vintages." I have included this for most red wines as well as for some whites and even a few sparkling wines that have shown a history of aging well. This will give you an idea of both the finest years for these wines, as well as an idea of how they mature.

As the emphasis of the book is on specific wines, I have not arranged the entries in alphabetical order according to producers (there is an index at the end of the book to facilitate finding a particular producer). I listed the wines the way I did to tell a story; for instance, the examples of Barolo in the chapter on Piemonte are grouped according to commune, so the Barolo from La Morra are together, followed by Barolo from Serralunga d'Alba and then Monforte d'Alba. For the chapter on Friuli, blended whites and reds are listed apart from their monovarietal counterparts; there are other such comparisons throughout the book (as in the chapter on Toscana). I believe this is a more interesting way in which to organize the individual chapters and tell the specific story of each Italian wine I have written about.

Piemonte

Principal Varieties

White:
Arneis, Cortese, Erbaluce, Timorasso, Moscato,
Riesling Renano, Chardonnay, Favorita

Red:
Barbera, Dolcetto, Nebbiolo, Vespolina, Ruché, Freisa,
Grignolino, Brachetto

———

MATTEO COREGGIA ROERO ARNEIS

This is a model estate in Canale d'Alba that is managed with the utmost care in every step of the process, from the vineyards to the cellar. There are several notable wines including a wonderful Roero Rosso Riserva (D'Ampsej) made from 100% Nebbiolo, but I have selected the regular bottling of Arneis, largely for its identity as a calling card for the Roero district where the finest versions of this variety are produced. Grown on sandy hillside soils, the grapes are fermented in steel and the wine is matured in steel with six months on the lees. Medium-full, this is always quite rich on the palate, while it can be fat and lush in the finest vintages. The aromas are of pear, lemon and almond and there is very good acidity and excellent persistence. The wine is approachable upon release and can drink well for five to seven years.

MALVIRÁ ROERO ARNEIS "TRINITÀ"

Roberto Damonte is one of the very best producers of Roero Arneis; in many vintages he will produce as many as four bottlings. The Trinità is aged primarily in steel tanks with a small percentage matured in small French oak barrels. Medium-full with a graceful entry on the palate, the aromas are of pear, hawthorn and melon; there is excellent persistence and good acidity with a light touch of minerality. Approachable upon release, the wine typically drinks well for three to five years.

GIANNI VOERZIO LANGHE ARNEIS "BRICCO CAPPELLINA"

While the best known examples of Arneis come from the Roero district across the Tanaro River from Barolo and Barbaresco, there are many excellent versions from within the Langhe. Several Barolo producers make a Langhe Arnies; one of the best is from Gianni Voerzio in La Morra. Displaying rich aromas of pear, melon and peony, this is quite rich – almost fat – on the palate and has a long finish with excellent persistence and precise acidity with a light touch of minerality. Matured solely in steel tanks, this has amazing varietal purity and is absolutely delicious! Quite rich, this can stand up to most white meats; enjoy upon release or up to five years after the vintage.

GHIOMO LANGHE ARNEIS "IMPRIMIS"

Giuseppino Anfossi is a man of simple tastes, someone who makes wines to please himself and his friends. At his small, but ideally situated estate in Guarene, very close to the Tanaro River, he specializes in crafting Arneis of great purity and richness. Although his vineyards are technically in the Roero zone, his village is one of only a few that cannot be desginated as such, therefore his wines must be labeled as Langhe Arneis (just a typical examples of the vagaries of Italian wine laws!). His most accomplished Arneis is "Imprimis", in which the grapes are cold soaked and aged on their lees for several months. Displaying seductive aromas of melon, pear, acacia and magnolia flowers, the wine has lovely texture and very good acidity; the finish is quite long and the overall balance is impeccable. Instantly appealing upon release, this drinks well for five to seven years without a problem and can in the best years, age for a decade. **BRV**: 2010, 2009, 2008, 2006.

VIGNETI MASSA TIMORASSO "STERPI"

There are approximately two dozen estates that work with the Timorasso variety in the province of Alessandria; Walter Massa has become the acknowledged leader. He produces three versions in most years, each aged solely in stainless steel. These are not powerful wines, but rather, wines of great subtlety and complexity. The finest is "Sterpi"; some 500 cases are produced per year. Aged solely in stainless steel, the wine displays a golden yellow color and aromas of grapefruit, dried pear and even a note of flint. Medium-full, the wine has beautiful texture and a lengthy finish with a note of dried honey. Although some have compared this to a Chenin Blanc from the Loire Valley, this truly is one of a kind. While enjoyable early on, it is often at its best six or seven years after the vintage date. **BRV**: 2009, 2008.

MARTINETTI "MARTIN"

Franco Marinetti moved from the world of advertising to wine almost forty years ago and today produces wines from several zones in Piemonte. He produces two versions of Timorasso: one labeled Biancofranco that is steel aged, the other called Martin, fermented and aged in French barriques. Low yields for this wine (about 20% less than the tank-aged example) means this has the richness and texture to stand up to the wood. Vanilla, custard and pineapple notes highlight the aromas and there is excellent complexity and length in the finish. This is a lush, very seductive style of Timorasso, rather different from most examples, but quite stylish and well made for peak consumption at three to five years of age.

MICHELE CHIARLO GAVI "ROVERETO"

This veteran Piemontese firm produces a wide variety of excellent local wines, especially with Barbera d'Asti and cru Barolo. Their whites are just as well crafted, especially Arneis and Gavi. There is a regular bottling of Gavi that is clean and quite typical of the zone, but this Rovereto offering, named for a small district in

Gavi, is outstanding. The soils of the selected vineyards are rich in magnesium, which lends a definitely minerality to the wine; small yields also ensure excellent depth of fruit as well as impressive texture. Another secret to the quality of this wine is that a portion of the grapes undergoes cryo-maceration, a process that preserves the lovely citrus, pear and melon perfumes of the Cortese grape. The acidity is healthy, but not high and there is a wonderful freshness to the wine along with a nicely structured finish. Enjoyable upon release, this is at its best some three to seven years after the harvest, depending on the quality of the growing season. **BRV**: 2010, 2009, 2008, 2006.

BERGAGLIO GAVI "MINAIA"
Nicola Bergaglio established his winery in 1945 in Rovereto, one of the premier sites in the Gavi commune; today Gianluigi and his son Diego manage the estate. There is a white label Gavi that is excellent; I have selected the "Minaia" bottling, which has a bit more richness on the palate and also tends to need a bit more time to flesh out. Aged only in steel tanks, this has distinct aromas of dried pear, chamomile, white flowers and herbs such as romsemary. This herbal edge tends to be a bit more pronounced after a few years in the bottle, although there is excellent freshness; the 2007 tasted in mid-2012 was showing beautifully, promising another two to three years of drinking pleasure. There is a flinty edge to the finish, which adds to the wine's complexity and intriguing qualities.

BROGLIA GAVI "BRUNO BROGLIA"
Gavi, produced entirely from the Cortese variety in the province of Alessandria, has generally been known for its fresh fruit, medium-body and clean finish, a wine meant for early drinking. The Gavis from Broglia, however, lend quite a different identity to this wine. This offering, from vines planted between 1953 and 1955, has tremendous richness on the nose and palate with a lenghty finish. The aromas are quite exotic, combining Anjou pear, kiwi and magnolia and the acidity is quite good. This is a mouthful of wine, aged only in steel tanks,

that can be enjoyed for three to five years, even from average growing seasons, while it drinks well for a decade from the best vintages.

MAGDA PEDRINI GAVI DI GAVI "LA PIACENTINA"

Magda Pedrini, who has lived in the Gavi area since she was a young
child, purchased the Ca' di Meo firm and began production of several
styles of Gavi in 2006. Her finest wine, a selection of the best Cortese
bunches from her estate plantings, is called La Piacentina, named for
the eponymous vineyard in Gavi. The winemaking here – lees aging
in steel tanks – is straightforward and minimal in nature, which results
in a wine of lovely varietal purity and cleanliness; I love the notes
of spearmint, quince and lemon zest in the aromas, while I am also
impressed with the lovely texture of this wine. Enjoy this wine upon
release (in the spring after the harvest) or over the following three to
five years.

ELVIO COGNO ANAS CËTTA

Nascetta or Anas Cëtta, as it is called by Elvio Cogno, is a rare indigenous
variety grown by only five producers in the Langhe at the moment. Valter Fissore at Cogno makes the most famous example from five acres
of vines in Novello, near the southern end of the Barolo zone. Fissore
ferments part of the wine in steel and part in small barrels and ages the
wine in the same manner. Medium-bodied, this has expressive citrus
fruit aromas with subtle herbal notes of thyme and rosemary. The acidity is healthy, but not exceedingly high and the finish has very good
persistence and freshness. While this is generally consumed within
two to three years of the harvest, this is a wine that can age as 12 and
15-year old versions taste out beautifully. **BRV**: 2010, 2009, 2008, 2006.

ETTORE GERMANO "HERZU"

Dry Riesling in Piemonte? Yes, there are a few intrepid souls who per-
severe with this variety – technically Riesling Renano - and do it well.
Vajra produces a lovely version called Pétracine that has dazzling
aromatics, while Sergio Germano crafts a richer, slightly more intese
version from his vineyards in Ciglié near Dogliani. There are five acres

of Riesling planted here, with the oldest vines dating back to 1995. The wine offers aromas of stone fruits – peaches and apricots – along with notes of geranium. Medium-full, the wine is tank fermented and aged for six months on its lees. There is notable freshness and acidity along with subtle mineral notes; the wine tends to age for three to five years, with a few of the finest examples drinking well for another two to three years.

ORSOLANI ERBALUCE DI CALUSO "VIGNOT S. ANTONIO"
Erbaluce is an indigenous variety from area around the town of Caluso in the province of Torino. Many of the vineyards are quite old (40-50 years), with most still planted in the pergola training sysyem. Gian Luigi Orsolani produces a regular, steel-aged Erbaluce as well as this single vineyard version, fermented and aged in oak. Offering beautiful aromas of rosemary, sage, almond and lemon rind, there is excellent depth of fruit and persistence; this drinks well for five to ten years of age. **BRV**: 2009, 2008, 2007.

CIECK MISOBOLO
Cieck is one of the leading estates working with Erbaluce, producing various examples, from sparkling to dry table wine to *passito*. My favorite is the table white "Misobolo," a 100% Erbaluce from 40 year-old vines that shows the complexity and structure of wines made from this variety. Offering aromas of ripe pear and golden apple with a hint of sage, this is medium-full with lively acidity, excellent persistence and a light touch of minerality. This is at its best at three to five years of age.

LA CAUDRINA ASTI SPUMANTE "LA SELVATICA"
Lest you think that Asti Spumante is a slightly sweet, cloying beverage that reminds you more of soda pop than wine, I invite you to try the La Caudrina version. Winemaker Romano Dogliotti is a specialist with the Moscato grape, producing both Moscato d'Asti (*frizzante*) and Asti Spumante. This is 100% Moscato from a single vineyard near the winery close to the town of Castiglione Tinella. Sporting

irresistible apricot, lemon peel and ginger aromas, this is off-dry and simply delicious! Drink within 12-15 months of release, which is usually six months after the harvest.

GIANNI VOERZIO MOSCATO D'ASTI "VIGNA SERGENTE"

This celebrated Barolo producer puts everything into all of his wines; this Moscato is prime evidence. Textbook aromas of white peach, apricot and mandarin orange along with a lovely hint of ginger, this has excellent depth of fruit and a long, enticing finish with just a trace of sweetness. This is a delicious dessert offering! Typical of this wine, this is best consumed with 12-18 months of the vintage date.

SARACCO MOSCATO D'ASTI "MOSCATO D'AUTUNNO"

This is a special bottling from this famous Moscato d'Asti producer. The main difference here is that this wine is made from a blend of musts – not finished wines – that Paolo Saracco makes once a year in March. This has the typical peach, apricot and honey aromas of the regular Saracco bottling, but there is greater freshness and complexity. Enjoy this lightly sweet wine with fresh peaches or strawberries over its first one or two years.

FORTETO DELLA LUJA MOSCATO D'ASTI "PIASA SAN MAURIZIO"

Forteto della Luja is a small producer in the Asti province that specializes in wines made from the Moscato variety. Dozens of producers in this area make a pleasing Moscato d'Asti, the light as a feather dessert, slightly sparkling (*frizzante*) wine that comes in at 5.5% alcohol. This version from Forteto della Luja has the same lovely peach, orange zest and lemon aromas as the others, but there is just a little more concentration with this wine; the structure means this can be enjoyed three years after the vintage.

BRAIDA BRACHETTO D'ACQUI

Brachetto d'Acqui is the red response to Moscato d'Asti. The Brachetto grape can be produced in various fashions, but it is most often made in a *frizzante*, slightly sweet style with very low (5.5% alcohol). The Braida version is one of the most typical and successful, with aromas of fresh strawberries and pink and red roses; medium-bodied with a clean, refreshing finish, the overall effect is one of delicacy and charm. This is a wonderful partner for fresh strawberries or even bitter chocolate. There's no need to age this wine – just drink it as fresh as possible with a slight chill.

MARENCO BRACHETTO D'ACQUI "PINETO"

At their estate in Strevi, just north of Acqui Terme in the province of Alessandria, the Marenco family produces lovely versions of Moscato d'Asti and Brachetto d'Acqui, both as a slightly sparking wine as well as a *passito*, made from naturally dried grapes. Their "Pineto" Brachetto is one of the best of its type, with raspberry and strawberry fruit, with just a hint of cinnamon in the nose. Lightly sparkling with a hint of sweetness, this is meant to accompany fresh peaches or strawberries or many types of chocolate desserts. This is at its best fresh – usually within a year of the harvest – although it can drink well up to a second year.

ELIO PERRONE "BIGARÒ"

I absolutely love the simple pleasures of Moscato d Asti as well as Brachetto d'Acqui, so the notion of making a wine that combines the best of these two products seemed like a winner to me. That is exactly what Elio Perrone has done with "Bigarò," a 50/50 blend of Moscato and Brachetto. Bright cherry in appearance, this is a *frizzante* wine with heavenly perfumes of yellow peaches, musk oil and raspberries. It has only 5.5% alcohol and is as light as a feather on the palate and finishes clean with a trace of sweetness- what a delightful wine! Enjoy it at its freshest with a simple serving of fresh fruit or even on its own.

FORTETO DELLA LUJA "FORTETO DELLA LUJA"

Here is a glorious version of Moscato; a blend of 95% Moscato and 5% Passula, this is harvested late so that the berries can be affected by botrytis. As the vineyard was planted in 1938, the yields are small but the flavors are remarkably concentrated. About 15% of the grapes are dried on mats (*passito*), with fermentation taking place in small oak casks for two years – the cold temperatures of the cellar dramatically slow this process down. Very rich and lush with medium sweetness, this has aromas and flavors of apricot, dried pear, honey and a distinct nuttiness. This ages beautifully, often for as long as 10-12 years. **BRV**: 2009, 2008, 2007, 2005, 2004, 2001.

ORSOLANI ERBALUCE DI CALUSO PASSITO "SULÉ"

Erbaluce, with its naturally high levels of acidity, is a variety that can be used to make several types of wines. Orsolani, like several other producers in this area, produces a dry white, a sparkling version and also a passito. This wine is named Sulé, which refers to the room (attic) where the Erbaluce grapes are taken to dry. This is a gorgeous dessert wine, with enticing aromas of chamomile tea, apricot and a hint of nuttiness. Quite lush on the palate, this is medium-sweet, but not cloying, as there is beautiful balancing acidity. This is really quite a special wine, one that can be enjoyed seven to ten years after the vintage. **BRV**: 2005, 2004, 2002, 2001.

BRAIDA BARBERA D'ASTI "BRICCO DELL'UCCELLONE"

At his estate in Rocchetta Tanaro in the province of Asti, Giacomo Bologna was one of the first producers to think that the everyday Barbera variety could make a world-class wine. So back in the late 1970s, he decided to let the grapes at this vineyard ripen a bit longer and then opted to age the wine in barriques, something unheard of at this time for Barbera; the result was an unqualified success. Today, Giacomo's daughter Raffaella has taken over production from her father who passed away in the 1990s. While Braida today produces three different single vineyard wines from Barbera, it is still the Bricco dell'Uccellone that is arguably the finest. Deep ruby red/light purple with aromas of blackberry, clove, tar and tobacco, this is a medium-full wine with excellent concentration and outstanding persistence; still aged in barriques, the oak is noticeable, but does not overwhelm. The wine is appealing upon release, but it improves with two to three years in the bottle and is generally at its best some seven to ten years after the vintage. **BRV**: 2009, 2008, 2007, 2006, 2004.

MICHELE CHIARLO BARBERA D'ASTI NIZZA SUPERIORE "LA COURT"

The Nizza sub-district of Barbera d'Asti is a zone with stricter requirements mandating lower yields and longer aging before release than
a Barbera d'Asti *normale*. One of the finest wines from here is the
"La Court" bottling from Michele Chiarlo; the La Court vineyard was
planted in 1973. The wine is fermented in large (65hl) French oak
casks and then half of the wine is matured in these casks while half is
aged in barriques. The finished wine has a deep ruby red color with
ripe aromas of blackberry, black cherry, licorice and tar and offers
excellent depth of fruit and persistence with good, but not exceedingly high acidity. A bit tight when released, give this a few years in
the bottle; it displays its best qualities four to five years after the harvest, while the best vintages can be enjoyed after seven to ten years.
BRV: 2009, 2008, 2007, 2006.

LA GIRONDA BARBERA D'ASTI NIZZA SUPERIORE "LE NICCHIE"

Located in Nizza Monferrato, La Gironda is a Barbera specialist, producing both Barbera d'Asti and Barbera Monferrato versions. What I
admire about the wines here is the understated approach, which
stands in contrast to some local producers. The "Le Nicchie" Barbera
from the restricted Nizza sub-zone is a perfect example of the grace of
this estate's Barberas. It is a modern wine with vanilla aromas joined by
notes of black cherry, plum and strawberry jam, but there is an overall sense of balance and ideal ripeness; this is not a showy wine. The
tannins are quite light, there is good acidity and a subtle note of dark
chocolate in the finish. Enjoy from three to five years of age.

TENUTA GARETTO BARBERA D'ASTI "FAVÀ"

Alessandro Garetto heads this unique winery in Agliano Terme,
one that specializes in various styles of Barbera d'Asti. Garetto
produces a simple Barbera called "Tra Neuit e Dì" ("between night
and day") a steel tank-aged Barbera meant for pizza and simple
pastas that is reminiscent of this wine from decades past. A second Barbera named "In Pectore" has some barrique aging, while

Favà is aged for 12-14 months in French barriques, almost totally new. Sourced from a small vineyard in the Nizza zone, this Barbera is a modern interpretation of the variety with black plum, black raspberry, clove, tar and vanilla aromas. Medium-full, this is quite ripe with good acidity (though lower than a traditional Barbera) with a round, satisfying finish with excellent persistence. This wine is appoachable upon release, but is generally at its best four or five years after the harvest. **BRV**: 2008, 2007, 2006, 2004.

CASCINA LA GHERSA BARBERA D'ASTI "VIGNASSA"

Under the leadership of Massimo Pastura, this small winery in Moasca has become an important player among Barbera d'Asti producers. There is a lovely everyday Barbera called Piagé that is a pure delight; the finest Barbera however is the "Vignassa," a Nizza Barbera d'Asti Superiore. Vignassa is the name of the first vineyard planted by Massimo's ancestors after phylloxera hit this area at the end of the 1800s; that was in 1925, making these vines more than 80 years old. The Vignassa name was first used for this wine in the 1989 vintage; aged in barriques for three years, this is one of the more restrained and better balanced versions of Barbera d'Asti today. I have tasted this wine back to 1999 and it is clear that the source of the fruit is wonderful and the winemaking is first-rate; this wine can drink well for a decade after release from all but the lightest vintages. **BRV**: 2008, 2007, 2006, 2004, 2001, 1999.

BERSANO BARBERA D'ASTI "COSTALUNGA"

One of the best respected producers of Barbera d'Asti is Bersano, established in 1907 by Arturo Bersano and today owned by the Massimelli and Soave families. Situated in Nizza Monferrato, the firm produces several examples of Barbera d'Asti, including a Nizza bottling that is quite modern in its approach. On the opposite end of the spectrum is their "Costalunga" Barbera, a wine that reminds us what a typical Barbera d'Asti used to taste like back in the 1960s and '70s. Aged in large Slavonian oak casks, this has beautiful blackberry and currant fruit, very good acidity and moderate tannins; balance and varietal focus are the

11

highlights of this wine. Here is a Barbera that is not overly ripe or showy, but one made for the dinner table. This is best consumed from three to five years of age.

PICO MACCARIO BARBERA D'ASTI "LAVIGNONE"

Pico Maccario and his brother Vitiliano have established a modern winery in the province of Asti; while they produce a bit of white wine, they are Barbera specialists. There are several offerings made in various manners; for me, the oak aging is a bit strong on a few of their wines, so I prefer the steel-aged Barbera, most notably the "Lavignone." Deep garnet upon release with attractive aromas of red cherry, red currant and coriander, this is medium-bodied with very good acidity, light tannins and best of all, lovely Barbera purity. This is a delightful wine meant for consumption upon release (about a year after harvest) and for another two to three years after that.

BOROLI BARBERA D'ALBA "QUATTRO FRATELLI"

While Barbera d'Asti tends to be a bit flashy at times, most examples of Barbera d'Alba are more restrained. The "Quattro Fratelli" from Boroli, named for the four brothers of this Alba family is a precise example of a Barbera with nice freshness, moderate tannins, good acidity and appealing bing cherry and plum flavors, nicely meshed in a harmonious wine meant for lighter pastas and meats or even simple *salumi*. It's got more weight than some similar wines, so it will drink well for at least three years and perhaps as long as its fifth or sixth birthday. Sometimes it's nice to taste a wine that aims only at being true to its varietal heritage.

CASCINA ROCCALINI BARBERA D'ALBA

While this is a new estate, proprietor Paolo Veglio has been in the local wine industry for several years, working with tenant farmers at his family's property at the Roccalini *sottozona* of Barbaresco. His first wine was a 2005 Barbaresco, but it was with the 2007 and 2008 vintages that Veglio produced superior wines, thanks to his teaming up with Dante Scaglione, then winemaker for Bruno Giacosa. Scaglione was leaving Giacosa and starting his own consulting business (he has since returned to winemaking duties at Giacosa); as he had purchased grapes from Veglio for the Giacosa wines, he decided to make Cascina Roccalini his first client. The Barbera d'Alba is simply stunning, aged solely in steel tanks, the wine explodes with luscious aromas of myrtle, black plum and tar. Medium-full, with a generous mid-palate and outstanding persistence, this is ultraclean winemaking that emphasizes varietal purity and ideal balance. This has a finish that seems to go on forever; given the pure pleasure of this wine, you wish it would! Although only a few vintages have been produced, based on tasting the 2008 and 2009 versions of this wine, I would estimate anywhere from seven to ten years of aging potential with this wine. **BRV**: 2009, 2008.

CA' VIOLA BARBERA D'ALBA "BRIC DI LUV"
Giuseppe (Beppe) Caviola has become one of the most in-demand enologists in Piemonte; he also works with producers in regions such as Sardegna and Toscana. He also finds the time to produce his own wines at his estate in Dogliani. This Barbera, from a cru with a Piemontese dialect name that means "hill of the wolf," is about 95% Barbera with small percentages of Nebbiolo and/or Pinot Nero. This is a ripe, lush, modern Barbera, aged primarily in barriques, yet the oak does not dominate. This is a delicious wine with good freshness; the 2005, tasted in 2012, seemed much younger. This is generally at its best from five to ten years of age. Note that before the 2007 vintage, this wine was labeled as a Langhe Rosso. **BRV**: 2009, 2008, 2007, 2005, 2004.

VIETTI BARBERA D'ALBA "SCARRONE VIGNA VECCHIA"
As the Alba area is most famous for Barolo and Barbaresco made from the Nebbiolo variety, the Barbera grape usually takes a secondary role in this zone. However that's not always the case as this wine at Vietti proves. Located in Castiglione Falletto, the Scarrone vineyard is situated on a steep slope just behind the Vietti winery. Luca Currado,

son of Alfredo Currado who made wines here for several decades, follows in the tradition of his father by producing two bottlings from this site.

One is from sections of the vineyard that average 60-65 years, while this Vigna Vecchia (old vine) offering is from vines that are at least 85 years old! You can imagine the concentration as well as the flavor intensity in this wine! The aromas are almost hypnotic with notes of ripe blackberry, black raspberry and licorice; the mid-palate is very rich with an extremely long finish with tremendous fruit persistence. This is a lush, indulgent, hedonistic wine if there ever was one! Absolutely delicious upon release, the wine improves over the course of 10-15 years. **BRV**: 2009, 2008, 2007, 2006, 2004.

MASSA BARBERA COLLI TORTONESI "SENTIERI"

There are a handful of producers who are so famous for one type of wine that few pay attention to their other offerings. That is clearly the case with Walter Massa, who has become celebrated for his work with Timorasso in the Colli Tortonesi zone in southeastern Piemonte, near the border with Lombardia. Massa also works with Barbera in this area; of the two produced, I favor the non-oak aged "Sentieri." Offering delightful bing cherry and red poppy aromas, this is medium-bodied with excellent acidity that gives the wine a zesty, zingy quality; tannins of course are quite light and the overall effect is one of elegance and pure red cherry and plum fruit. Enjoy this wine from two to five years of age. **BRV**: 2010, 2009, 2008.

PIO CESARE DOLCETTO D'ALBA

This famous Barolo and Barbaresco producer also makes a first-rate Dolcetto d'Alba from their hillside vineyards in Treiso. Bright scarlet in color, this has zesty aromas of black raspberry, cranberry and violets with juicy, ripe fruit, light tannins and good acidity. This is one of the most typical versions of Dolcetto d'Alba and it's also one of the most harmonious and elegant; it's also one of the most consistent, as I've enjoyed this wine every year for more than two decades. Consume within two to three years of the vintage date, although five years is not out of the question.

ROCCHE COSTAMAGNA DOLCETTO D'ALBA "RÙBIS"

While most Barolo producers also make a Dolcetto d'Alba, few release one quite as special as the "Rùbis" offering from Rocche Costamagna. Of course, it helps that properietor Alessandro Locatelli – a true Piemontese gentleman – sources the grapes from a 55 year-old vine-yard near the highest elevations in La Morra, some 1200 feet above sea level. At these heights, yields are naturally low (about 1 kg/vine), hence the resulting wine has excellent depth of fruit and a generous mid-palate. This is a ripe, zesty Dolcetto with appealing black rasp-berry and black plum fruit, moderate tannins and very good acidity. It's so tasty and effusively fruity upon release, but after two to five years in the bottle, it settles down a bit. Only a little more than 300 cases are produced each year, so it's not easy to find, but it's definitely worth the search.

GIUSEPPE MASCARELLO DOLCETTO D'ALBA "SANTO STEFANO DI PERNO"

Here is another excellent Dolcetto from a famed Barolo producer, Giuseppe Mascarello of Castiglione Falletto. The grapes are sourced from the family's estate vineyard in Monforte d'Alba where the Dol-cetto vines were planted in 1994.

Matured in cement tanks to give the wine a clear varietal focus, there are aromas of currant and plum, but the fruit notes are toned down here; there is also a noticeable savory edge on the nose. Medium-full, this offers medium-weight tannins and impressive complexity with good acidity and balance. Enjoy this upon release and for up to five years of age –perhaps longer from the finest vintages.

PECCHENINO DOGLIANI "SIRI D'JERMU"

The town of Dogliani, a little south of Barolo, is known for the Dolcetto grape. This variety produces fruit-forward wines with moderate acidity and tannins that can be enjoyed upon release; in fact, most examples of Dolcetto are meant for consumption within the first two to three years. However the examples of Dolcetto from Dogliani, unlike versions of this grape made in Alba or Asti, are more "serious" bottlings of Dolcetto, wines that can be enjoyed for some 7-10 years (in rare instances) after the harvest. The Dogliani style is so famous that the finest wines from here (DOCG) are not even labeled as Dolcetto di Dogliani, but merely as Dogliani as with this wine.

Pecchenino is a family-run estate, now in the hands of brothers Attilio and Orlando, who oversee production from their twenty-two hectares in Dogliani. They produce several examples of Dolcetto, including "San Luigi" (Dolcetto di Dogliani DOC) as well as "Bricco Botti" and "Siri d'Jermu" (Dogliani DOCG). This wine sports a bright purple color with aromas of black plum, licorice and black raspberry. Medium-full and deeply concentrated, the wine is aged in 25HL oak casks for one year. The middle weight, nicely polished tannins, good acidity and impressive persistence combine to yield a lovely wine.

LUIGI EINAUDI DOGLIANI "VIGNA TECC"
Back in 1897, Luigi Einaudi purchased an estate at San Giacomo near the town of Dogliani; in 1948, Einaudi became Italy's first president. Today his great grandson Matteo Sardagna manages various estates in Dogliani as well as in Barolo. Their Vigna Tecc, a 100% Dolcetto, is sourced from vineyards that were planted in 1937 and 1941, resulting in a very concentrated wine with impressive structure. Steel aged to preserve the charms of the Dolcetto grape, this has appealing black raspberry fruit with a hint of tar and clove and excellent grip. Enjoy for three to five years after the harvest.

MARZIANO ABBONA DOGLIANI "PAPÀ CELSO"
One of the most delicious, varietally pure examples of Dogliani is the "Papà Celso" offering from Marziano Abbona. Sourced from a single vineyard with vines ranging from 40-60 years of age, this offers attractive black cherry and plum fruit flavors along with the typi-

cally medium-weight tannins found in Dolcetto from this commune. Aged solely in steel tanks, the emphasis here is on the freshness and luscious traits of the variety. The forward nature of this wine gives it an instant appeal, but it tends to drink best at three to five years of age.

FONTANAFREDDA DOLCETTO DI DIANO D'ALBA "LA LEPRE"

Diano D'Alba, just a few kilometers from Serralunga D'Alba is another small town known for Dolcetto. However unlike Dogliani, the examples of Dolcetto from here are much more typical of the grape, as the wines are soft and quite drinkable upon release.

The La Lepre bottling from Fontanafredda is an outstanding example of the charm of Dolcetto from this tiny hamlet. Named for the wild rabbit that runs through the vineyards, La Lepre has a deep purple color with intense fruit aromas of black raspberry and black cherry preserves along with notes of licorice. Medium-full, this has a generous mid-palate loaded with varietal fruit. The persistence is excellent and there are medium weight tannins and moderate acidity, as is typical for Dolcetto. Aged solely in steel tanks so as not to take away from the beautiful Dolcetto fruit, this is quite simply a delicious wine! Drink this within two to three years of the vintage date for optimum enjoyment.

DACAPO RUCHÈ DI CASTAGNOLE DI MONFERRATO "MAJOLI"

Ruchè is one of Piemonte's most distinctive varieties, a red with very good acidity and medium weight tannins that produces traditional, rustic wines. At DaCapo, owners Paolo Dania and Dino Riccomagno craft one of the loveliest examples of this wine. Sourced from a single vineyard in the commune of Castagnole Monferrato in the province of Asti, the wine is aged only in steel tanks and offers intriguing aromas of rhubarb, wild strawberry and nutmeg. Medium-bodied, this has an elegant entry on the palate backed by tannins that sneak up on you in the finish. Enjoy this from two to five years of age, depending on the intensity of the vintage.

GIUSEPPE MASCARELLO FREISA

Freisa is a Piemontese variety that yields a light red – sometimes made in a *frizzante* style – that is pleasant, but hardly memorable. But let a great producer such as Giuseppe Mascarello work with this grape and the results are remarkable! Sourced from the estate Toetto vineyard in Castiglione Falletto planted in 1989, this has much greater weight and complexity than you could ever expect from a Freisa. Matured for fifteen months in Slavonian oak, there are striking aromas of Asian spice (hoisin), lacquer and dried currant. As typical of this variety, the tannins are light, while acidity is high; atypically there is a rich finish of very good persistence. This wine is really worth a search; it certainly is a fitting inclusion here as one of Italy's most distinctive wines The 2006 tasted in mid-2012 had at least five years of life ahead of it – unheard of for a Freisa!

VAJRA FREISA "KYÉ"

This veteran producer situated just outside the town of Barolo also makes an accomplished version of Freisa. The word "kyé" in Piemontese dialect means "who is that person?" Aldo Vaira has, in this case, used this term to mean "what is Freisa?" Deep garnet; displaying aromas of currant and a delicate note of cinnamon, this has very good concentration, modest tannins, very good acidity and light tobacco notes on the finish, which offers notable persistence. This is a stylish wine to be enjoyed from three to seven years of age.

CRIVELLI GRIGNOLINO D'ASTI

At his 20-acre estate in Castagnole Monferrato in the province of Asti, Marco Crivelli has been producing a range of lovely regional wines since 1986. His Ruché is a splendid example of that wine, but I am focusing on his Grignolino. Pale garnet in color, as is typical, there are pure varietal aromas of wild strawberry, currant and floral notes (carnation). Medium-bodied, this has very light tannins, high, rather tart acidity and a pleasing earthiness which adds to the pleasure of this wine, especially when served with *salumi* or lighter pasta. It's important to note that not every red wine from Piemonte is meant to age for 25 years; there is a place for a charming, lighter red such as Grignolino, especially when made as beautifully as this! This can be enjoyed immediately upon release – less than a year after the harvest – and is best from two to three years of age.

PRODUTTORI DEL BARBARESCO BARBARESCO "RIO SORDO"
PRODUTTORI DEL BARBARESCO BARBARESCO "MONTESTEFANO"

If I had to choose only one producer of Barbaresco for this project, it would be Produttori del Barbaresco. I say that as the wines produced here take Barbaresco to a level few producers can match, as these are wines of tremendous varietal purity as well as evidence of local terroir. Under the leadership of Aldo Vacca, the wines here – aged solely in the traditional *grandi botti* – are routinely outstanding, thanks in no small part to the growers in the town of Barbaresco that are also members of this cooperative. Each year, there is a Barbaresco *normale*, which is a lovely wine that drinks well for 10-12 years from the finest vintages. For the best years, Vacca will bottle nine separate crus, all of them from sites within the Barbaresco commune. I have selected two of the nine to represent the winery, but the fact is that all of them are quite special wines.

The Rio Sordo displays lovely aromas of red cherry, strawberry, currant and a hint of nutmeg backed by excellent concentration and a lengthy finish with elegantly styled tannins along with finely tuned acidity. The Montestefano tends to be the most tannic, longest-lived of the nine crus, offering perfumes of red cherry, strawberry and cinnamon. Medium-full with a generous mid-palate, there is excellent persistence. All of the cru bottlings are released at the same time, generally five years after the vintage. The Rio Sordo is generally at its best within seven to twelve years of the vintage, while the Montestefano can be enjoyed 15-25 years after the harvest. **BRV**: 2007, 2005, 2004, 2001, 1999, 1996.

CASCINA DELLE ROSE BARBARESCO "RIO SORDO"

Here is another gorgeous Barbaresco produced in a traditional method. This tiny estate, located at the Rio Sordo vineyard in the

Barbaresco commune, is managed by the husband and wife team of Italo Sobrino and Giovanna Rizzolio, who take great care in every step of the process from grape to vine. This is a medium-full wine offering textbook aromas of red cherry, orange peel and sandalwood backed by excellent depth of fruit and impressive persistence. Aged solely in *grandi botti*, the wood notes are quite subtle and there is very good acidity along with graceful tannins. This is an outstanding example of what the terroir of Barbaresco is all about! The wine generally is at is best some 12-15 years from the vintage. **BRV**: 2009, 2008, 2007, 2006, 2005, 2004, 2001.

Note: Italo and Giovanna also produce a second Barbaresco from the Rio Sordo site known as "Tre Stelle"; they were the first producers to use this designation after the Rio Sordo site was divided in two parts, creating this new cru in 2005. Aged for a few months less than the Rio Sordo offering (again, solely in large casks), this Barbaresco is also a first-rate representation of this site.

PIER VINI BARBARESCO "RIO SORDO"
Pier Paolo Grasso manages this small family estate in Treiso in the Barbaresco zone; reds such as Barbaresco and Langhe Nebbiolo are highlights. The "Rio Sordo" from the famous cru in the commune of Barbaresco, is a subdued offering with textbook cherry, currant, cedar and tar aromas; medium-full, this has beautiful acidity and distinct notes of oregano and sage in the finish. This is a low-key, traditionally aged Barbaresco that emphasizes finesse and elegance. **BRV**: 2009, 2008, 2007.

RATTALINO BARBARESCO "QUARANTADUE 42"
Massimo Rattalino is in love with Barbaresco, so much so that he made himself a bet that he could leave his job in the construction business and start his own winery. He purchased a vineyard in Barbaresco and began realizing his dream when he produced his first wines in 2002. His first Barbaresco was from the 2005 vintage; the term Quarantadue or 42, is the name of the plot on the zoning

map of the area. Traditionally matured in large casks, this is a classically styled Barbaresco; I first tried the 2008 vintage in 2011 and was quite impressed with the dried cherry and currant fruit aromas along with a touch of oregano and subtle red spice. There is a rich mid-palate, very good acidity, excellent persistence, subtle wood notes and round tannins; the 2008 should peak in another 12-15 years. I am thankful that Rattalino decided to pursue his passion; he is definitely a producer worth watching! **BRV**: 2009, 2008, 2007, 2006.

Nebbiolo Vineyards below the town of Barbaresco

FIORENZO NADA BARBARESCO "ROMBONE"

Bruno Nada, one of several producers with this surname in the Barbaresco area, is the winemaker at this excellent estate in Treiso. The Rombone Barbaresco is his most famous wine, an offering that is undeniably modern in its approach, but one that maintains a fine sense of terroir. Deep garnet with aromas of red cherry, persimmon and orange pekoe tea, this is quite ripe and rich with distinct small oak notes, very good acidity and young, firm tannins. Offering excellent complexity and a gentle hand with the winemaking, this wine tends to need some time to settle down upon release and is generally at its best seven to ten years after the harvest, while a few of the best examples drink well at twelve or fifteen years of age. **BRV**: 2009, 2008, 2007, 2006, 2004.

RIZZI BARBARESCO "BOITO"
The Rizzi family – father Ernesto and son Enrico – make lovely traditional Barolo at their supremely situated estate in Treiso. Everything here, from the Barbaresco *normale* to the cru bottlings is quite special and is made with great care. The Boito vineyard, a small section of the larger cru Rizzi, is located some 800-1000 feet above sea level and is comprised largely of white clay soil, which definitely adds a sense of terroir to the wine. Aged solely in large oak casks, this is a supple Barbaresco with gorgeous red cherry, strawberry and red spice aromas, excellent concentration, polished tannins and very good acidity. This wine tends to peak at ten to fifteen years after the harvest. **BRV**: 2009, 2008, 2007, 2006, 2005, 2001.

FONTANABIANCA BARBARESCO "SORI BURDIN"
At the Fontanabianca estate in Neive, Aldo Pola crafts Barbaresco in various styles, with the Serraboella bottling aged in botti, while the Sori Burdin is barrique-aged. This is a powerful Barbaresco, offering ripe cherry and blackberry fruit along with notable spice and tobacco notes. Displaying excellent persistence and fine grip, the oak is noticeable, but tends to not overwhem the fruit, while there is almost always good acidity. This tends to drink well at seven to ten years of age and as long as twelve years from the best harvests. **BRV**: 2009, 2008, 2007, 2006, 2004, 2001.

BRUNO GIACOSA BARBARESCO "ASILI RISERVA"
Here is one of the most renowned producers of Barbaresco – as well as Barolo – who continues to produce small lots of deeply concentrated wines that are among the very finest of their type. There are

several bottlings of Barbaresco including a regular Asili, from the famed cru in the commune of Barbaresco. The Riserva Asili, which is bottled with the red label – the highest designation for Giacosa - is made from vineyards between 10 and 15 years of age; the wine is matured in Allier oak barriques for 24 months. Displaying aromas of roses, red cherry, geranium and brown spice, this is a massive, powerhouse Barbaresco with very good acidity, firm tannins and nicely integrated oak notes, along wth excellent persistence and outstanding complexity. A wine such as this needs several years to settle down and display its charms, but the patient drinker is greatly rewarded as this is wine that peaks sometime between 15 and 30 years, depending on the vintage. **BRV:** 2007, 2004, 2001, 1996.

MARCHESI DI GRÉSY BARBARESCO "MARTINENGA CAMP GROS"

Just on the outskirts of the town of Barbaresco, the Marchesi di Grésy estate is one of the area's most consistent and time-honored producers. Alberto di Grésy oversees production, which originated with the initial wines in 1973. The Martinegna vineyard is the source for three outstanding Barolos; Martinenga, Gaiun and Camp Gros, these last two from older sections of the vineyard. The Camp Gros is made from a small section of this site that was planted in 1965; this is the northeastern sector of Martinenga and is comprised of blue marl soils, typical for this area. Aged in French barriques for six months and then *botti* for 24 months followed by 15 months of bottle aging before release, this is a magnificent Barbaresco with truffle and red cherry aromas with hints of balsamic emerging after a few years. Medium-full with a generous mid-palate, this has delicate brown spice notes and rich, balanced tannins along with a finish highlighted by excellent persistence and very good acidity. First produced from the 1978 vintage and only made in the finest years, Camp Gros has an enviable track record for aging, as it displays it best qualities at 10-12 years of age, though it often drinks well for 15-20 years. **BRV:** 2007, 2006, 2005, 2004, 2001.

GAJA SORI SAN LORENZO

Angelo Gaja is arguably Italy's most famous wine producer; he is certainly the most visible personality among his country's vintners, at least as far as marketing. Gaja has followed in the footsteps of his father and has always sought out the finest vineyards to produce the finest wines. It is not a stretch to say that he made Barbaresco a household name during the 1970s and '80s, producing wines of impressive complexity, powerful depth of fruit and unmistakable terroir.

While Gaja continues to produce Barbaresco, since the 1996 vintage, he has labeled his single vineyard offerings from Barbaresco such as Sori San Lorenzo and Sori San Tildin as Langhe Rosso, as he now makes the wines from 95% Nebbiolo and 5% Barbera (Barbaresco must be 100% Nebbiolo). This wine, from a cru just outside the town of Barbaresco was the first single vineyard Barbaresco from Gaja and one of the first from any producer. The aromas are of cherry, licorice, coffee and brown spice when it is young, changing to more balsamic and truffle notes after a decade in the bottle. Full-bodied with outstanding complexity, the wine has well integrated oak – it is aged first in barriques and then in large casks – as well as very good acidity and young, firm tannins. Even from a lesser vintage, this wine can age 20 years and usually the wine is at its best some 30-40 years after the harvest. Though not technically a Barbaresco, it is certainly one of the most extraordinary wines of this zone. Indeed, this wine is so famous and was such a history-making effort, a book was written about it! **BRV**: 2008, 2007, 2006, 2004, 2001, 1999.

BARTOLO MASCARELLO BAROLO

Here is a Barolo that represents the history and tradition of this zone as well as any wine. Today when cru Barolo – a Barolo coming from a single vineyard – is the norm, the Bartolo Mascarello Barolo harkens back to the model of the 1950s and '60s, when Barolo was blended from vineyards in more than one commune. This tradition is continued today by Maria Teresa, daughter of Bartolo, who passed away in 2005. Bartolo was known not only for his unshakable faith in tradition when it came to producing Barolo – aging solely in *botti* – but also for his sly sense of humor, most notably on a label he designed that read "No Barriques, No Berlusconi." Unlike some of today's Barolos with very ripe fruit and emphatic notes of oak, the Bartolo Mascarello Barolo is a more subdued wine with herbal over-tones, rich, but balanced tannins and very good acidity. The finest bottlings tend to show well after a decade in the bottle and can be enjoyed on their 40th birthday. **BRV**: 2008, 2007, 2006, 2005, 2004, 2001, 1999.

COGNO BAROLO "VIGNA ELENA"

At their gorgeous small estate in Novello, Nadia Cogno and her wine-maker husband Valter Fissore produce elegantly styled versions of Barolo. Their source is the Ravera cru, which is situated immediately below the winery; this is one of the most underrated of all Barolo cru. There is an excellent Ravera bottling and in the finest years, Fissore produces a wine called "Vigna Elena" from some of the oldest sections of the Ravera vineyard. The primary feature of this wine however, is that these vines are planted to the rosé clone of Nebbiolo, a strain rarely seen anymore in Barolo. As you can imagine from the name, the rosé clone yields a more perfumed style of Nebbiolo, one reminiscent of red and orange roses. Valter and Nadia named this wine for their daughter Elena; they give this wine the utmost care, aging it in large Slavonian oak casks for three years – one year more than their Ravera bottling.

On their website, the proprietors write that this is "an uncompro-mising wine, strictly for Barolo purists…" I would heartily agree, as this is a distinctive Barolo with striking perfumes of orange peel, currant, dried cherry, tar and the aforementioned roses. Medium-full with excellent concentration, this is an extremely elegant Barolo with silky tannins and a seductive earthiness in the finish that beautifully expresses its specific terroir. Barolo is often referred to as the "wine of kings" and certainly as a "masculine" wine; here is a "feminine" Barolo that stands tall amidst the big boys. This is somewhat approachable upon release, some five years after the harvest, but it clearly opens up and reveals more of its charms slowly over the course of fifteen to twenty years. Of all the Barolos I taste every year, there are few examples I look forward to with greater anticipation that this marvelous wine. **BRV**: 2007, 2006 (outstanding), 2005, 2004, 2001, 1999 (these last three vintages all outstanding).

CAVALLOTTO BAROLO "BRICCO BOSCHIS RISERVA SAN GIUSEPPE"

The Cavallotto family founded their winery in Castiglione Falletto in 1948; today brothers Alfio and Giuseppe along with their sister Laura manage operations. Their most celebrated Nebbiolo vineyard for production of Barolo is Bricco Boschis, a vineyard at the far eastern sector of their property. The section reserved for the Riserva San Giuseppe Barolo is 2.45 hectares facing south and east; the average age of the vines here are just over 50 years of age. The wine is aged solely in *grandi botti* for four or five years and then in bottle for one year before its release. While there is also a Bricco Boschis Barolo *normale*, which in itself is a lovely traditional Barolo of excellent breeding, the San Giuseppe is a wine that captures the essence of the Nebbiolo variety as well as this particular terroir with superb grace. Medium-full with excellent concentration, the aromas open slowly to notes of red cherry and currant along with hints of thyme, sandalwood, cedar as well as the classic tar and rose profile. The mid-palate is beautifully defined, the oak notes are very subtle and there is excellent persistence and very good acidity. The finish is quite long with polished, silky tannins and notes of brown spice. A wine of remarkable elegance and class, this is an outstanding Barolo that is among the finest, traditionally made or not. The wine generally drinks best some 12-20 years after the vintage, with some wines at peak 25-40 years after the vintage. **BRV**: 2006, 2005, 2004, 2001, 1999 (outstanding), 1998 (a wonderful wine from a very underrated vintage), 1996.

CERETTO BAROLO "BRICCO ROCCHE"

Ceretto is one of the great names in the Langhe, producing outstanding examples of both Barbaresco and Barolo. The estate was founded in 1937 by brothers Bruno and Marcello Ceretto who were among the first in their area to specialize in single vineyard wines; to that end, they established wineries in both the Barbaresco and Barolo zones. Their main cellars are located just outside of Alba, where a splendid visitors' center was opened to the public in 2010.

Today, Marcello's son Alessandro is the winemaker, producing cru Barbaresco (Asili and Bernardot) and Barolo (Brunate, Prapó, Cannubi, Bricco Rocche). While the Prapó is always an excellent – sometimes outstanding wine – it is the Bricco Rocche that is the most famous wine produced at Ceretto. The Rocche vineyard is located in Castiglione Falletto in the heart of the Barolo zone; the Ceretto family owns 4.5 acres and as their rows are at the top of this vineyard, the wine is labeled as Bricco Rocche. Aged in small and medium-sized French oak, the wine offers aromas of dried cherry, currant and cedar backed by impressive concentration and persistence. The acidity is at a good level – certainly the elevation of the vineyard (1025-1115 feet above sea level) helps preserve a healthy natural acidity - and the tannins are nicely tuned. This is a powerhouse Barolo built for the long haul – lighter vintages drink well after 20 years, while the finest examples are at peak after 40 years – yet the wine has a finesse and balance that keeps everything in check. This is an outstanding wine as well as an exemplary example of local terroir. **BRV**: 2008, 2007, 2006 (outstanding), 2005, 2004, 2001, 1999.

VIETTI BAROLO RISERVA "VILLERO"

The Vietti winery is known for several cru Barolos produced each vintage, such as Brunate from La Morra, Lazzarito from Serralunga and Rocche from Castiglione Falletto, adjacent to the winery. In the finest years, they also produce a *riserva* Barolo from the Villero vineyard in Castiglione Falletto, situated just north and at a slightly lower elevation than Rocche. The 2004 is the latest release;

the vines from the small Vietti plot (just over two acres) were 37 years old that vintage. Winemaker Luca Currado ages the wine in large Slavonian casks for three years and the final result is, in a word, sublime. Medium-full with outstanding concentration, there are classic aromas of red cherry, orange peel, tar and a note of balsamic. Quite rich in the mid-palate, this has a very long finish with great persistence, while the tannins are perfectly balanced and the acidity is precise. This is a Barolo of great complexity and class and Vietti rightfully assigns a different artist to create a special label for each new release. This is a Barolo that will be in peak condition anywhere from 20-25 years for a year such as 2004 to perhaps 35-40 years for a phenomenal vintage such as 1996. **BRV**: 2004, 2001, 1997, 1996, 1990.

BRUNA GRIMALDI BAROLO "BRICCO AMBROGIO"

Like many of their counterparts, Bruna Grimaldi and her husband Franco Fiorino aim to make wines that ideally reflect their origins, nothing more, nothing less. So it's fascinating to taste the three cru Barolos from Grimaldi, as each is a terroir-driven wine of impeccable balance. Her most famous wine is the Vigna Regnola, located quite near the Falletto vineyard of Bruno Giacosa in Serralunga. She also produces a Barolo from the Camilla cru of Grinzane Cavour and for the first time in 2007, produced a Barolo from Bricco Ambrogio in Roddi, in the far northeastern reaches of the Barolo zone. Sourced from 40-year old vines and aged for 30 months in *tonneuax*, this is a beautifully crafted wine with aromas of strawberry, raspberry and roses. There is excellent persistence and very good acidity with stylish tannins and delicate spice notes. As this is from Roddi and not Serralunga, this is not as powerful a wine as her Regnola Barolo, but it is a well made, appealing wine of lovely varietal character that will be at its best at 15-20 years of age. **BRV**: 2008, 2007.

FRATELLI ALESSANDRIA BAROLO "MONVIGLIERO"

Situated in the town of Verduno in the northern reaches of the Barolo zone, this firm produces as many as four different examples of Barolo each vintage; my favorite is the "Monvigliero" from a site most producers believe is the finest in this commune. The family's portion of this vineyard is more than thirty years old and has an ideal southern/ southwestern exposure, some 1050 feet above sea level. Aged for six months in *tonneaux* and then twenty four months in large casks, this is a supple, elegantly styled Barolo with gorgeous aromas of strawberry jam, orange pekoe tea, cedar and a hint of marjoram. There is excellent persistence, bright fruit, very good acidity, subtle wood notes and a long finish; this is a lovely expression of terroir. The winemaking here is precise and honors the site, so that the 2006 was very rich and a bit closed upon release, while the 2007 from a warmer growing season was more approachable and charming at the same stage. This is at its best anywhere from twelve to twenty years. **BRV**: 2008, 2007, 2006, 2005, 2004, 2001.

RENATO RATTI BAROLO "ROCCHE"
RENATO RATTI BAROLO "CONCA"

Renato Ratti was a man in love with Barolo the wine, but perhaps even more with Barolo, the land. Establishing his winery in 1965, Ratti produced wines from small areas of La Morra in the heart of the Barolo zone, crafting wines that emphasized varietal character along with notable expression of place. Ratti was interested in terroir across the Barolo zone and as he researched soils as well as conditions such as exposure, sunshine and wind, he developed a greater understanding of the Barolo zone as a whole. He produced a map of the crus of Barolo; this was among the first serious zonation studies of this wine zone and indeed this map is still highly regarded today.

In the early 1970s, a few years after producing his first cru Barolo from Marcenasco, he then made wine from two additional vineyards in La Morra, namely Rocche and Conca. These have been a splendid success for the winery since the first production and today, Renato's son Pietro (the elder Ratti passed away in 1998) continues to refine these cru Barolos in their new multi-million dollar, state of the art facility on a hill just below the town of La Morra (the exact location is a *frazione* called Annunziata). The Conca vineyard – conca meaning "shell", which describes the ampitheater-like shape of this site – was first sourced for a Ratti Barolo from the 1971 vintage; today, after various replantings, the vines today average 15 years of age. The Rocche, which is situated closer to Barolo than Conca, was first bottled as a Ratti cru from the 1971 vintage; the average age of these vines is 50 years.

Both wines today are aged initially in barriques for one year and then in large casks for a second year. Each features inviting fruit aromas of red cherry and plum; the difference among the two is that there are more spice notes – such as sage and cumin – in the Rocche. Both wines are quite rich on the palate with beautifully integrated oak and firm, but silky tannins. Both wines are quite powerful, yet elegant in a classic La Morra style and age extremely well with the Conca generaly showing its best some 20-25 years after the harvest, while the Rocche from the same vintage can often peak an additional five to seven years later. These are two regal Barolos that are not only supreme examples of La Morra terroir, but are also wines that are a tribute to the devotion and hard work of Renato Ratti and his son Pietro. **BRV**: (for both wines) 2008, 2007, 2006, 2005, 2004, 2001 (outstanding), 1999, 1998.

PAOLO SCAVINO BAROLO "ROCCHE DELL'ANNUNZIATA RISERVA"

Established in 1921 in Castiglione Falletto by its namesake, the Paolo Scavino winery is without doubt one of the most distinguished Barolo houses. Paolo's son Enrico took over after his father's death and today he has been joined by his daughters Enrica and Elisa. The Rocche dell'Annunziata Riserva from the famous cru in La Morra, is the company's most sumptuous and sleek Barolo. The family acquired a section of this vineyard in 1990 with some of the vines that are still producing today dating back to 1942. This is a modern Barolo, matured in barriques, yet the oak treatment in this wine takes a back seat to the perfectly ripe fruit, precise acidity and polished tannins. This is a true *riserva* in every sense of the word, a wine that displays the extraordinary qualities of its site as well as particular growing season. This has the structure to drink well for 25 to 40 years. **BRV**: 2005, 2004, 2003, 2001 (exceptional).

ROCCHE COSTAMAGNA BAROLO "BRICCO FRANCESCO"

The famed La Morra cru Rocche dell'Annunziata is the source of this Barolo from Rocche Costamagna. Francesco is the name of the son of the founder of the firm, the great grandfather of current proprietor Alessandro Locatelli. Bricco Francesco is sourced from a small part of the Rocche vineyard; the vines average 35 years of age and are farmed to very small yields. Aged in large casks, this is a Barolo that expresses its origins; the aromas are of balsamic, dried cherry, nutmeg and cedar, while there is good natural acidity and excellent persistence. This is a refined, classy Barolo with beautiful complexity and grace. Made only in the finest years, this typically is at peak from 12-20 years of age. **BRV**: 2006, 2005, 2004, 2001, 1999, 1998.

ROBERTO VOERZIO
BAROLO "SARMASSA"
BAROLO "CEREQUIO"
BAROLO "BRUNATE"
BAROLO "ROCCHE DELL'ANUNZIATA TORRIGLIONE"

Since the early late 1970s and early 1980s, there have been producers of Barolo that have moved away from the traditional aging of their wines in *botti grandi* to a more international style of maturing their Barolo in French barriques. Today, some of these producers have now settled upon the use of both small and large casks for aging purposes. But for Roberto Voerzio, who made his first Barolo in 1986, barriques have always been the preferred option for aging his various cru bottlings. However, what truly makes these wines so remarkable are not the barrels, but instead the outstanding quality of the grapes. Voerzio sources fruit from several vineyards in the communes of La Morra and Barolo (Brunate, Cerequio, Sarmassa) that other producers also use, but it is the way that Voerzio farms these plots that makes all the difference. Trimming fruit from the bunches several times during the growing season, Voerzio works with final yields that are less than half of what is legally permitted with the Barolo DOCG regulations.

Voerzio produces as many as six different bottlings of Barolo per year; for me, it is impossible to select one, so I have opted for four different cru bottlings, each of which is routinely outstanding. Each of the wines has tremendous depth of fruit and excellent persistence along with slightly different flavor profiles. The Cerequio has caraway and cumin notes to go along with the red currant and orange peel fruit, while the Brunate has more black plum fruit along with hints of violets in the aromas. The Rocche dell'Annunziata – made from 50-55 year old vines – has more of a marmalade and balsamic profile, while the Sarmassa displays notes of truffle and caramel to go along with the textbook cherry and red currant perfumes. These are Barolos produced in a modern style and the spice from the new oak does add another dimension to these wines, but there is more than enough fruit to balance the wood. These are wines that will peak in 15-20 years in lighter vintages, while the wines from the finest vintages should drink well for 25 years plus. **BRV**: 2008, 2007, 2006, 2005, 2004, 2001, 1999.

MARCARINI BAROLO "LA SERRA"
MARCARINI BAROLO "BRUNATE"

Here is a Barolo producer that should be much better known, given the quality of the wines as well as the consistent track record. The cellars are located in the town of La Morra (on top of the hill); the owners source fruit from two of this commune's most famous vineyards: La Serra and Brunate. The former is located just above Brunate, which explains the La Serra – "greenhouse" – name – as this vineyard receives a touch more sun that Brunate and attains ripeness first. There are lovely notes of fruit, such as red cherry, in the aromatic profiles of these wines, along with cedar and truffle. Medium-full, these wines tend to be a bit shy upon release, but display wonderful complexities about five to seven years later and tend to be at their best 15-20 years after the vintage. If you want the most full-bodied, most highly extracted examples of Barolo, you will need to look elsewhere. But if it is subtlety, finesse and elegance you seek in a Barolo, the wines from Marcarini are for you! **BRV:** 2008, 2007, 2006, 2005, 2004, 2001, 1999.

CORDERO DI MONTEZEMOLO BAROLO "BRICCO GATTERA"
This historic estate in the La Morra *frazione* of Annunziata (very close to the Renato Ratti winery) is one of the most beautiful in all of the Barolo zone. This family holding is today managed by Alberto and his sister Elena, who are the grandchildren of Paolo Cordero di Monteze-molo who took over the estate in the early 1940s. There are three sep-arate bottlings of Barolo most vintages; the Bricco Gattera is from the estate vineyard with the famous Lebanon cedar, arguably the most visibly recognizable tree in all of the Barolo zone.

Sourced from old vines some 1000 feet above sea level, this is a rich, modern Barolo matured for 18-20 months in French oak; the aromas are of ripe red cherry, red roses and vanilla, with hints of truffle, as the wine ages. Offering impressive concentration, very good acidity and rich, youthful tannins, this is characterized by its sweet young fruit and excellent persistence. This is a bit more tight upon release than a typical La Morra Barolo, so give this time to settle down; peak enjoy-ment is often from 15-25 years. **BRV**: 2008, 2007, 2006, 2005, 2004, 2001.

GIUSEPPE RINALDI BAROLO "LE COSTE"
Giuseppe or "Beppe" Rinaldi, as he is more commonly known, is one of the best-loved and well-respected vintners in Barolo. Producing Barolo since 1970, this is an ultra traditional house where the wines are aged in big casks. There are two Barolos produced: the Canubi San Lorenzo Riserva and the Le Coste, from the cru in the commune of Barolo. Medium-full, this has substantial aromas of myrtle, currant, orange peel and licorice along with haunting notes of cedar. The wine is aged for 36 months in large casks and the wood notes here are beau-tifully integrated, while the finish is quite long with polished tannins

and very good acidity. This wine tends to peak some 20-25 years after the vintage, with a few bottlings drinking well upon their 40th birthday. Simply a sublime version of traditional Barolo! **BRV**: 2008, 2007, 2006, 2005, 2004, 2001, 1999.

FRANCESCO RINALDI BAROLO "BRUNATE"

This ultra traditional Barolo producer in Barolo is run by Luciano Rinaldi, who is in his 80s, along with his niece Paola. There are three versions of Barolo produced here: a regional Barolo, made from fruit from Barolo and La Morra; Cannubio, from the famous Cannubi hill and Brunate, from the cru that is located in both the Barolo and La Morra communes. Right away, you realize that the Brunate bottling from Francesco Rinaldi is a traditional, *botti*-aged Barolo by looking at the color, which is pale garnet, even light pink; this is about the lightest color you will ever see in a Barolo. This is a sensual Barolo that is anything but a fruit bomb, as the aromas are of cedar, dried herbs, oregano and dried cherry. Medium-full with an expansive mid-palate, this is supple and refined with polished tannins, very good acidity and very subdued wood notes. The finish is ultra long with excellent persistence and there is a distinct herbal character to this wine, both in the aromas and in the finish. This is a lovely expression of terroir and is routinely one of the three or four finest examples of Brunate Barolo. This wine shows beautifully upon release, but displays greater complexities with time in the bottle. The lighter vintages of this wine are at peak some 20 years after the vintage, while the finest offer great pleasure at 35-40 years after the harvest. **BRV**: 2008, 2007, 2006, 2005, 2004, 2001, 1999.

G. D. VAJRA BAROLO "BRICCO DELLE VIOLE"

Aldo Vaira and his wife Milena are among the friendliest, most gentle people you will meet in any profession; in a land populated by gracious farmers, they are among the most congenial. Their charm translates into all their wines, from a dry Riesling to a delicate, delicious Moscato d'Asti to this cru Barolo. From the "hill of the violets" just outside the town of Barolo, this is a traditional wine aged solely in large casks that combines floral and fruit notes with polished tannins and impeccable varietal purity. This is definitely not a powerful, assertive style of Barolo, but one that enchants you with its finesse and poise. The 2005 version of this wine, from a vintage not that well celebrated, was a seamless wine and clearly one of the finest of that year. Vaira often releases this wine six to twelve months after other producers' Barolos, believing the wine needs extra bottle age to come together. This generally shows its best at 15-20 years of age, though some bottles are in fine shape for a few years longer. **BRV**: 2008, 2007, 2006, 2005, 2004, 2001.

MICHELE CHIARLO BAROLO "CEREQUIO"

The Cerequio vineyard, which is situated in both the La Morra and Barolo communes, has been identified as one of the very finest of all Barolo crus for more than a century. Located on a gently sloping hill visible from the main road that leads from Barolo to Alba, the site is in the midst of the high-rent district, next to the crus of Brunate and La Serra. This is clearly the finest Barolo produced by the Chiarlo family, one of the Langhe's most renowned wine estates for the past five decades. The wine is somewhat vigorous upon release, so it clearly drinks better after five to seven years in the bottle, but it is always a harmonious Barolo, one displaying classic dried cherry, cedar and orange peel aromas along with firm tannins and good acidity. Matured in special mid-size barrels (700 liters, or slightly more than three times the size of a barrique), this beautifully reveals the mineral aspect of the Cerequio plot. This is at peak from 15-25 years of age, depending on the strength of the vintage. **BRV**: 2007, 2006, 2005, 2004, 2001, 1999 (note that the family made the decision not to bottle this wine from the 2008 vintage.)

MASSOLINO BAROLO VIGNA RIONDA RISERVA

Established in 1896, this family estate is now managed by brothers Franco and Roberto Massolino. This small cellar (100,000 bottles per year), located in the middle of the town of Serralunga d'Alba, specializes in Barolo from this commune, although a cru Barolo from Castiglione Falletto called Parussi was added to the lineup as of the 2007 vintage. The winemaking here for the various examples of Barolo is traditional with aging solely in large casks (Parafada, a cru Barolo used to receive some barrique aging, but that has been changed as well, so all the Barolos here are matured in *grandi botti*). The Vigna Rionda Riserva, from a hillside vineyard just below the cellars, is the most powerful Barolo from Massolino; certainly the vine age – ranging from 25-45 years – has much to do with that. This is a true *riserva*, as the wine is aged for a total of six years- three and one-half in Slavonian oak casks and two and one-half in the bottle before release. Sporting aromas of red cherry, currant, orange peel and cedar, there is excellent concentration and persistence as well as ideal structure and very good natural acidity. The tannins are rich, but nicely balanced and the wood notes, as might be expected, are quite subtle. This wine generally starts to display its complexities a decade after the vintage date and tends to peak 25-40 years after the harvest. **BRV**: 2006, 2005, 2004, 2001, 1999.

GIOVANNI ROSSO BAROLO "CERETTA"
At this tiny cellar just outside the old section of Serralunga d'Alba, Davide Rosso produces several Barolos from several esteemed local vineyards. Given his traditional, minimalist style of enology, each wine beautifully displays its unique terroir. My favorite, year in and year out, has been the Ceretta Barolo, from a hilltop site situated near the Baudana zone. This is a Barolo with beautiful ripe red cherry, red plum and carnation aromas backed by notable depth of fruit, very good acidity and silky tannins. While this is a bit rounder and more approachable than many examples of Serralunga Barolo, this does exhibit the stuffing and structure that will see it through 15-20 years in most vintages and longer in great years such as 2008 and 2006. **BRV**: 2008, 2007, 2006, 2005, 2004.

Note that with the 2007 vintage, Rosso started to produce a special Barolo from a small parcel of 60-year old vines in the highly esteemed Vigna Rionda cru in Serralunga. Rosso inherited this plot and has named the wine after the previous owner, Tommaso Canale. Canale previously sold grapes from this vineyard to Bruno Giacosa;

now as Davide Rosso takes his rightful place with this great site, he has made two splendid wines from the 2007 and 2008 vintages. Barely 1000 bottles of each were produced, making this one of the most highly sought after Barolos of all.

FONTANAFREDDA BAROLO "LA ROSA"

Fontanafredda represents a story of a famous producer that has reinvented itself. For years, this gorgeous estate in Serralunga d'Alba turned out respectable examples of Barolo, but ones that rarely realized their potential. Then general manager Giovanni Minetti hired Danilo Drocco as winemaker, who immediately began to improve the overall quality of the wines, especially with the La Rosa bottling. The La Rosa vineyard is the beautifuly situated ampitheather that surrounds the winery and is owned exclusively by Fontanafredda. The wine, aged partly in barriques and partly in *botti* is quite floral with lovely perfumes of red cherry, strawberry and red roses. Medium-full, the wine has beautifully integrated oak notes, very good to excellent depth of fruit and a long, pleasing finish with silky tannins. This is one of the best balanced, subtle and complex examples of Barolo you will find. This is generally at peak some 15-25 years after the vintage. **BRV**: 2008, 2007, 2006, 2004, 2001, 1999, 1998.

E. MIRAFIORE BAROLO "LAZZARITO"

Just as there were some major changes at Fontanafredda in the 1990s, so too in the first decade of the 21st century, a new direction was put in place here, as Oscar Farinetti, owner of the famous food market Eataly, purchased the winery. One of his most important decisions was to introduce the "Mirafiore" line; as Mirafiore was a former name of this estate, the wines with this marque would represent a link to the traditions of the 19th and early 20th century at this estate. In short, the wines would display the style of past decades and thus would be aged in large barrels – no barriques for the Mirafiore wines. There is an excellent Dolcetto d'Alba as well as a marvelous Barbera d'Alba, but it is the Lazzarito Barolo that is the star in this lineup. Winemaker Danilo Drocco had made this wine into arguably the finest Barolo each vintage from Fontanafredda, aging the wine in both large and small barrels and expressing its power. But now with the fruit from this vineyard going solely to the Mirafiore project, this wine is aged only in *grandi botti*. Medium-full to full-bodied, the aromas are of dried cherry, plum, tobacco, cumin and tar. The tannins are quite rich, yet well balanced and the acidity is very good. The wine is quite robust on the palate, yet it is never over the top and displays a wonderful harmony of all components. This wine should peak in 20-25 years after the harvest. **BRV**: 2007, 2006, 2004.

PAOLO MANZONE BAROLO "MERIAME"

There's no hidden agenda with Paolo Manzone the man or with his wines; the focus is clear. Manzone produces the typical range of local wines with his cru Barolo from the Meriame vineyard being his finest product. Situated below many of other cru of Serralunga, the vineyard sits in a bowl, giving it ideal exposure to the sun, ensuring ideal ripeness. The vines here are 60 years old, resulting in a deeply concentrated wine that is matured in mid-size oak casks. This is a classic Serralunga Barolo with big red fruit and spice notes, excellent concentration and firm tannins with very good acidity. Displaying impressive complexity no matter the vintage, this is a wine that tends to peak between 15-25 years of age. **BRV**: 2008, 2007, 2006, 2005, 2004, 2001.

MAURO SEBASTE BAROLO "PRAPÒ"

It's been a real pleasure witnessing all the hard work of Mauro Sebaste over the past decade pay off with such a wonderful variety of red and white wines from the Langhe and Roero districts. He produces three different examples of Barolo, each from a highly regarded cru: a *riserva* from Brunate in La Morra, one from Monvigliero in Verduno and this exquisite wine from Prapò in Serralunga. The wine is aged primarily in large casks (1600 liter) of French oak with a small percentage in smaller 400-liter barrels; total aging in wood is 36 months. From the initial aromas of currant, dried cherry, cedar and balsamic to the elegant tannins and precise acidity, this is a classy Barolo that expresses its terroir in a graceful manner. It's made in a style that offers aproachablity upon release, as it's not a tightly wrapped wine, yet it clearly will offer greater complexity at twelve years of age and older; the best vintages will drink well for as long as 25 years. **BRV**: 2008, 2007, 2006, 2005, 2004.

PIO CESARE BAROLO "ORNATO"

The firm of Pio Cesare is one of the most historic in all of the Langhe. The cellars, located in the center of the town of Alba run right up against old Roman walls and hold some remarkable wines. Current director Pio Boffa, a direct descendant of Pio Cesare, sees to it that every wine produced here from the everyday Gavi to the various bottlings of Chardonnay, an excellent Dolcetto d'Alba and the offerings of Barbera are as well crafted with as much attention given to them as the cru bottlings of Barolo and Barbaresco. The cru Barbaresco "Il Bricco" is a marvelous wine with impressive depth of fruit and structure, but for this report, I am singling out the "Ornato" Barolo. The vineyard itself is a superb site, located next to the famous Falletto cru of Bruno Giacosa in Serralunga d'Alba. The wine is definitely a modern style of Barolo, but is not over the top as with some small barrel-aged Barolos. Fermented in stainless steel and given 15 days skin contact, the wine is matured for 36 months, with 70% of the wine going into new French barriques and 30% aging in 25-hectoliter casks. Deep garnet in color, the inviting aromas are of red cherry, orange peel and caraway; there is a generous and well-defined mid palate. Generally this wine needs several years after release to show its best, although in a warm year such as 2007, the wine is more forward and somewhat approachable at an early age. The wine has a marvelous track record and generally peaks at 20-25 years after the vintage. **BRV**: 2008, 2007, 2006, 2004, 2001 (outstanding), 1999.

ETTORE GERMANO BAROLO "LAZZARITO RISERVA"

At this ultra consistent property in Serralunga d'Alba, Sergio Germano produces Barolos of impressive structure from local crus Ceretta and Prapò. He recently added another Barolo, this one a *riserva* offering from the Lazzarito vineyard. This renowned vineyard, located just below the town of Serralunga, is also the source for Barolo from producers such as Fontanafredda and Vietti. Germano farms about one and one-half acres of this site; the vines were planted in 1931. He ages the wine for thirty months in 2000-liter casks; along with classic orange peel and dried cherry aromas there are also notes of tobacco, a signature of this site. There is very good acidity and the tannins are polished; this has the concentration to drink well for 15-20 years. **BRV**: 2007, 2006, 2005.

ASCHERI BAROLO "SORANO – COSTE & BRICCO"
As you drive through the commune of Serralunga d'Alba from the Fontanafredda estate toward the town itself, you will climb a few hills along the way. Tucked into a small plot on the left of one small hill is the Sorano cru of Ascheri. Matteo Ascheri, whose cellars are located in the nearby town of Bra, produces two versions of Barolo from this site. Both the regular Sorano Barolo as well as the Coste e Bricco are treated in similar fashion in the cellars – aging for 28 months in Slavonian oak – but the grapes themselves make the difference in these two wines. Coste & Bricco refers to the vines from the top of this hillside vineyard (Bricco) as well as the vines that face southwest and catch the late afternoon sun (Coste). This is a classically oriented, traditional Barolo that I love for so many reasons; the aromas of red cherry, cedar, orange peel and red roses, the precise acidity, the impressive depth of fruit, the impeccably balanced tannins and of course, a beauiful sense of terroir. This is a classy – and classic – Barolo that should be better known. This tends to be at peak drinking condition from 12-25 years, depending on the vintage. **BRV**: 2008, 2007, 2006, 2004, 2001.

ELIO GRASSO BAROLO "GINESTRA CASA MATE´"
ELIO GRASSO BAROLO "GAVARINI CHINIERA"
Here are two examples of traditional Barolo from estate vineyards of Elio Grasso. Elio has been one of the kindest, most gracious vintners in the Barolo zone for many years, always willing to impart wisdom to another grower or take the time to answer questions from a journalist.

Today, Elio continues his work in the vineyards and has largely passed on the winemaking duties to his son Gianluca. These two wines share much in common, with aromas of red cherry and currant, often with a hint of truffle. Medium-full, they offer excellent depth of fruit and persistence along with a typical sense of Monforte d'Alba terroir, with a distinct herbal edge and a powerful finish of great complexity. These wines tend to need some time to round out – the Casa Maté is generally a bit more approachable – and are at their best some 20-25 years after the vintage. **BRV** (both wines): 2008, 2007, 2006, 2005, 2004, 2001, 1999, 1998, 1996.

GIOVANNI MANZONE BAROLO "LE GRAMOLERE"

The examples of Barolo from Monforte d'Alba are rugged wines, ones that have big tannins and a muscular mid-palate; these are wines that require patience. The best of these Barolos are from producers that emphasize elegance as well as a sense of place in their wines; Giovanni Manzone does it as well as anyone in this commune. The Gramolere Barolo is a special product for this family, as Giovanni's grandfather (also named Giovanni) and later his father, purchased sections of this vineyard; today they own 12 acres of this site. Matured for two years in large casks, this has a dazzling array of perfumes (roses, bitter chocolate, dried cherry, mandarin orange), excellent persistence and firm, beautifully managed tannins. Give this time to display its best qualities; it is generally at its best from 15-25 years of age. **BRV**: 2008, 2007, 2006, 2005, 2004, 2001, 1999.

ODDERO BAROLO BUSSIA SOPRANA "VIGNA MONDOCA"

The Oddero family has been producing first-class, terroir driven examples of Barolo for several decades, long before cru Barolo became popular. The wines have always represented balance and a sense of place and their structure has assured a long life. The best evidence of that for me was tasting their 1964 Barolo at the winery in Santa Maria (a *frazione* of La Morra) in May, 2011; this was a wine that displayed extraordinary finesse and varietal character - as well as remarkable freshness – at forty-seven years of age.

Over the years, Oddero - today under the management of Mariacristina Oddero - has assembled an excellent range of cru Barolo, from sites such as Rocche and Villero in Castiglione Falletto, Brunate in La Morra and Vigna Rionda in Serralunga d'Alba. While each wine is beautifully made and an exemplary representative of its origins, I am featuring the Bussia Soprana "Vigna Mondoca" for this book, as it is arguably the most distinctive of the Oddero Barolos. The family purchased a small section of this vineyard in the late 1970s and has never replanted, meaning the vineyards are at least 35-40 years of age. The soils are more limestone than clay with the top of the hill (almost 1200 feet above sea level) looking like "lunar soil," Mariacristina once told me. This is a muscular Barolo with hefty tannins, so powerful that Oddero has made the decision to release the wine one year later than their other Barolos, in order to let the wine shed at least some of its youthful bitterness. Yet the tannins are well balanced – thirty months of aging in botti of Austrian oak aide in that – and there is tremendous depth of fruit. Even the 2007 version of this wine, from a forward, somewhat international vintage, is quite brawny and much more tannic than most Barolos from this year. This needs quite a few years to settle down and is generally at peak from 15-25 years, although a few great bottles from the finest years drink even longer. **BRV**: 2007, 2006 (outstanding), 2005, 2004 (outstanding).

ALDO CONTERNO BAROLO "GRAN BUSSIA"

Here is one of not only Barolo's greatest wines and not just one of Italy's finest wines, but to put it simply, one of the world's greatest wines. Gran Bussia is a blend of the three Barolo crus at this magnificent estate in Monforte d'Alba; the three vineyards are Romirasco (which provides the majority of the fruit for this wine), Colonello and Cicala. These are vineyards that have an average age of 40-45 years for the Colonello and Cicala and 50-55 years for the Romairasco. An important note about this wine is that is it only produced in great vintages and only when all three vineyards provide sufficient fruit of the highest quality. Thus in a great year such as 2004 there will not be a Gran Bussia bottling, as the Cicala vineyard was heavily affected by hail that year (hailstorms are an all too-often problem in this part of the Barolo zone). To date, then the wine has only been produced 14 times, from vintages such as 1999, 1998, 1996, 1990, 1985 and 1979.

The 2001 which I tasted at the winery in 2011, is a wine that leaves me searching for the proper adjectives. This is a massively concentrated wine, yet one that has amazing elegance and lightness. Displaying aromas of dried cherry, fig, cedar and hazelnut, the wine is perfectly balanced with very good acidity, firm but round tannins and very subtle oak – the wine is aged solely in *grandi botti*. This is as complex a Barolo as I have ever tasted – in fact, I am not certain I have tasted a wine of greater complexity from anywhere in the world! This is a brilliant statement about how to craft a Barolo that has superb varietal character along with amazing structure as well as being a first-rate expression of terroir from the Bussia hill of Monforte d'Alba. I estimate that this 2001 will peak in 50 years; this is an estimate beyond any I have ever made in more than 30 years of tasting wine from around the world. Thank you to the Conterno family for showing us what a truly great Barolo is all about!

BORGOGNO LANGHE NEBBIOLO

The Borgogno firm, located in the town of Barolo, has been in operation since 1761, making this one of Piemonte's most historic wine producers. Traditional Barolo, matured in Slavonian oak, has been this company's calling card for more than 150 years; even today there are several vintages of Barolo that are more than twenty years old that are available for sale at the winery. Their Langhe Nebbiolo is a lovely example of what this winery's philosophy is all about – producing wines in a traditional manner that represent a sense of place. This is basically a declassified Barolo; this is a 100% Nebbiolo from the same vineyards where their Barolos are sourced. Looking at and smelling this wine might certainly lead you to believe you are tasting one of Borgogno's top wines, as this has textbook dried cherry, cedar and sandalwood aromas, subtle wood notes and very good acidity. This is of course, lighter in body than Barolo, but this is a lovely substitute when you choose not to spend the money for that wine. Enjoy this for five to ten years after the vintage. **BRV**: 2009, 2008, 2007, 2006.

ENRICO SERAFINO NEBBIOLO D'ALBA "DIAULERI"
Nebbiolo d'Alba – 100% Nebbiolo from hills in the Roero and Langhe that are not set aside for Barolo or Barbaresco – is a nice alternative to those two famous wines; while this wine will not age as long, it is more approachable upon release and is priced at less expensive levels than its famous counterparts.

One of the most focused examples of Nebbiolo d'Alba I have tasted is from Enrico Serafino, an historic estate founded in 1878 that is now part of the Campari group of wineries (along with Sella & Mosca from Sardegna, e.g.). The company produces a few dozen wines, with the specialty wines under the Cantina Maestra label representing their finest products from their best vineyards. The Nebbiolo d'Alba "Diauleri" – a word in Piemontese dialect that means "devil" in a positive sense, that is "good chap" or "crafty individual" – is sourced from vineyards both in the Roero and Langhe districts. Medium-bodied with aromas emphasizing fresh cherry and currant fruit, this is an elegant Nebbiolo, with moderate levels of youthful tannins, good acidity and subtle wood notes (the wine is matured both in wood and steel). Enjoy this wine from three to seven years after the vintage. **BRV**: 2009, 2008, 2007.

MALABAILA DI CANALE ROERO ROSSO "BRIC VOLTA"
While Roero Arneis has become a very well known wine, Roero Rosso is still an unfamiliar product for most wine lovers. This is a shame, as it is a 100% Nebbiolo that is much more approachable than a Barolo or Barbaresco upon release and is certainly much more affordable. There are a few dozen producers that make notable examples; Malabaila di Canale crafts some of my favorites. The "Bric Volta" from vineyards in Canale (across the Tanaro River from Barbaresco) is

medium-full with appealing dried cherry, tobacco and tar aromas backed by a nicely balanced finish with very good persistence and a subtle herbal edge. As with most versions of Roero Rosso, this is about balance and drinkability, not power. The wood notes are delicate (the wine spends only eight months in oak) and in most vintages, there is very good acidity. Enjoy this from three to seven years of age. **BRV:** 2009, 2008, 2007.

BRANDINI LANGHE ROSSO

Located just outside the town of La Morra, the Brandini winery is owned jointly by New York restaurateur (and proprietor of his own winery in Friuli) Joseph Bastianich and Eataly founder Oscar Farinetti. Several local wines, such as Arneis, Dolcetto and Barolo are produced; one of their best efforts is their Langhe Rosso, a blend of 70% Nebbiolo and 30% Barbera. Extremely aromatic with perfumes of currant, red cherry and hints of tobacco, this is medium-full and quite elegantly styled, as there is very good acidity, subtle oak and impressive persistence. Above all, this is a food wine that is a pleasure to drink; it will improve over the course of five to seven years, but it can be enjoyed when released at two years of age. **BRV:** 2010, 2008, 2007, 2006.

TRAVAGLINI GATTINARA RISERVA

The Travaglini family is one of the leading producers of Gattinara, a 100% Nebbiolo (the grape is locally referred to as Spanna) from a small zone in northeastern Piemonte. They are an important producer if only for the fact that they own appoximately half of the vineyard land in this area, but the quality of their wines ensures this firm's role as ambassador for Gattinara. Soils here at elevations of 900-1400 feet are rocky and similar to the soil composition of the Alps with granite, quartz and ferous minerals, which give a reddish appearance to the earth. This terroir is expressed in the Travaglini wines, especially in the *riserva*, aged for three years in Slavonian *botti*. Medium-full, this is a traditional style of Nebbiolo that matures slowly as the youthful tannins need time to soften. As this wine is only produced in the finest vintages, the quality of the fruit as well as the wine's structure is superior (acidity is very high for a red). This is priced similar to some cru Barolos, but the comparison is a worthy one. Give this highly original wine plenty of time – ten to twelve years at least – and if you have the patience (as well as good fortune) try a twenty or twenty-five year old bottling for one of the finest examples of Nebbiolo you will ever find! **BRV**: 2006, 2005, 2004, 2001 (exceptional).

LE PIANE BOCA

The Boca wine zone in northern Piemonte, a bit north of Gattinara, is one of Piemonte's smallest. Swiss wine importer Christoph Künzli fell in love with this area and in 1998, purchased the estate of local grower Antonio Cerri, taking over his treasured inventory of wines as well; he has also purchased other local vineyards as well for production of two other wines. His Boca is a blend of Nebbiolo (Spanna) and Vespolina, a variety that brings some exotic spice and acidity to the wine; there is also a tiny percentage of Bonarda in the mix. Medium-full, this is a rich, sensual wine that ideally reflects the local terroir. Matured for eighteen months in large casks and then another sixteen months in bottle before release, this offers currant, cherry, sandalwood and balsamic aromas with rich, refined tannins, very good acidity and marvelous persistence. I have enjoyed this wine in Piemonte with *dentice*, a Mediterranean fish; the texture of the fish and the wine were a perfect match! Yet, I could also imagine this working well with veal or roast pork in a nebbiolo sauce. In a region known for its distinctive reds, this is one of the most singular! Enjoy this from five to twelve years of age. **BRV**: 2007, 2006, 2005, 2004, 2001, 1999, 1998.

SELLA LESSONA "OMAGGIO A QUINTINO SELLA"

Located just north of the Boca wine zone, the Lessona wine district – named for the eponymous town – is primarily the entity of one producer, Sella. This is an historic family in this small town, owning vineyards here since 1671; one of their estate vineyards in Lessona has been planted with vines since 1436! Several wines are produced by the family, including an Erbaluce as well as a Bramaterra red, but the finest wines here are the Lessona DOC reds. The "Omaggio a Quintino Sella" bottling, named in honor of the family member of the mid 19th century who was an engineer and economist, is a marvelous wine that rivals some of the finest examples of the more famous Piemontese reds, such as Barolo and Barbaresco.

Sourced from 50 year-old vines situated almost 1100 feet above sea level, this is a blend of 85% Nebbiolo and 15% Vespolina; made in a traditional approach, the wine is aged for anywhere from 36 to 48 months in Slavonian oak casks of 25hl. The color is beautiful – a pale garnet for the 2005, opened in 2012 – and the aromas are quite haunting with notes of orange peel and cherry; the generous mid-palate leads to a beautifully structured finish of great length and complexity. The wood notes are quite subtle and the acidity is finely tuned - you want to enjoy another glass immediately after your first. The balance is perfect and the sense of the local terroir is ideally expressed. This is a first-class, memorable, singular wine! Only a little more than 3000 bottles are produced each vintage, so this is not easy to find, but if you want to discover this gem of a wine from this special land, you should make the search! Like most great examples of Nebbiolo, this improves with several years in the bottle; this should drink well at various stages from five to twenty years. **BRV**: 2006, 2005, 2004.

Pairing the wines and foods of Piemonte – A Chef's Perspective

Carne cruda; tajarin; plin; ravioli gnocchi; ragù di salsiccia; stinco arrosto; Brasato al Barolo; cardi; bagna cauda; lingua in salsa; polenta; fonduta; tartufo. In the autumn days the perfumes permeate the roads of our little Langhe countryside and we awakenen our heart and stomach!

These are plates of long preparations from a warehouse of the ingredients and fruits of the recipes handed down from the keepers, the housewives of the families, from secrets never uncovered.

Walking in autumn along the roads of our little Langhe countryside, we take in the odors of the musts and esters of the wine. Amidst the roads, the perfume is entwined to the voices of the wholesalers of grapes and *tartufi*. And while for some, it is the hour for *caffè* or *cappuccino*, for others in the streets of the market of Alba, it is already time for the first *panino* of *salumi* and butter or a bowl of tripe to enjoy with a glass of Dolcetto.

The bonds between food and wine in the cuisine of the Langhe is inseparable; it is part of the familiar roots and it is evolved in the true and proper eno-gastronomy.

And after these digressions, we understand that wine should accompany our traditional dishes. I always recommend never beginning without an Arneis, especially if it is welcome as a fruity aperitif, served with a *focaccia* and local *salumi*, raw *salsiccia di Bra* and traditional herbed *lardo*. A Dolcetto di Dogliani, today a DOCG wine known as Dogliani, pairs with traditional *antipasti*.

And between a mouthful of *cruda* and a share of *vitello tonnato*, one certainly should move on to a Barbera d'Alba of structure for the *tajarin* with a meat sauce and finally, so we are not lacking, a Barolo to enjoy with braised beef, which can be appreciated with all the vegetables stewed with the beef.

But the menu does not always have to be so vast to be able to support such a tasting; thus for a simple dish at lunchtime, with a plate of meat ravioli (*plin*) and a mixed garden of bitter vegetables, I recommend a glass of Nebbiolo. For an excellent

Piemontese dessert, I recommend *semifreddo* of nougat and *amaretti* paired with a fresh, cold Moscato.

And then we remember the flavors, the perfumes and the odors of our land that make us remember that this combination of food and wine is something simple, everyday and so familiar!

Chef Maria Cristina Rinaudi
Ristorante Le Torri, Castigione Falletto

Valle D'Aosta

Principal Varieties

White:
Prié Blanc, Petite Arvine,
Muscat, Chardonnay

Red:
Fumin, Petit Rouge, Cornalin, Premetta,
Picotendro (Nebbiolo), Syrah, Pinot Nero, Gamay

———

LES CRÊTES CHARDONNAY "CUVÉE BOIS"

While the Valle d'Aosta region in far northwestern Italy is a relatively unknown wine territory, the Les Crêtes wine estate in Aymavilles has become quite famous, especially for this lovely white. Produced from 15-year old vines situated more than 2000 feet above sea level, this is a ripe, toasty Chardonnay fermented and aged in 300-liter French barriques. Spicy with a distinct nuttiness, this is richly textured and can age for five to seven years in most vintages. The fact that this wine from this unheralded region has been recommended by many as the finest Chardonnay produced in Italy is a great testament to proprietor Constantino Charrère.

CAVE DU VIN BLANC BLANC DE MORGEX ET DE LA SALLE "RAYON"

Founded in 1983, Cave du Vin Blanc is this region's best known cooperative winery. Situated in Morgex in western Vallee d'Aosta, they are well known for their dry white known as Blanc de Morgex et de La Salle, produced entirely from the Prié Blanc variety. They name this steel-aged version "Rayon," a synomym for Prié Blanc. Medium-full, the aromas on a young version of this wine are apple with light traces of stone fruit; this changes dramatically after a few years, as the 2008 tasted in mid-2012 was more endowed with apple cider perfumes. There is excellent persistence and lively acidity and the earthy, minerally aspects of the wine emerge when mature. A distinct, fascinating wine to be enjoyed anywhere from three to ten years of age.

LA CROTTA DI VEGNERON CHAMBAVE MUSCAT
Founded in 1980, La Crotta is a cooperative winery situated near the town of Chambave in the northeastern reaches of the Valle d'Aosta DOC zone. The Muscat, named for the town, is very dry with aromas of spiced pear, yellow flowers and applesauce. Aged only in steel tanks and in contact with its lees for several months, this is a Muscat with good weight on the palate. It also ages well, as the 2007 bottling of this wine I tasted in early 2012 displayed lovely freshness.

LES CRÊTES PETITE ARVINE
Petite Arvine is an indigenous white variety of Valle d'Aosta that is also found in Switzerland; indeed the grape is also referred to as Swiss Valais. The Les Crêtes version, sourced from vineyards in Amayvilles some 1800 to 2100 feet above sea level is a typical non-oak aged version that offers aromas of yellow peach, kiwi and yellow flower notes.

The mid-palate is quite rich with a slight oiliness, thanks to several months of lees aging, while the finish is very dry with good acidity and an earthy, almost resinous finish. Best enjoyed in its youth, the wine offers optimum drinking at three to five years of age.

OTTIN PETITE ARVINE
After working with a local cooperative for years, Elio Ottin decided to produce his own wines at his estate at Porossan Neyves, a bit north of the town of Aosta. Petite Arvine, from vineyards more than 1900 feet above sea level, has become a specialty. Displaying a straw/light copper color with aromas of mango, mandarin orange and dried pear. Medium-

full with a slight oiliness on the palate, along with good acidity and beautiful varietal character. Meant to be consumed fresh, this is at its best from two to four years.

LO TRIOLET PINOT GRIS

Marco Martin, a grape grower by trade, founded Lo Triolet in 1993; today he produces approximately 42,000 bottles per year, split among varieties such as Pinot Gris, Gewurztraminer, Fumin and Gamay. His Pinot Gris is from a vineyard near Introd in the northwestern reaches of the region; these vines are at an elevation of more than 2900 feet, making them what surely must be the highest altitude planting of this variety in the world! Fruit from this high an elevation tends to be highly aromatic, while acidity is usually quite bright. The perfumes are lovely, focusing on apricot, red apple and pear; there is a lovely mouthfeel and there is lively acidity and admirable persistence and harmony. This is definitely an Alsatian style Pinot Gris – quite dry with plenty of white spice notes. This is not a big wine, so don't wait too long to drink this – up to three years for most vintages is recommended – but this is stylishly made!

LES CRÊTES BRUT ROSÉ "NEBLÚ"

Constantino Charrère started experimenting with a classically made sparkling version of the local red variety Premetta a few years ago; the results have been quite good. Displaying a light copper color and pear, cherry and strawberry aromas, this has a light creaminess and tart acidity with a pleasing note of bing cherry in the finish. This is a delicate sparkling wine to be enjoyed with *antipasti* or lighter poultry upon release and for another year or so. More than a curiosity, this is a less acidic, rounder sparkling wine than most examples from this region.

CAVES COOPERATIVES DU DONNAS ROSÈ "LARMES DU PARADIS"

Donnas or more formally the Cave Coooperatives de Donnas was founded in 1971; today this cooperative producer has twenty members. This is a Nebbiolo rosé made in the *salasso* ("blood letting") method, also known as *saignée* in France; basically, this is free-run juice that delivers lovely fresh fruit. The aromas are of bing cherry and watermelon; medium-bodied, this is dry and delicate with good acidity. It's not a big rosé, but it's quite pleasant with a salad on a hot day; enjoy within its first twelve to eighteen months.

DI BARRÒ FUMIN

Fumin is an indigenous red variety of Aosta, with deep color and zesty fruit that is reminiscent of a Dolcetto from Piemonte. One of the best examples is made by Elvira Rini and Andrea Barmaz at Di Barrò, located in Saint-Pierre, not far from the town of Aosta. The winery's name has a double meaning; the first is a combination of letters from the last names of the founders, BARmaz and ROssan, while the second connotation refers to the word *barile*, local dialect for a large wooden cask used in area winemaking. Sourced from vineyards perched at an elevation of 2000 feet, this is a widely appealing wine, given its beautiful aromas of black plum, myrtle, blackberry and licorice; the wine ages solely in stainless steel, so as to highlight the perfumes. Fruit-forward with elegant tannins, this is enjoyable upon release and is at its best from five to seven years of age.

LO TRIOLET GAMAY

There's nothing terribly complicated about this wine; it's Gamay, steel aged with lovely freshness. But it's also very appealing with beautiful perfumes of wild strawberry, currant and dried rose petals; no doubt the bright aromatics are the result of fifteen year-old vines situated between 1900 to 2900 feet above sea level. Medium-bodied, this has pleasing tart acidity and very light tannins. Nicely balanced, this is a pleasure on its own or paired with lighter poultry dishes or very young cheeses from one to three years of age.

LES CRÊTES SYRAH "CÔTEAU LA TOUR"

As you might expect, many examples of Syrah in this far northwestern zone of Italy have Rhone-like characteristics; here is one of the best. Produced from the eponymous vineyard near Amayvilles, each vintage displays admirable ripeness, with aromas of blueberry along with notes of cinnamon and nutmeg. Aged in slightly larger than normal French barriques, the wine has lovely complexity, balance and texture and can certainly be enjoyed at seven to ten years of age, while a few top vintages drink well for another few additional years. This wine was originally labeled as "Côteau la Tour" for several years, as there was no D.O.C. designation for Syrah in the region. Regulations were changed a few years back and now this wine is labeled both with the grape type and the vineyard name. **BRV**: 2009, 2008, 2007, 2004.

DIDIER GERBELLE TORRETTE SUPERIEUR "VIGNE TSANCOGNEIN"

Torrette is one of the region's best-known reds; the wine must contain a minimum of 70% Petit Rouge. This version, made by young Didier Gerbelle at his family's estate, is from a single vineyard at Amayvilles, some 2100 feet above sea level. Blended with 30% of a mix of Cornalin, Premetta and Fumin, this is an intriguing and instantly appealing wine with its perfumes of blackberry, mulberry and charred meat. The mid-palate is quite elegant, the tannins are silky, the wood notes are slight and there is very good acidity. The big plum fruit flavors in the finish only add to this wine's overall pleasure; this is at its best from five to ten years of age. **BRV**: 2007, 2006.

DONNAS "NAPOLEON"

The red wine "Napoleon" from the Caves Cooperatives du Donnas, named for the time in 1800 when Naploeon visited this small region, is a beauty! 100% Nebbiolo, also locally known as Picotendro, is a *selezione* of their finest grapes; aged for twelve to eighteen months in mid-size casks. This has classic Nebbiolo aromas of orange peel, sandalwood, dried cherry, currant and cedar notes; offering impressive depth of fruit along with very good acidity and subdued wood notes; it tends to be at its best from five to seven years of age. **BRV**: 2007, 2006, 2004.

Lombardia

Principal Varieties

White:
Chardonnay, Pinot Bianco, Sauvignon, Turbiana,
Trebbiano di Lugana

Red:
Pinot Nero, Chiavennasca (Nebbiolo), Merlot, Marzemino,
Cabernet Franc, Cabernet Sauvignon

———

CA' DEL BOSCO FRANCIACORTA "CUVÉE ANNAMARIA CLEMENTI"
Franciacorta is Italy's finest sparking wine type, in my opinion. Actually the term Franciacorta refers to the wine itself as well as the production method (based on the classic method of Champagne where the secondary fermentation is in the bottle) and the area where the vines are planted in low-lying hills not far from Lago Iseo in Lombardia's province of Brescia. One of the very best estates in Franciacorta is Ca' del Bosco, managed by Maurizio Zanella. Every offering he produces is noteworthy, with the Cuvée Annamaria Clementi the most complete and complex. A blend of 55% Chardonnay, 25% Pinot Bianco and 20% Pinot Noir from vineyards that were planted in 1974, the wine is aged for 77 months on its own yeasts! Full-bodied with outstanding persistence, the wine is on the austere side with vibrant acidity and has an impressive perlage. The flavors are of dried pear, biscuit, peach and honey and the wine has amazing complexity and depth. This is a great wine - clearly one of the very finest sparkling wines made in Italy! This wine is generally at its best six to eight years

after the release (the release is usually eight years after the vintage). **BRV**: 2004, 2003, 2002, 1999, 1998.

BELLAVISTA FRANCIACORTA "GRAN CUVEE PAS OPERE´"

Established in 1977, Bellavista is one of the giants of Franciacorta, both in terms of size as well as quality. The style here is one of elegance, with the wines being less austere than many other producers in Franciacorta. There is a regular Brut bottling which is excellent; then there is the Gran Cuvée level, of which there are several wines. One of the very best is the Pas Operé, a blend of 60% Chardonnay and 40% Pinot Nero, produced from twenty year-old vineyards. Aged on its own lees for 60 months, the wine sports lovely aromas of pippin apple, lime and a hint of yellow peach along with a distinct yeastiness. There is lively acidity and a long, round finish with excellent persistence. The best bottlings drink well for ten to twelve years. **BRV**: 2004, 2003, 2000, 1999.

BELLAVISTA FRANCIACORTA "VITTORIO MORETTI"

This cuvée is named for Bellavista founder Vittorio Moretti; produced only on special occasions, the 2004 was only the seventh bottling of this wine. A blend of 52% Chardonnay and 48% Pinot Nero, a total of 35% of the wine was barrel fermented; the wine then spent six months in old oak barrels. The mousse and perlage are very impressive and the overall sensation is one of elegance and lightness amidst all the power. Full-bodied, the aromas are of yeast, lemon rind, quince, dried pear and biscuit.

The finish is extremely long with outstanding persistence. This is generally released seven years after the harvest and while tantalizingly delicious upon release, it will drink well for an additional 10-15 years. While many producers of Franciacorta tend to frown upon any comparison with Champagne, as they prefer that their products stand on their own, I liken this wine to the Taittinger Comtes de Champagne. Winemaker Mattia Vezzola is one of the top enologists in all of Italy and this is a great wine, easily one of the finest in the entire country! **BRV**: 2004, 2002, 1995, 1991.

CA' DEL BOSCO "CUVÉE ANNAMARIA CLEMENTI" ROSE´

Given the success of the Annamaria Clementi Franciacorta Brut, it is no surprise that Maurizio Zanella decided to add a rosé bearing this name to his lineup. Of course, this would have to be a very special rosé and indeed, this is something quite extraordinary. 100% Pinot Nero, this is one of the most deeply colored sparkling rosés I have ever experienced, displaying a deep pink, almost garnet appearance.

Once poured into a glass, the perlage simply explodes! This has a rich, meaty nose with notes of red plum, ripe strawberry and a hint of pepper. There is excellent concentration, very good acidity and outstanding persistence. The finish is extremely dry; this is an Extra Brut, as there are only five milliliters of *dosage* liqueur per bottle. Wonderfully full and complete, this is a sensational wine that is truly memorable; I believe this is among the ranks of the world's finest sparkling rosés. The 2004 bottling, released in 2012, should drink well for another three to five years. **BRV:** 2004, 2003.

Ca' del Bosco winery

LE MARCHESINE FRANCIACORTA ROSE´ MILLESIMATO

The Biatta family produces several cuvées at Le Marchesine; my favorite is the vintage-dated Rosé. A blend of Chardonnay and Pinot Nero, this is a full-bodied rosé with excellent persistence and a rich mid-palate and finish. Deeply fruity with excellent structure and lively acidity, this is a delicious wine that combines a beautiful bright strawberry color with lovely freshness as well as a beautiful combination of richness on the palate and delicacy in the finish. Vintage dated, this drinks well for five to seven years after its release.

RONCO CALINO FRANCIACORTA ROSE´ "RADIJAN"

Here is a sparkling rosé made exclusively from Pinot Nero, a bit of a rarity in Franciacorta. Displaying a lovely bright copper color, the aromas are very pretty and delicate with notes of strawberry, pear and geranium; medium-full, this has a very light feel on the palate and in the finish. The acidity is very good, but not too high and there is impressive persistence while the lengthy finish is quite elegant. Here is what finesse is all about with a sparkling wine; this is not a wine to lay away for four of five years, but what a classy offering to be enjoyed upon release and for another year or two with a variety of foods from sautéed duck breast to veal medallions.

MIRABELLA FRANCIACORTA ROSE´ "CUVÉE DEMETRA"

While I love a sparkling rosé, it's generally because the blend is primarily Pinot Noir. Here is the exception to my rule, as this cuvée has only 20% Pinot Nero with 40% Pinot Bianco and 40% Chardonnay. Aged for four years on the yeasts and then another six months after disgorgement before release, this has a lovely deep pink color, aromas of bing cherry, strawberry and dried pear and a generous mid-palate. There is impeccable balance and lively acidity; overall the wine has beautful finesse and delicacy. Enjoy for two to three years after release.

ELISABETTA ABRAMI FRANCIACORTA ROSE´

Elisabetta Abrami produced her first wines from Franciacorta in 2006 and currently produces 30,000 bottles per year. Her Rosé, a blend of

70% Pinot Nero and 30% Chardonnay, is a delightful wine, medium-bodied with good freshness and impeccable balance. This has good length and persistence in the finish, which is quite clean. This is not the most intense rosé from Franciacorta, but it is very refreshing with an elegance that I admire; this is best paired with salmon, tuna, lighter red meats or game.

IL MOSNEL SATÈN BRUT MILLESIMATO

Satèn in Franciacorta – literally "satin" or "silky" – is characterized by two things: first it must be produced exclusively from white varieties (Chardonnay, Pinot Bianco), while secondly, it is bottled under less pressure than other examples of Franciacorta, giving it a rounder, softer taste in the finish. Most of the best examples, such as the vintage-dated offering from Il Mosnel are made entirely with Chardonnay. This version, bottled after a minimum of thirty months on the yeasts, is one of my favorite examples of Satèn, with enticing lemon peel and quince aromas, excellent concentration, very good acidity and wonderful complexity. Don't let the fact that this is made entirely with Chardonnay mislead you, as this can age for up to five years after the vintage date. **BRV**: 2007, 2006.

RICCI CURBASTRO FRANCIACORTA SATÉN BRUT

Along with heading the organization that oversees rules and regulations for DOC wines, Riccardo Ricci Curbastro produces sublime examples of Franciacorta at his small estate near Capriolo. One of my favorites is the Satén, a 100% Chardonnay that is fermented in oak barrels. Medium-full, this has aromas of dried pear, lemon peel, biscuit and a light toastiness. The finish is long, the mousse is persistent and the balance is excellent. This is best consumed within three to five years after the release of the wine.

RICCI CURBASTRO FRANCIACORTA EXTRA BRUT MILLESIMATO

While the Curbastro Satén is charming and restrained, his Extra Brut is a powerful, austere sparkling wine. The cuvée is 50/50 Pinot Nero/Chardonnay; the wine remains on its lees for three and one-half years, while the dosage is extremely low (only 2/g per liter). The perlage is visually impressive in its persistence and the aromas are of dried pear, biscuit and a light nuttniess. Full-bodied, this has excellent persistence, lively acidity, a very dry finish and outstanding complexity. This can drink well for five to seven years after the vintage date - sometimes even longer. **BRV**: 2007, 2005.

ENRICO GATTI FRANCIACORTA MILLESIMATO BRUT
Established in 1975, the Enrico Gatti estate is small, producing a little more than 100,000 bottles of Franciacorta per year. The quality level is very impressive, be it the regular Franciacorta, the Satén bottling or the Rosé. My favorite is the vintage-dated Brut, a 100% Chardonnay that ages for five years on its yeasts. Medium-full, this has aromas of pear, lemon and a light herbal character (chervil, thyme) and sports a long finish with excellent balance and persistence. This is an outstanding wine and in my opinion, is more complex than many of the more expensive bottlings of Franciacorta from other producers. **BRV**: 2006, 2005, 2004.

LA MONTINA FRANCIACORTA EXTRA BRUT MILLESIMATO
Brothers Vittorio, Gian Carlo and Alberto Bozza are the proprietors at this medium-sized estate in Monticelli Brusati in the central eastern section of the Franciacorta wine zone. They produce several examples of Franciacorta, including an unusual Rosé Demi-Sec; their most accomplished cuvée has been the Extra Brut Millesimato, which is made only from the best years. A blend of 55% Chardonnay and 45% Pinot Nero, the wine is aged in oak barrels and spends sixty months on the lees. Medium-full with a very fine stream of bubbles, this has expressive aromas of quince, apples and passion fruit, lively acidity and a light minerality in the lengthy, beautifully structured finish. Offering marvelous complexity, this can improve for two to three years after its release. **BRV**: 2006, 2005.

MONTE ROSSA FRANCIACORTA BRUT "CABOCHON"
The Rabotti family established Monte Rossa in the 1970s; today, the winery is recognized as one of the finest and most consis-

tent in Franciacorta. The wines are rich, extremely well balanced and very flavorful. Their best wine is the vintage-dated Cabochon, a blend of 60% Chardonnay and 40% Pinot Nero, all from estate vineyards. The wine spends 40 months on its yeasts and is matured in small oak barrels. The aromas are of dried pear, honey and vanilla, the mid-palate is extremely rich and the complexity is striking. This is generally best from five to seven years after the vintage. **BRV**: 2008, 2005, 2004.

GUIDO BERLUCCHI FRANCIACORTA "PALAZZO LANA EXTREME"

Founded in 1961, the Guido Berlucchi firm is one of the oldest in Franciacorta. The Palazzo Lana line is relatively new for this firm; it represents the finest they can produce. The Extreme bottling is a vintage-dated 100% Pinot Nero, partly fermented in small oak barrels; the wine spends 48 months on its yeasts. The aromas are of sour cherry, currant and a hint of blackberry and while quite rich on the palate, this offers a great deal of finesse and a long, flavorful, delicate finish.

ANDREA ARICI FRANCIACORTA "DOSAGGIO ZERO" MILLESIMATO

This new project from businessman Andrea Arici is restricted to wines that receive no dosage. The vintage-dated wine is 100% Chardonnay from older vineyards that were formerly abandoned; Arici worked with local farmers to have them brought back to life. This is a particular wine, offering the strong toasty flavors, very high acidity and austerity of a classic Champagne such as Bollinger. This is a notable bottling of Franciacorta that is at its best three to five years after release. **BRV**: 2008, 2005.

FERGHETTINA FRANCIACORTA EXTRA BRUT MILLESIMATO

The Gatti family has made this estate into one of the benchmarks of Franciacorta. The Extra Brut is a blend of 80% Chardonnay and 20% Pinot Noir that ages for 72 months on its yeasts! This is a toasty sparkling wine with aromas of pear, candied fruit and almond. Full-bodied with a delicate mousse and very fine bubbles, this is a powerful Franciacorta that can age for five to six years after its release. This is a sublime sparkling wine that shows how complex and refined Franciacorta can be when given the utmost care. **BRV:** 2006, 2005, 2004.

CAMOSSI FRANCIACORTA BLANC DE NOIRS MILLESIMATO

Brothers Claudio and Dario Camossi produced their first sparkling wines at their small cellar in Erbusco in 1996. There are several cuvées made here, ranging from a delicious Rosé and Satèn to the more full-bodied examples of Brut and Extra Brut. The Blanc de Noirs is a new wine here; I tasted the 2008 bottling at a visit to the winery in the fall of 2012. Produced entirely from Pinot Nero, this has a lovely brilliant copper color and very fine bubbles, with beautiful aromas of plum and sour cherry. The rich mid-palate leads to a long, slightly earthy finish of very good freshness and impressive length. Look for this to be drinking well for another two to three years.

SAN CRISTOFORO FRANCIACORTA PAS DOSE´
BRUT MILLESIMATO

Founded in 1992 by Bruno Dotti and his wife Claudia Cavalleri, San Cristoforo is an example of a Franciacorta winery that should be better known. Every product is well made, with fine balance and structure. The Pas Dosé, which has no dosage, is made entirely from Chardonnay, and features aromas of ripe apple, vanilla and white spice. Medium-full, the acidity is lively and the finish is quite flavorful. The wine is at its best five to seven years after the vintage date.

MAZZOLINO BRUT BLANC DE BLANCS / CRUASE´

Franciacorta is not the only notable sparkling wine in Lombardia; the *metodo classico spumanti* of Oltrepò Pavese from the southwestern reaches of the region are lovely wines. I have chosen two from the esteemed producer Mazzolino, located in Corvino San Quirico. The Brut Blanc de Blancs, made entirely from Chardonnay is medium-bodied with appealing apple peel, lemon and white flower aromas with very good ripeness and acidity. The finish is beautifully structured and the mouthfeel is impressive.

Even better is the Cruasé, a 100% Pinot Nero sparkler; the name comes from the words "cru and "rose"; this is a specialty of Oltrepò Pavese. The Mazzolino version, sporting a lovely pale salmon color, spends eighteen months on the lees and delivers beautifully pure bing cherry and strawberry fruit perfumes along with a touch of honey. Medium-full with a frothy mousse and very good acidity and persistence, this is quite complex, nicely balanced and remarkably delicious! Enjoy upon release and over the next two years.

RAINOLDI VALTELLINA SUPERIORE "INFERNO"

The Valtellina wine producing zone is located in far northern Lombardia, not far from the Swiss border. The principal grape is Nebbiolo, which is known locally as Chiavennasca. Vineyards are generally located on steep terraces in order to give the vines moderate growing conditions, as the morning and afternoon sun in this area can be quite scorching. The name Inferno gives you an idea of how hot temperatures here can get; this is one of the sub-zones of Valtellina and the soils are among the rockiest. The aromas are of cherry, plum and black spice and the wine is medium-full with rich tannins, as is usual for the variety. These are more approachable examples of Nebbiolo as compared with Barolo; this wine is at its best ten to twelve years after the vintage. Rainoldi ages this wine for fifteen months in barriques, yet the wood notes are quite subtle. This is a wine of excellent complexity as well as richness and power. **BRV**: 2006, 2005, 2004, 2002.

SANDRO FAY VALTELLINA SUPERIORE VALGELLA "CARTERIA"

Sandro Fay established his winery in 1973 and today is considered one of the cutting edge producers of Valtellina. This wine is produced from Nebbiolo grapes sourced from the Cateria vineyard in the Valgella sub-zone; the plantings are situated at an elevation of 1500 feet. The wine goes through malolactic fermentation in barriques and is then matured for twelve months in similar barrels. Medium-full with ripe aromas of licorice, cherry, paprika and pepper, the wine has a long, flavorful finish with firm tannins and good acidity. This is at its best starting seven years after the vintage and can age as long as twelve to fifteen years from the finest years. **BRV**: 2007, 2006, 2004, 2002, 2001.

AR.PE.PE VALTELLINA SUPERIORE SASSELLA "ROCCE ROSSE RISERVA"

Ar. Pe. Pe refers to Arturo Pelizzatti Perego, who founded this firm in 1984. This is an ultra traditional producer, aging the wines in large casks. This particular wine ages in cement and steel tanks for five years and then chestnut barrels for a period of three to four years! Produced solely from Nebbiolo, the wine has a beautiful deep garnet color and offers aromas of dried cherry, currant, cedar and truffle. Medium-full, the wine has a long finish with velevety tannins and very good acidity. The wine is at its best anywhere from 10-20 years after the vintage. **BRV**: 1999, 1997, 1996.

MAMETE PREVOSTINI SFORZATO DI VALTELLINA "ALBAREDA"

While a Valtellina Superiore is produced in a fashion much like most red wines the world over, Sforzato (sometimes known as sfursat – loosely translated as "forced"), is produced using the *appassimento* process, as in Amarone, where the grapes are naturally dried for several months in special temperature and humidity controlled rooms. In Valtellina, these rooms are actually small buildings known as a *fruittaio*. This wine from Prevostini is produced from grapes sourced from the Grumello and Sassella sub-zones; drying of the berries lasts until the end of January; the wine is aged in barriques for eighteen months. Medium-full, the aromas are of blackberry, coffee, tar and licorice. The tannins are firm, but well balanced and there is a distinct herbal note in the finish. This generally drinks well for ten to twelve years after the vintage. **BRV**: 2007, 2006, 2004.

NINO NEGRI SFURSAT DI VALTELLINA "CINQUE STELLE"

Founded at the end of the 19th century, Nino Negri is one of the reference points in terms of Valtellina estates. The winery produces as many as three different versions of Sfursat each vintage; the Cinque

Stelle ("five stars") is their most refined. This is a selection of the finest Chiavennasca grapes from the best sub-zones of Valtellina; the grapes are dried for three months and the wine is aged for a period of sixteen months in new French barriques. Medium-full, this is as elegant and as polished a Sforzato as you will find, but more, it is a wine of outstanding complexity and style. There is a vast array of flavors, from cherry and berry fruit to coffee, balsamic and licorice and the overall sensation is one of finesse, as the finish is quite long with polished tannins. The wine is quite approachable upon release, but optimum enjoyment is from seven to ten years after the vintage. **BRV**: 2007, 2006, 2003, 2001.

FRECCIAROSSA CROATINA
Frecciarossa represents a great deal of history in the Oltrepò Pavese district, dating back to 1920, when wine was sold not in bottles, but rather in barrels and demi-johns. Margherita Odero, a descendant of the founders of the estate, is the current proprietor and she has upgraded and modernized the cellars and vineyards. Her version of Croatina – also known as Bonarda in this zone – is a delightful wine, one with aromas of black raspberry, black plum, tar and dark chocolate aromas. Medium-full with an elegant finish displaying moderate tannins and good acidity, this has subtle oak influence, despite the fact that is was matured for eighteen months in small and mid-size French oak. I love the balance and purity of this offering; it's not a powerful wine, but one that caresses you! Enjoy this from five to seven years after the vintage date.

CASTELLO DI LUZZANO BONARDA "CARLINO"
At this beautiful estate in Rovescala not far from the border of Emilia-Romagna in southern Lombardia, Giovanella Fugazza oversees production of wines from two DOC zones: Colli Piacentini and Oltrepò Pavese. This wine made from Bonarda (also locally referred to as Croatina) is not the typical Oltrepò wine, but it is quite special. Aged only in steel tanks and displaying aromas of wild strawberry, currant and rhubarb, this has very good acidity (a signature of this variety),

modest tannins and a light earthiness in the finish. This is a nicely balanced wine with a light rustic edge that is a delight to enjoy, especially paired with local *salumi* or lighter pastas. Drink from three to five years of age.

Veneto

Principal Varieties

White:
Garganega, Trebbiano di Soave, Glera, Pinot Bianco,
Chardonnay, Sauvignon

Red:
Corvina, Rondinella, Corvinone, Molinara,
Cabernet Sauvignon, Merlot

———

ADAMI VALDOBBIADENE PROSECCO SUPERIORE BRUT "BOSCO DI GICA"

For years, Prosecco from the Conegliano Valdobbiadene area of the Veneto has been a light, refreshing sparkling wine meant for immediate consumption. Produced from the Glera variety (almost exclusively, though small percentages of other varieties are allowed) and produced according to the Charmat method, Prosecco has gained great popularity around the world. Recently however, several dozen producers in this zone have refined their production methods, crafting special bottlings of Prosecco that offer more expressive aromas as well as greater complexity. One of the best producers of high quality Prosecco is Adami. Their Bosca di Gico offering displays lovely aromas of white peach, honey, jasmine and madarin orange backed by a rich mid-palate and a finish with good length and impressive persistence. This is first-rate, reasonably priced Prosecco with a lot of style!

VILLA SANDI VALDOBBIADENE SUPERIORE CARTIZZE "VIGNA LA RIVETTA"

One of the prized vineyards – actually a large hill – in the Valdobbiadene zone is Cartizze, which is recognized as something of a grand cru for Prosecco. There are several dozen owners of this 250-acre site, each producing a few hundred to a few thousand bottles of Cartizze, almost always in an Extra Dry style. One of the most renowned is that of Villa Sandi, one of the area's best-known producers. Straw in appearance with good persistence in the perlage, there are golden apple and citrus fruit aromas, a clean, elegant entry on the palate and very good complexity. Drink this over 12-18 months after the release.

BISOL VALDOBBIADENE SUPERIORE CARTIZZE

Bisol has been one of the leading producers of Prosecco from the Valdobbiadene area for many years and their range of products is one of the most varied in this zone. Their Cartizze is from a plot on this famous hill approximately 1000 feet above sea level, which ensures good structure as well as beautiful perfumes from the cool temperatures. The aromas are quite exotic, with notes of lemon oil, magnolia blossoms and grapefruit; medium-full, this is round with very good persistence and a lightly sweet finish. Unlike most Prosecco, this can drink well for two to three years after release. **BRV**: 2010, 2009.

SORELLE BRANCA PROSECCO "PARTICELLA 68"

The sisters Branca produce exemplary versions of Prosecco, the finest being this offering from a hill in the town of Colbertado. Particella 68 refers to the official plot number of this hill where the grapes are grown. Made from a blend of 90% Prosecco, 5% Bianchetta and 5% Perera, this has textbook Prosecco aromas of white peach and pear along with notes of acacia flowers and hawthorn and is medium-bodied and dry with very good persistence. There is lovely texture and a mid-palate that offers more depth than most bottlings of Prosecco. While this needs to be consumed at an early age, this will be in fine shape within a year or two after release, thanks to its structure, balance and concentration.

MEROTTO PROSECCO VALDOBBIADENE SUPERIORE RIVE DI COL SAN MARTINO MILLESIMATO BRUT "CUVEE DEL FONDATORE GRAZIANO MEROTTO"

While it may be a bit difficult to remember this name, one taste of this wine will make the effort quite memorable! The Merotto winery dates back to 1936; today Graziano Merotto produces several top cuvées at his winery in Col San Martino in the heart of the Prosecco Valdob-biadene zone. This bottling is a *millesimato* – vintage dated – and has a beautiful appearance with lovely, frothy foam. The white peach and lemon peel aromas are quite charming and there is very good depth of fruit and a long, satisfying dry finish. The best Prosecco seem to me to be weightless; this offering fits that manner beautifully. This is best consumed within 12-18 months after release.

ASTORIA PROSECCO VALDOBBIADENE SUPERIORE MILLESIMATO RIVE DE REFRONTOLO "CASA VITTORINO" BRUT

Giorgio and Paolo Polegato established Astoria in the town of Refron-tolo in the center of the Prosecco zone near Valdobbiadene back in 1987. Their success both in the cellars as well as in the marketplace has been quite notable, as Astoria Prosecco is seen in events ranging from the Giro d'Italia bicycle race to film festivals. Lest one think that they are merely reaching for publicity, try a glass of their Brut "Casa Vittorino." Offering intense aromas of peach and lemon peel, this has very good concentration, lovely freshness and is dry with a slight bit-terness not often found in most examples of this wine. This is a deli-cious sparkler on its own, or enjoyed with risotto with vegetables. **BRV**: 2011, 2010.

PERLAGE PROSECCO "ANIMAE"

This artisan producer of Prosecco has been certified organic since 1985 and starting in 2005, has been a Demeter-certified farm. Their most distinctive wine is the "Animae" which is believed to be the first-ever Prosecco made without added sulphites; it also has extremely low sugar – around 3 grams per liter, similar to a Pas Dosé style of Franciacorta. Sourced from vines averaging eighteen years of age some 800 feet above sea level, the must is fermented for four to six months, much longer than most examples of Prosecco. This does not display the simple white peach and citrus aromas of most Prosecco, rather this offers notes of herbal tea, caramel, dried pear and brown sugar on the nose; medium-full, this has lively acidity and excellent complexity. Enjoy this upon release and for another one to two years. **BRV**: 2011, 2010.

NINO FRANCO PROSECCO BRUT "RIVE DI SAN FLORIANO"
Today in America and other countries, Prosecco is a smashing success, as there are dozens, perhaps hundreds of labels that fill the shelves of markets. But a little more than a decade ago, it wasn't like that as Prosecco was unknown to most consumers. It took the work of a few key producers to introduce this wine abroad; one of the most prosperous was Primo Franco, third generation of his family to manage the Nino Franco estate in Valdobbiadene. The wine that paved the way for this producer was their "Rustico," a delightful, so typical Prosecco that is still quite popular today.

A few years ago, Primo introduced a new cuvée entitled "Rive di San Floriano," a 100% Glera from the eponymous vineyard. Medium-full and quite dry, this has lemon peel and ginger aromas; after a few years, a slight vegetable note (green beans) can also be detected in the nose. Offering excellent complexity and structure, this has become one of the finest examples of the new direction of Prosecco. Enjoy this upon release or over the course of four or five years after the vintage date.

MIONETTO SPUMANTE EXTRA DRY "SERGIO"
Mionetto has been one of the producers that has put Prosecco on the map, especially in the United States. There are several products

of varying levels of sweetness as well as price. The Sergio bottling, though not technically a Prosecco, is from this same area and is their winery's version of the heights that sparkling wines of this zone can achieve. Produced primarily from the Glera grape (formerly known as Prosecco) along with other local varieties, this has white peach, apple and floral aromas, medium-body and an off-dry finish. The complexity and freshness are quite something on this wine, as is the beautiful bottle design. Here is a sparkling wine with beautiful roundness and expressive flavors that makes for a lovely aperitif or an accompaniment to lighter seafood.

LE VIGNE DI ALICE ROSATO BRUT "OSÉ"

"La vita per noi é una bollicina" – "Life for us is a sparkling wine" (or bubble, if you will); this is the motto of Cinzia Canzian and Pier Francesca Bonicelli, proprietors of Le Vigne di Alice a few miles north of Conegliano. Named for Alice, the grandmother of Cinzia, this is a solid producer of Prosecco Superiore and a few other bubblies. I admire the winemaking here and am delighted with the quality, especially with the Extra Dry, which is much drier than most Prosecco of this designation. But I'm really a fan of their rosé named "Osé", a blend of 90% Glera and 10% Marzemino. It's technically not a Prosecco, but it is a beautifully made wine with strawberry, pear and *frutti di bosco* flavors, lovely complexity and a dry, delicate finish. This is not a wine to be laid away for several years; rather, enjoy it upon release by itself or even with lighter white meats or duck breast.

VIGNALTA PINOT BIANCO "AGNO CASTO"

Founded in 1980, Vignalta is an attractive winery producing charming whites and reds from the Colli Euganei area of Veneto, a bit south of Padua. The name of the wine is derived from an ancient vine that grew in the botanic garden of Padua for more than 500 years. A blend of 90% Pinot Bianco and 10% Incrocio Manzoni, this is produced only in the finest vintages. Steel aged, this offers aromas of white peach, yellow flowers and a note of thyme. Medium-bodied, there is a light touch of minerality;

enjoy this within two to three years of the vintage, though it sometimes is fine at five years of age.

ZENATO LUGANA RISERVA "SERGIO ZENATO"

The Lugana DOC zone is located in the western reaches of Veneto, with vineyards in the shadow of Lake Garda. The primary grape is Trebbiano di Lugana, while small amounts of other varieties may be used. The Zenato estate at Santa Cristina specializes in Lugana, producing both a steel-aged version as well as this lovely barrel-fermented and matured offering. The wine has a golden yellow appearance and rich aromas of Anjou pear, pineapple and hints of apricot. Medium-full, this is quite lush on the palate with excellent complexity and beautiful texture. This is best consumed within five to seven years of the harvest.

MONTE DEL FRÁ CUSTOZA SUPERIORE "CÀ DEL MAGRO"

Custoza or Bianco di Custoza is a Venetian white that has a little of this and a little of that; in fact, it's difficult to find a local white variety that's not part of these blends. The production area is southeast of Lake Garda and the basic varieties are Garganega and Trebbiano; this version from Monte del Frá also includes Cortese, Malvasia, Chardonnay, Riesling Italico and Incrocio Manzoni (I told you there were a lot of varieties in this wine!). This particular bottling is from a 40 year-old vineyard and displays intriguing aromas of quince, cinnamon, yellow poppies and a hint of fig. Aging on its lees in steel tanks for four months gives this wine a rich mid-palate and extends the finish; there is very good acidity and lovely freshness. Owner Marica Bonomo is proud of this wine and rightfully so! I would love this wine with a simple vegetable risotto; enjoy from three to five years of age.

INAMA SAUVIGNON "VULCAIA"

While Stefano Inama is best known for his single vineyard offerings of Soave, he also produces excellent Sauvignon Blanc. The regular Vulcaia bottling is made from Sauvignon grapes grown in the Soave area; the clones are from the Loire Valley. Steel tank fermented and aged, this is a very rich dry white with vibrant acidity and lovely fresh pear and spearmint flavors. This is a cleaner, more fruit-driven version of Sauvignon than found in Friuli or Alto Adige; drink within two to three years of the harvest.

CANTINA DEL CASTELLO SOAVE "CARNIGA"

This winery, situated directly in the shadow of the famed Soave castle, is headed by Arturo Stocchetti, one of Soave's true gentlemen. He produces three bottlings of Soave Classico, each made with the two principal grapes of the district: Garganega and Trebbiano di Soave. As this acreage of this latter variety is shrinking in Soave, as growers are not replanting it due to various reasons (it is not as resistant to mold as Garganega, e.g.), you see fewer examples of Soave containing Trebbbiano di Soave in the final mix. This is a shame as the variety has exotic aromas of honey and kiwi that work beautifully with the honeydew melon and cherry blossom aromas of the Garganega variety.

The Cantina del Castello Soave Classico normale has 10% Trebbiano in the blend; steel-aged, this is one of the best examples of this wine type each year. The "Pressoni" from the vineyard of the same name, located just east of the town of Soave, has 20% Trebbiano to go with the 80% Garganega. This vineyard is farmed in the traditional pergola system, where the canopy is overhead and provides shade for the clusters. Medium-bodied, this is a delicious wine with a light minerality. The Carniga is from a vineyard situated just west of the town; unlike Pressoni, this site is farmed according to the more modern Guyot system used throughout much of the world. This is a blend of 80% Garganega and 20% Trebbiano di Soave and offers more exotic aromas of hibiscus, pineapple and quince, no doubt a reflection of the site. Medium-full, with very good acidity, persistence and complexity, this wine also has a nice touch of minerality in the finish. This is generally at is best five to seven years after the vintage – yes Soave, when made from the best grapes by the best vintners ages beautifully! **BRV**: 2010, 2009, 2008, 2007, 2005.

CA' RUGATE SOAVE CLASSICO "MONTE ALTO"

Ca' Rugate in Monteforte d'Alpone has some of the most beautiful pergola vineyards in Soave Classico. Organically farmed, the vineyards are the source for several excellent bottlings of Soave, including the basic San Michele bottling as well as the Monte Fiorentine offering. The Tessari family that manages these vineyards has been producing Soave since 1986 and today winemaker Michele Tessari does a brilliant job crafting various styles of Soave, be they steel-aged or barrel-fermented and matured.

The Monte Alto, like the other wines is 100% Garganega, but this wine differs as it is aged in oak barrels unlike the other cuvées that are steel-aged. The Monte Alto is also fermented in oak barrels, both in barriques of 225 liters as well as *botti grandi* of 20 hectoliters. While most examples of Soave are not oak aged, this wine is an outstanding example of how wood can be integrated with the finest Garganega bunches to produce a Soave Classico of great complexity and structure. Here is a wine that displays typical varietal aromas – pear and melon - along with subtle vanilla notes; there is a creaminess on the palate and a long, sensual finish with a slight nuttiness. This generally needs at least two or three years after release to show its best qualities. The wine ages beautifully, often showing well after a decade. **BRV**: 2010, 2009, 2008, 2006, 2005, 2004.

AGOSTINO VICENTINI SOAVE SUPERIORE DOCG "IL CASALE"

Not every notable Soave comes from the Classico zone; here is proof of that. Agostino and Teresa Vicentini own 30 acres of land in Colognola ai Colli, west of the Classico area where they grow grapes for the production of Soave and Valpolicella as well as some delicious cherries. The couple produce a very fine Soave (non DOCG) named "Vigneto Terre Lunghe" from estate fruit that has 10% Trebbiano di Soave and sports textbook melon and white peach aromas. The Il Casale, a richer, more complex wine, is a Soave Superiore DOCG, aged solely in steel tanks, that is released a year later than the Terre Lunghe. The wine is a sheer delight, a 100% Garganega of beautiful varietal purity with aromas of yellow peach, Bosc pear and acacia flower backed by lively acidity and impressive concentration and persistence. This wine typically is at its best three to five years after the harvest. **BRV**: 2010, 2009, 2008, 2006.

PIEROPAN SOAVE CLASSICO "CALVARINO"
PIEROPAN SOAVE CLASSICO "LA ROCCA"

Leonildo Pieropan is arguably the most renowned vintner in Soave. His wines represent the Garganega variety and the Soave Classico area as brilliantly as any producer. The Pieropan estate was established in 1890; today Leonildo is aided by his wife, Teresita and their two sons, Andrea and Dario. There are three Soave Classicos produced: a *normale*, Calvarino and La Rocca. Calvarino is sourced from a single vineyard at an elevation of 650-1000 feet above sea level; the soils are of clay and basalt and the training system is pergola. First produced in 1971, Calvarino is a blend of 70% Garganega and 30% Trebbiano di Soave; a mix that harkens back to decades ago when the latter variety made up a large percentage of most examples of Soave. The vines at Calvarino ("little Calvary", referring to the difficulty of farming this plot) are between 40 and 60 years old and are low-yielding, delivering wines of great concentration. Fermented and aged in glass-lined steel tanks – this wine sees no wood aging – there are enticing aromas of honeydew melon, Bosc pear and lilacs. Medium-full, this has excellent persistence, lively acidity and beautiful structure. Here is a Soave than can age 15-20 years from the finest vintages! I recall tasting the 1989 version of this wine with Teresita Peropan at the winery in 2004; the wine had amazing freshness and complexity and seemed to me to have enough character and stuffing to drink well for another ten years.

La Rocca is made from the similarly-named vineyard on the Monte Rocchetta hill, just below the Soave castle. Situated some 650-1000 feet above sea level, the soils are a mix of clay and chalk and the training system is the modern cordon spur. First produced in 1978, La Rocca is different from Calvarino in several ways; first, it is produced entirely from Garganega and those grapes are picked later than normal, generally at the end of October. Also, the La Rocca is given wood aging, first with a short maceration in 25- hectoliter barrels and then maturation for one year in barrels ranging in size from 500 to 2000 liters. Deep yellow with exotic aromas of golden apples, Anjou pear, magnolia and mango, this is medium-full with excellent concentration, superb persistence and beautifully defined acidity. While the La Rocca may not age quite as long as the Calvarino, 10-12 years is fairly common for this wine. Best recent vintages for both the Calvarino and La Rocca include the 2010, 2009, 2008 (especially brilliant), 2005, 2004 and 2001. Incidentally, Pieropan has recently produced his first offerings of Amarone; his version of this powerful Veronese red is among the most elegant you will find, which should come as no surprise to anyone who recognizes the harmony in every bottle of his Soave.

GINI SOAVE CLASSICO "CONTRADA SELVARENZA VECCHIE VIGNE"

Anyone who doubts that Soave can age needs to taste this wine from the Gini brothers, Sandro and Claudio. A blend of 90% Garganega and 10% Trebbiano di Soave, the wine is fermented in wooden casks and then matured in barriques for six months. The aromas display notes of Anjou pear, heather and lilacs and there is excellent depth of fruit and well as outstanding persistence and lively acidity. Rather than overwhelm the fruit, the oak aging merely adds some texture to this wine along with subtle spice. While quite enjoyable upon release, this is much better with time and generally at its best 7-10 years after the vintage; in some cases, 12-15 years. **BRV**: 2009, 2008, 2006, 2005, 2004.

FILIPPI SOAVE CLASSICO "MONTESERONI"

Filippo Filippi is one of a small group of artisan producers in Soave that are crafting offerings that are several steps above the light, refreshing wine many people still associate this area with. Filippi is constantly experimenting with various styles- some of his wines are made from late harvest grapes – and the results are quite special. I first encountered his wines when I tasted his 2008 Castelcerino Soave, which had a chalkiness in the finish that was very similar to a first-rate Chablis: it was then I knew I had to visit theis estate and find out more about this winemaker and his products. The Monteseroni Soave Classico is sourced from vines planted in the 1950s and has vibrant aromas of Bosc pear and acacia flowers with impressive concentration and a strong sense of minerality. This is best consumed five to seven years from release. **BRV**: 2009, 2008, 2006.

FATTORI SOAVE "MOTTO PIANE"

Antonio Fattori is a wonderful winemaker, but first and foremost, he is a thoughtful man who continues his family tradition (he is a third generation vintner) of crafting the most elegant examples of Soave that he can. What I like about him is his lack of ego, preferring to talk about his wines, the vineyards he works with and the winemaking decisions he encounters. The results are quite special for his various versions of Soave as well as his Recioto di Soave. The dry offering of Motto Piane – there is also a Recioto di Soave labeled as Motto Piane – is made from 100% Garganega grapes that have been dried for 40 days. Deep yellow with aromas of Anjou pear, golden apples and magnolia flowers, the wine has excellent concentration and a generous mid-palate. The finish is quite lengthy and the wine overall has lovely balance as well as deep varietal purity and impressive complexity. An additional five to seven years of cellaring after the release will bring forth greater complexities. **BRV**: 2011, 2010, 2009, 2008.

ANSELMI CAPITEL FOSCARINO

Roberto Anselmi marches to a different drummer than most of us. A rebel, he does things his way and his results as a winemaker have been pretty spectacular. Back in the 1990s, he decided to stop using the term Soave for his wines as he believed that the regulations to produce this wine were too broad, resulting in too many dull, one-dimensional wines. To Anselmi's thinking, Soave had an inferior image, so he elected not to be associated with the Soave consorzio, labeling his wines with proprietary names under the IGT Veneto Bianco banner. The Capitel Foscarino is from a famed cru in the Soave Classico area; this wine is a blend of 90% Garganega and 10% Chardonnay. The secret to the complexity in this non-oak aged offering is that Anselmi lets the wine age for six months on its own lees in steel vats. Medium-full, here is a lovely white with beautiful texture and richness as well as very good acidity. The optimum drinking period is five to seven years. **BRV**: 2010, 2009, 2008, 2005.

Vineyards at Castelcerino, Soave Classico zone

COFFELE RECIOTO DI SOAVE "LE SPONDE"

While the beginnings of viticulture for the Coffele family in Soave date back to 1928, the modern history started in 1971, when they first produced wines under their own label. Today, winemaker Alberto Coffele and his sister Chiara, run the business on an everyday basis, along with their parents Giuseppe and Giovanna. The entire range of Soave offerings are produced here, from the traditional dry Soave Classico to Soave Spumante, both dry and sweet. Among the finest wines each year is the dessert wine, "Le Sponde" Recioto di Soave. Produced entirely from Garganega grapes sourced from their estate in Castelcerino, this is the traditional wine made by a process of hanging clusters of grapes in a special temperature and humidity controlled room for several months and letting them dry naturally (this is the *appassimento* process, as also practiced in Valpolicella for the production of Amarone and Recioto della Valpolicella). The grapes are then put into small oak barrels, fermented and aged for 10-12 months before bottling. Medium-sweet, the wine is quite rich on the palate with a distinct nuttiness in the finish that accompanies flavors of apricot, honey, caramel and Scotch whiskey. The wine is appealing upon release, but clearly becomes rounder and more complex after five to seven years in the bottle, while it peaks as long as ten to twelve years after the harvest. **BRV**: 2009, 2008, 2006, 2004, 2001.

CA' RUGATE RECIOTO DI SOAVE "LA PERLARA"
Most Soave producers make a Recioto di Soave, but few do it as well as Ca' Rugate. Certainly the grapes from the winery's estate vineyards in Monteforte d'Alpone have much to do with the wine's success, but it is also expert handling of these grapes in the cellar by winemaker Michele Tessari. The Garganega bunches are dried naturally for a period of six to seven months, as they shrivel and intensify in flavor. They are then fermented in barriques, where the wine stays in contact with its own lees. The resulting product is medium-full and slightly lush with rich aromas of pineapple, apricot and almond; medium-sweet, there is very good natural acidity to keep all the components in harmony. This is ultra appealing and delicious upon release, but is displays its finest sensations some seven to ten years after the harvest. **BRV**: 2009, 2008, 2006, 2004, 2001.

FATTORI RECIOTO DI SOAVE "MOTTO PIANE"
Along with his Soave "Motto Piane" (mentioned earlier), Antonio Fattori also produces a Recioto di Soave with the Motto Piane label. Produced entirely from Garganega from vines averaging fifteen years of age, the grapes are dried for five to six months and are fermented in a combination of oak barrels and stainless steel tanks. Medium-full with gorgeous aromas of pineapple, apricot and herbal tea, the wine has a lush mid-palate and a lengthy finish with beautiful acidity and

ideal balance. From the best years, the wine should drink well seven to ten years after the harvest. **BRV**: 2009, 2008, 2005, 2004.

LA CAPPUCCINA RECIOTO DI SOAVE "ARZIMO"

I've known Sisto Tessari and his sister Elena of La Cappuccina for about ten years; they are warm, gracious people who always have a smile on their face and are happy to have you try their wines, especially at the restaurant of their brother Simone! They produce some very impressive versions of Soave, but I just love this *recioto*; deep amber gold with appealing aromas of honey, apricot and marzipan, this is medium-full and slightly lush with very good structure and acidity. This is best enjoyed with almond or honey-based pastries on just on its own; peak drinking is generally from seven to ten years of age. **BRV**: 2009, 2008, 2007, 2006.

PIEROPAN RECIOTO DI SOAVE "LE COLOMBARE"

Recioto di Soave comes in various styles, ranging from lightly sweet to rather lush and full-throttle. Here is one of the most delicate and elegant bottlings. Produced from Garganega grapes from a vineyard planted in 1980, the wine is made from grapes dried on bamboo racks in a special room known as a *fruittaio* and then fermented and aged in 25 HL *botti*. Medium-full, this displays aromas of apricot, mango, lemon oil and a hint of almond. This is lightly sweet with a lovely freshness and there is cleansing acidity that keeps everything in check. Best consumed seven to ten years after the harvest. **BRV**: 2009, 2008, 2005, 2004, 2001.

MONTE DEL FRÁ BARDOLINO

Bardolino is the delightful red wine produced from vineyards that abut Lake Garda. Made from similar varieties as in Valpolicella to the east – Corvina, Corvinone, Rondinella and others such as Molinara and Dindarella – this is a wine meant to charm and enchant, one fashioned for early consumption. The Monte del Frá version, made from a blend of Corvina, Rondinella and a small amount of Sangiovese, is a typical offering with its fresh red cherry fruit, soft tannins and good acidity. It's nicely balanced and is really quite a tasty young red wine that is a nice alternative to the big reds of the Veneto as well as the rest of Italy.

LE FRAGHE BARDOLINO

"I don't want to make wines to discuss, just to drink," says proprietor Matilde Poggi of Le Fraghe. Given that, I hope she'll forgive me as I point out the beauty of her estate Bardolino, a wine she has been making from her family's vineyards since 1984. A blend of 80% Corvina and 20% Rondinella – a much higher percentage of Corvina than the typical Bardolino – this has intriguing aromas of black pepper, blueberry and cocoa. Medium-full with notable persistence, very good acidity and lovely focus, this is a complex Bardolino that always remains gentle on the palate – nothing is forced with this wine, which is what you would expect from this charming and graceful woman. Enjoy this from three to five years of age.

COSTADORO BARDOLINO CHIARETTO BRUT

My, how the producers of Bardolino along the shores of Lake Garda have fun! They produce Bardolino, a charming red, from the same grapes used for Valpolicella and of course, they also make one of Italy's finest *rosati*, Bardolino Chiaretto. To top if off, they also make a sparkling Bardolino Chiaretto. This has a deep strawberry color and expressive mousse; the aromas are of dried cherry and pear with notes of rye. Medium-bodied, this is dry and the finish offers very good persistence and freshness. This is not a wine to lay away for five years or more, but it does drink well a year or two after release. This *spumante* from the estate of Giovanni and Valentino Lonardi will surprise you with its richness and complexities!

ZÝMĒ VALPOLICELLA "REVERIE"

Here is a lovely wine from a remarkable producer. Celestino Gaspari is the son-in-law of the late Giuseppe Quintarelli, one of the most renowned vintners in Italy. Gaspari worked at his cellars in Negrar for more than a decade; he used that experience to establish Zýmē in nearby San Pietro in Cariano in 2003. This humble Valpolicella, a blend of Corvina, Rondinella, Corvinone and Oseleta, is made in the style of easy-drinking Valpolicella of days past, when the aim of a producer was to make a wine for youthful consumption – how nice that Gaspari has recalled that time! Sourced from young vines and aged only in steel, this has inviting aromas of currant, wild strawberry and nutmeg; medium-bodied with modest tannins and good acidity, there is a light note of pepper in the finish. Enjoy this charming wine with *salumi* or lighter pastas from one to three years of age.

VILLA BELLINI VALPOLICELLA CLASSICO SUPERIORE "TASO"

How's this for a novel approach? At her estate in San Pietro in Cariano, Cecilia Trucchi decided to stop producing Amarone after ten years in order to focus on Valpolicella. Her reasoning? "I wanted to redeem Valpolicella in order to give this historic wine its due, as it was being overwhelmed by Amarone." As you might imagine, her Valpolicella is something quite special, with rich black plum, myrtle and Queen Anne cherry aromas, excellent depth of fruit and a lengthy, beautifully structured finish. Traditionally aged in large casks, this is a marvelous example of how complex and ageworthy Valpolicella can be. Enjoy this up to seven years after the vintage. **BRV:** 2009, 2008, 2007, 2006.

Cecilia Trucchi

VENTURINI VALPOLICELLA CLASSICO SUPERIORE

There are so many elegant and delicious wines made at this small winery in San Floriano that I wasn't sure which wine I would select. While the regular Amarone is outstanding in most years, I opted for the Valpolicella Classico Superiore, in part as it represents this wine style as well as that of any of the area's producers. The grapes are sourced from vines averaging 30 years of age, which are planted entirely in the pergola system. A blend of Corvina, Rondinella and Molinara, the wine is aged in oak barrels for twelve months, followed by six months in bottle before release. Offering lovely perfumes of Queen Anne cherry and strawberry jam, this is medium-bodied, with moderate tannins and very good acidity. This is an understated, supple Valpolicella with excellent freshness and wonderful typicity. Enjoy this within three to five years of the vintage.

TEDESCHI VALPOLICELLA CLASSICO SUPERIORE "LA FABRISIERA"

Few producers give as much attention to a Valpolicella wine as does Tedeschi. This historic family estate in Pedemonte in the Valpolicella Classico district specializes in Amarone as well as Valpolicella Classico. The La Fabrisiera Valpolicella is sourced from grapes in the western reaches of the Classico zone; traces of limestone are intermixed with clay soils. The grapes are left to ripen a bit later and combined with very low yields (akin to an Amarone), this results in a wonderfuly concentrated Valpolicella, a wine that has much more weight and complexity than a typical Valpolicella Superiore. Bing cherry, herbal tea and dried plum aromas lead into a wine of excellent persistence and notable spice along with very good acidity. This is not a Ripasso wine, as are many examples of a Valpolicella Superiore, but rather a rich Valpolicella that stays true to its heritage while delivering impressive complexity. This drinks best three to seven years after the vintage.

CA' LA BIONDA VALPOLICELLA CLASSICO SUPERIORE "CASAL VEGRI"

Owned by the Castellani family, Ca' La Bionda is situated in Marano in the heart of the Valpolicella Classico zone. Sitting down with Alessandro

Castellani is quite an experience, as he tells you about his vineyards and production methods; he does not utter a word about points or ratings, preferring to let the wines speak for themselves. Every wine here is given great attention, especially this single vineyard Valpolicella Superiore. It is important to note that Ca' La Bionda does not produce a Ripasso, so this is a true Valpolicella, made according to traditional methods. A blend of 70% Corvina, 20% Corvinone and 10% a mix of Rondinella and other local varieties, the wine is matured primarily in *grandi botti* while about 10% is aged in barriques. The aromas are of fresh cherry along with notes of cedar and tar; medium-full, the wine has excellent persistence, medium-weight tannins and a light hand with the oak. Generally this wine is at its best some five to seven years after the harvest. Recently the winery released the 2001 after ten years in wood, labeling it as "Decenalle." Tasted in early 2012, the wine was notable not only for its elegance and traditional Valpolicella style, but also its amazing freshness. **BRV:** 2009, 2008, 2007, 2006, 2005, 2004.

ROMANO DAL FORNO VALPOLICELLA SUPERIORE "MONTE LODOLETTA"

In every wine zone throughout Italy, there are a few individuals who have redefined greatness; in Valpolicella, Romano Dal Forno is one of those men. He produces meticulously crafted Valpolicella and Amarone from tiny yields from vineyards in the Illasi Valley, in the eastern reaches of the Valpolicella zone. He uses new oak exclusively for his wines, which are deeply concentrated and need years to show their best after release. For the Monte Lodoletta Valpolicella Superiore, Dal Forno dries all the grapes in the *appassimento* process, giving this Valpolicella the properties of an Amarone. The wine certainly has the body and intensity of most versions of Amarone; the aromas are of black raspberry, cassis and violet and there is extremely impressive concentration. Here is a Valpolicella that can easily age for a decade, perhaps as long as fifteen years from the finest vintages. This wine is not produced every year, so it is rare and somewhat expensive, but you owe it to yourself to try this wine if you want to experience the true potential of Valpolicella. **BRV**: 2006, 2004, 2000.

BUGLIONI VALPOLICELLA RIPASSO "IL BUGIARDO"

Mariano Buglioni has made a successful transition from the textile industry to that of a wine producer. He owns an estate in Cariano and produces a variety of wines, which he just also happens to sell in his *osterie* both in Verona and Negrar. One of his most successful wines is his Valpolicella Ripasso "Il Bugiardo"; *ripasso* being a wine in between a Valpolicella *normale* and an Amarone, both in weight as well as style. Grape skins from Amarone are used in the production of Ripasso, giving this special Valpolicella more intensity and spice. This is a blend of Corvina, Corvinone, Rondinella and Molinara, made in a style with big richness and ripeness with firm tannins and plenty of spice. The wine is most assuredly modern style, but it is nicely balanced with well-integrated wood notes. This can accompany game and roasts upon release, but it is better with an additional three to five years of cellaring. **BRV**: 2007, 2006, 2004.

NICOLIS VALPOLICELLA CLASSICO SUPERIORE RIPASSO "SECCAL"

The Nicolis family has been producing honest, well made versions of the typical wines of the Valpolicella district since 1951. One of their best products is their *ripasso* "Seccal" named for their eponymous estate vineyard. Matured for sixteen months in Slavonian oak casks, this is medium-full with red cherry, cedar and dark chocolate aromas; the finish has impressive persistence with round tannins. This is an elegant *ripasso*, one that is not as ripe as some, but is instantly recognizable for its type. Enjoy this from five to seven years of age. **BRV**: 2009, 2008.

ALLEGRINI "PALAZZO DELLA TORRE"

Under the leadership of Marilisa Allegrini, this family estate in Fumane has become one of Italy's most renowned wineries. Amarone and Valpolicella, the staples of this area, are produced by Allegrini, but it has been the production of several unique red wines that have earned the greatest attention at this firm. Among those wines are La Poja, a 100% Corvina (among the first of its type) from a single vineyard as well as La Grola, a blend of Corvina and Syrah. The Palazzo della Torre, classified as a Veronese IGT (as are La Grola and La Poja), is a blend of Corvina and Rondinella, along with Sangiovese. The latter two are fermented as traditional red wines, while the Corvina is dried in the *appassimento* method; this then is a Ripasso wine. Deep ruby red with aromas of black cherry, black plum, vanilla and a hint of raisins (from the dried Corvina grapes), this offers very good concentration, a rich mid-palate, good acidity and nicely integrated wood. This is at its best five to seven years after the vintage, though it may drink well for up to a decade or slightly longer. **BRV**: 2008, 2007, 2006, 2004, 2001.

BEGALI AMARONE DELLA VALPOLICELLA CLASSICO "MONTE CA' BIANCA"

Established in 1943, the quaint family winery of Begali is located in the tiny hamlet of Cengia, a *frazione* of San Pietro in Cariano in the Valpolicella Classico zone. The quality of all the wines is quite high here, even with the Valpolicella *normale*, which is one of the finest of this type I have tasted. This cru Amarone, a blend of Corvina, Corvinone, Rondinella and a small percentage of Oseleta, is refined for four years in a combination of large and small oak casks. The aromas of black raspberry, clove, black plum, chocolate and a hint of raisins grab you right from the start and there is excellent depth of fruit and persistence. This is a great example of how elegant Amarone, a wine normally considered a powerhouse, can be. Best consumed ten to fifteen years after the vintage, this is a sublime wine! **BRV**: 2007, 2006, 2004, 2001.

ANTOLINI AMARONE DELLA VALPOLICELLA CLASSICO "MORÒPIO"

Pier Paolo and Stefano Antolini produce exquisitely balanced versions of Amarone that display beautiful perfumes as well as ideal ripeness. From vineyards in Marano, they have two notable cru Amarone: the Ca' Coato, displaying lovely red cherry and wild strawberry aromas with very good depth of fruit and the Moròpio, a glorious bottle of wine. Produced from vines that are from 30-40 years old, the Moròpio is aged in both barriques and small cherry barrels. This has similar perfumes as with the Ca' Coato along while the mid-palate and finish are longer; this is approachable upon release and drinks beautifully for 12-15 years from the vintage date. **BRV**: 2008, 2007, 2006, 2004.

QUINTARELLI AMARONE DELLA VALPOLICELLA CLASSICO

Giuseppe (Bepi) Quintarelli was a man who treasured harmony and subtlety in all of his wines. He passed away in early 2012, leaving a legacy of more than 50 years of glorious Valpolicella, Amarone and Recioto that were true calling cards for this wine zone. Quintarelli was all about tradition, maturing his wines in large Slavonian oak casks, thus ensuring that wood was a supporting player in his wines and did not overpower the fruit or dominate the finish. One of the keys to his wines was the long time they remained in wood; instead of two years, Quintarelli would keep his Amarone in casks for more than six years. I visited the estate shortly after his death and tasted through the wines with his grandson Francesco, who is taking a key role at the winery. We tasted a 2000 Amarone as well as the 2003, which was going to be released later in 2012; contrast that with most producers who were getting ready to release their 2008 Amarone!

The 2000 I tasted that day was a memorable wine, offering perfumes of morel cherry, myrtle, turmeric and even a note of cough syrup. Medium-full, the wine had an elegant entry on the palate with layers of flavor and a long, long, graceful finish with precise acidity and outstanding persistence. I noted 15-20 years for its optimum drinking potential, but I was probably being a bit conservative. This is a benchmark Amarone, one that every other producer should measure their wine against. Expensive yes, but greatness is never something that is easily attained. **BRV**: 2003, 2000, 1999, 1998.

CORTE SANT'ALDA AMARONE DELLA VALPOLICELLA

For many, Marinella Camerani is the first lady of Amarone. She established her estate in Mezzane di Sotto in the eastern half of the Valpolicella zone in 1986 and has been among the most important Amarone producers ever since. She farms organically as well as biodynamically, giving her wines a lightness and subtleness on the palate. The soils here are limestone, which is typical of the Mezzane area; they are also rather poor. Given that, the primary variety here is Corvinone, a grape with larger berries than Corvina, which is the dominant grape used at most Valpolicella estates. Camerani does not produce Amarone ever year; for example, she declined to produce a 2007 bottling, as conditions were simply too hot that year. Her Amarone is medium-full with excellent acidity and structure; this is not the mouthful of wine you experience with other bottlings, but instead a restrained style of wine that sneaks up on you. Red plum, morel cherry and violets highlight the aromas, while the tannins are restrained. The wines stand the test of time, peaking at twelve to fifteen years for a lighter vintage to twenty years plus for the richest years. **BRV**: 2008, 2006, 2004.

MUSELLA AMARONE DELLA VALPOLICELLA RISERVA
At this beautiful property in the northeastern reaches of the Valpolicella zone, Emilio and Maddalena Pasqua have assembled an impressive range of local wines, from a very good Corvina rosé to a luscious Recioto. The Amarone Riserva, from estate vineyards ranging from ten to fifty years of age, is a lovely wine with appealing aromas of myrtle, black cherry, tobacco and tar; medium-full with very good acidity, excellent persistence and a long, long finish, this is an accomplished wine that beautifully represents what a well-made, elegant, approachable Amarone is all about. Enjoy this from five to twelve years of age – perhaps longer from the finest years. **BRV**: 2008, 2007, 2006, 2005, 2004.

MASSIMAGO AMARONE DELLA VALPOLICELLA
At Massimago, a lovely farm in Mezzane di Sotto, proprietor Camilla Rossi Chauvenet turned away from her family's work in the legal profession, as she clearly preferred wine for her life's pursuit. Her Amarone, first produced from the 2004 vintage, has been especially noteworthy as of late, as evidenced by the 2007 and 2008 releases. The former displays the ripeness of that warm growing season with its red cherry and strawberry flavors; there are also notes of wood from the aging in small and large casks. The 2008 is a more refined

wine, with less obvious oak and a better overall structure; this is an Amarone of admirable restraint. The Massimago Amarone can be appreciated upon release at four years of age, but it is clearly designed to be enjoyed from seven to twelve years of age. **BRV**: 2008, 2007.

Grapes undergoing *appassimento* drying process

VALENTINA CUBI AMARONE DELLA VALPOLICELLA CLASSICO "MORAR"

Giancarlo Vason and his wife Valentina Cubi took over a 18th century estate in Fumane in 1969; today they operate out of a state-of-the-art cellar at this location. Their "Morar" Amarone, aged in various sized oak casks, is an appealing, impressively concentrated wine that offers aromas of raspberry and cumin with a delicate raisiny note. There is good acidity and the tannins, while rich, are sleek and polished. This style is so inviting when young, but it would be a shame not to age this wine for a decade or so, when it rounds out and truly displays its breeding. **BRV**: 2008, 2007, 2006, 2005, 2004.

SPERI AMARONE DELLA VALPOLICELLA CLASSICO "VIGNETO SANT'URBANO"

This single vineyard Amarone is sourced from terraced hillside vineyards at a small plot above the town of Fumane; the terrain here is a mixture of volcanic and limestone soils, lending a distinct minerality to this wine. Aged for 36 months in a combination of mid-sized *tonneaux* and large Slavonian oak casks, this is a sensual Amarone that combines flavors of maraschino cherry and myrtle with herbal notes of oregano and tobacco. This is a seamless Amarone with bright fruit expression, precise acidity and round tannins; this has been one of the most consistent examples of Amarone for the past two decades. Approachable even upon release, it is generally at peak 12-15 years after the harvest. **BRV**: 2008, 2007, 2006 (exceptional), 2004, 2001.

STEFANO ACCORDINI AMARONE DELLA VALPOLICELLA CLASSICO "IL FORNETTO"

This winery is a true family affair with Stefano being joined by his sons Tiziano and Daniele, who serves as winemaker. The Il Fornetto Amarone represents their finest offering and is produced only from the best vintages. Sourced from a vineyard in Negrar, this has a modern edge to it, as it is aged for 36 months in barriques. Ripe and forward with black cherry, tar and tobacco notes, the mid-palate is quite generous, while there is excellent persistence along with ideal acidity. The complexity and balance of this wine are very impressive; this is a classically structured Amarone. Optimum drinking depends on the particular bottling, but twenty years is common. **BRV**: 2004, 2001, 2000, 1999.

LE RAGOSE AMARONE DELLA VALPOLICELLA CLASSICO

Back in 1969, Arnaldo Galli planted vineyards high above the Negrar Valley in the eastern reaches of the Classico zone; since then his sons and he have produced one of the most classic versions of this wine. The style here is one of fullness, yet not power, a wine of great complexity as well as balance and above all, distinctiveness. Sourced from plantings in clay and limestone soils, the grapes are put through a typical three to four month *appassimento* process and then fermented with indigenous yeasts; this is followed by one year in stainless steel tanks and then four to five years – much longer than the minimum aging required – in Slavonian oak *botti*. Displaying a marvelous set of aromas- blackberry, tar, black cherry, marmalade and iodine, this has a rich mid-palate and a beautifully structured finish with very good acidity and plenty of spice. Given its long aging in large casks, this is released later than many other examples of Amarone; it also needs more time to come around and display its gifts. How nice in 2012 to taste the current vintage of this wine from 2005, while other producers are releasing their 2008s! This is a great example of what the Italians refer to as a *vino da meditazione* – a wine to reflect on and savor. Enjoying this wine at less than ten years old is a shame and in reality, this is best consumed at 15-20 years of age. An outstanding wine that is a gem of traditional philosophy in the vineyards and in the cellar. **BRV**: 2005, 2004, 2001, 1999.

BERTANI AMARONE DELLA VALPOLICELLA CLASSICO

Bertani has been one of the most important names in Amarone for more than 50 years, as they first produced this wine in the 1958 vintage. As Amarone had only been in existence for a few years – the sweet Recioto was the wine that had been produced for centuries – Bertani was clearly a pioneer in how this wine would take its shape. The owners decided that they would age this powerful wine for a lengthy period in large casks, believing this would soften and tame its aggressive nature. During a recent visit to the winery, I was given a sample of an older bottling of Bertani Amarone and asked to guess the vintage; Having tasted some gorgeous older bottlings in previous years, I knew how well the wine aged. I tried a small portion and given the color and flavors, I guessed it was the 1978; imagine my pleasant surprise when I discovered this was the 1964 vintage (labeled back then as Recioto Valpolicella Amarone Classico Superiore).

That wine had spent 14 years in wood! The size of the barrels was enormous – 120hl or 12,000 liters. Given that much time in wood, my host at the winery noted there was no sediment when he opened the bottle, as over that long period of time, all the sediment had fallen to the bottom of the cask. The wine was in magnificent shape and I noted that the 1964 had at least another 12-15 years of life ahead of it; here was a wine some 47 years old that would be drinking well on its 60th birthday!

While Bertani Amarone has undergone some changes in terms of length of aging as well as the size of the oak casks, it still is a unique product. Current vintages are aged in 65 and 75hl oak casks for six years, a much longer time than is the practice at most other estates (two to three years in 20 to 30hl is common elsewhere). Thus in 2011, the 2004 Amarone was the current release at Bertani, while many other producers had issued their 2007 on the market. The aromas are of Queen Anne cherry, cedar and nutmeg; there is impressive weight on the palate and outstanding persistence with very good acidity and silky tannins. This is an ethereal Amarone, one that has amazing complexity and richness as well as delicacy and finesse. Depending on the strength of the vintage, Bertani Amarone peaks around 20-40 years of age. **BRV**: 2004, 2001, 2000, 1999, 1998.

TOMMASI AMARONE DELLA VALPOLICELLA CLASSICO
Business today at this venerable firm in Pedemonte in the heart of the Valpolicella Classico zone is as it has been since 1902, a family affair. Giancarlo Tommasi is the winemaker, while his siblings and cousins deal with the domestic and export markets. Winemaking, while implementing modern technology, is at heart, also a matter of tradition, as their standard Amarone is aged in very large casks for a period of three years. Medium-full, this has plenty of tobacco and spice notes (caraway, thyme) to accompany its cherry and currant fruit, while the wine displays admirable balance with good acidity and refined tannins. This is not a splashy, chewy, overly ripe Amarone, but one that

is elegant and subdued in the tradition of Giancarlo Tommasi who founded this company more than a century ago. This Amarone can be enjoyed over a lengthy time span, from five to twenty years of age. **BRV**: 2008, 2006, 2005, 2004, 2001, 1999.

TENUTA SANT'ANTONIO AMARONE DELLA VALPOLICELLA "CAMPO DEI GIGLI"

If you think about it, there's nothing really out of the ordinary concerning Tenuta Sant'Antonio in Mezzane in eastern Valpolicella. After all, this is a family estate, one of hundreds, if not thousands found throughout Italy. Four Castagnedi brothers: Armando,

Tiziano, Massimo and Paolo, who had worked with their father as grape growers in Valpolicella, purchased 50 acres of vines in 1989 and soon afterwards began to produce their own wines. So what makes their wines special is the attention and pride of the brothers, who produce beautifully detailed wines in several categories, from Soave to Amarone.

Their flagship wine has been the Amarone della Valpolicella Campo dei Gigli, a selection of their finest estate grapes from pergola vineyards averaging 40 years of age, situated some 1000 feet above sea level. Primarily Corvina and Corvinone with Rondinella and small amounts of Oseleta and Croatina, the wine is fermented in wooden barrels and then matured for three years in new French *tonneaux*. Medium-full, this wine oozes with beautifully ripe black fruits – cherry, raspberry and plum – and ends with a lengthy finish with good acidity and excellent persistence along with notes of licorice and tobacco. It is in many ways a "new" style of Amarone, but it is not an international wine. The Castagnedi brothers continue to refine their wines constantly; prime evidence of that is the new 2004 Riserva Amarone, just released in November, 2012. This at its best seven to ten years after the vintage. **BRV**: 2008, 2007, 2006, 2005, 2004.

BRUNELLI AMARONE DELLA VALPOLICELLA CLASSICO RISERVA "CAMPO DEL TITARI"

Established in 1936 in San Pietro in Cariano, this small firm is under the guidance of Luigi Brunelli and his wife Luciana. There are two special bottlings of Amarone made here; the couple point to the "Campo Inferi" as the wine of Luciana, as it is a more graceful, feminine offering. The "Campo del Titari," is a more masculine wine, one, as Luigi describes it, that "pulls no punches." Made only in the finest years, the grapes for this wine are sourced from an estate vineyard planted in the pergola system; soils are limestone with numerous rocks. Matured for three years in new French barriques, there are oaky notes in the aromas along with dark chocolate, dried cherry and notes of Asian spice, yet the tannins are graceful and the balance is quite impressive. This is modern in its approach, but has a fine sense of place and breeding. This is meant for optimum enjoyment from ten to twelve years of age. **BRV**: 2007, 2006, 2004.

TEDESCHI AMARONE DELLA VALPOLICELLA CLASSICO "CAPITEL MONTE OLMI"

Any study of Amarone from the Classico zone should include this cru from Tedeschi. Capitel Monte Olmi is situated on a hill near Pedemonte some 1000 feet above sea level; the vineyard has an ideal southwestern exposure with the vines currently averaging twenty years of age. While the 1964 vintage was the first labeled as Monte Olmi, the wine was probably made before that as well, as the family purchased this site in 1918. A blend of 30% Corvina, 30% Corvinone, 30% Rondinella and 10% assorted varieties in the vineyard, this is traditionally aged in Slavonian oak for a period of two to three years. Medium-full, with aromas of tobacco, black cherry, black plum and clove, there is excellent depth of fruit and an earthy finish with ripe fruit notes. This wine stands the test of time quite well, as the 1999 version, tasted in 2011, was a wine with ten to twelve years of life ahead of it; the 1991 tasted the same day was nearing peak, but would hold for another five to seven years. **BRV**: 2007, 2006, 2005, 2004, 2001, 1999.

ZENATO AMARONE DELLA VALPOLICELLA CLASSICO RISERVA "SERGIO ZENATO"

This family firm produces Amarone in a style that more producers should aim for; elegance, finesse and roundness. The *riserva* offering, named for the man who founded the winery back in 1960, is made from grapes at estate vineyards in Sant'Ambrogio in the western reaches of the classico zone and contains a small percentage of Sangiovese in the blend along with Corvina and Rondinella. *Appassimento* lasts for three to four months; the grapes are placed in small trays that are spaced so that there is proper air circulation for drying. After fermentation, the wine is aged in large Slavonian oaks casks for 48 months. Medium-full, this has a rich mid-palate with layers of flavor along with a lengthy finish with excellent persistence, silky tannins and very good acidity. This is an Amarone of uncommon grace and harmony even upon release, although the wine drinks well for as long as 20 years after the harvest. **BRV**: 2007, 2006, 2004, 2003, 2001.

MONTE DALL'ORA AMARONE DELLA VALPOLICELLA CLASSICO

At this small estate in San Pietro in Cariano, Carlo Venturini and his wife Alessandra craft lovely examples of Valpolicella, Amarone and Recioto from organically farmed vineyards. The Amarone is an especially splendid wine, a blend of Corvina (only 40%, much smaller than many other examples of Amarone from the Classico zone), Corvinone, Rondinella and Oseleta from estate pergola vineyards of limestone soil. Matured for three years in 25hl casks and then another year in the bottle before release on the market, the wine is complex, complete and quite refined. The lovely aromas are slightly high-toned in nature, with notes of currant, raspberry and Queen Anne cherry; medium-full with a rich mid-palate, this has very good acidity (especially the gorgeous 2008 version), lovely structure and ideal balance. What a pleasure to drink upon release, though it is heavenly after ten to twelve years of age. **BRV**: 2008 (outstanding), 2007, 2006, 2005.

ZÝMĒ AMARONE DELLA VALPOLICELLA CLASSICO RISERVA "LA MATTONARA"

Celestino Gaspari makes a lovely Amarone della Valpolicella about "seven out of ten years," as he says (the current release in 2012 was the 2004), but it is with this unique *riserva* bottling that he realizes his great potential. Certainly the years working for his father-in-law Giuseppe Quintarelli as well as with Romano dal Forno, witnessing first-hand two extremely different philosophies, has given him great insight into what Amarone can be; here is his ultimate offering to date. Gaspari produces this wine in only the very best years; meaning this wine is of higher quality than even his regular Amarone which is not produced every vintage – talk about strict quality control.

This is a traditionally crafted wine, fermented with indigenous yeasts in cement tanks and then matured in large Slavonian oak casks for *nine* years! Deep garnet/light ruby red in appearance, this has lovely aromas of maraschino cherry, damson plum, hints of raspberry and slight balsamic notes. Medium-full with excellent concentration, this has outstanding persistence and complexity, an ultra long finish and lovely finesse and charm. Celestino has made a great wine here, taming the beast that is Amarone and rendering it a sublime *vino da meditazione*. I tasted the 2001 in 2012 at the winery and was amazed; I expect this wine to drink well for another 12-15 years.

MASI AMARONE DELLA VALPOLICELLA CLASSICO "MAZZANO" "CAMPOLONGO DI TORBE"

Masi is arguably the most famous producer of Amarone; this firm has certainly done more than any other in terms of promotion of this iconic wine. Located in Sant'Ambrogio in the western reaches of the Valpolicella Classico district, this estate has for more than forty years been under the guidance of Sandro Boscaini, who has made Masi Amarone into one of Italy's most famous wines. Boscaini likes to say that his firm helped define the modern style of Amarone; this does not mean an international style with dominating oak and ultra ripe grapes, but modern in the sense of richness and well as cleanliness, as the wines display fullness and a sense of place while avoiding the oxidative notes that were common in versions of Amarone from the 1960s and '70s.

Masi produces several bottlings of Amarone, from a regular bottling named Costasera to a *riserva* to two separate cru bottlings, Campolongo di Torbe and Mazzano. These wines have been produced since the mid-1960s and age marvelously well. I participated in a special tasting of five decades of Masi Amarone at the winery in November, 2011; the oldest wine, the 1967 Campolongo di Torbe, was in excellent shape, as I noted that the wine could be enjoyed for another 7-10 years.

Both vineyards are in the commune of Negrar in the Classico zone; situated at 1000-1200 feet above sea level, these sites are a combination of clay and limestone (more limestone is present at Campolongo). The vines at both sites are on steep slopes and are supported by terraced walls. The wines are made with slight differences, as the drying process for the Mazzano is generally two to three weeks longer than that of Campolongo, in addition, aging takes place solely in French *tonneaux* for the Mazzano, while large Slavonian oak casks as well as French *tonneaux* are used for the Campolongo (three years of oak maturation is the norm). Both wines are very rich on the palate, offering expressive cherry and currant fruit with notes of tobacco and brown spice. The Mazzano has notes of bitter chocolate and licorice not found in the Campolongo; indeed if one were to define terroir for Amarone – a fleeting notion for a wine in which the grapes are dried for several months – one could point to the Mazzano bottling as one of the few Amarones in which there is a definite site identity.

The wines, while powerful, also have impeccable balance and in all but the warmest years, also have very good acidity, this a result of the elevation of the vines as well as the inclusion of a small percentage of Molinara in the wines, a grape Boscaini likes to use in Amarone blends to keep the wine drinkable. These wines regularly show well for 20-30 years after the harvest, with the finest bottlings drinking beautifully at 40-45 years. **BRV**: 2004, 2001, 1999, 1997.

IGINO ACCORDINI RECIOTO DELLA VALPOLICELLA CLASSICO

While Amarone has become the most famous wine of the Valpolicella zone, Recioto is the wine that has a much longer history behind it, as this is a wine that has been produced in this area for over 1000 years, as compared to slightly more than fifty for Amarone. Both wines are made according to the *appassimento* process, with similar varieties, but while Amarone is made as a dry red wine, Recioto is sweet.

The word recioto comes from *recie* meaning "ears", a reference to the tops of the grape bunches, which received the most sun and were thus riper. Today most Amarone producers also produce a Recioto, but the difference in sales is dramatic, as one producer told me that he sells ten bottles of Amarone for each bottle of Recioto. This is a shame as consumers who don't think they'd like a sweet red – or may not even understand the concept of such a wine – generally tend to love the wine once they try it.

The Recioto made at the Igino Accordini winery is just like his son Guido – honest and inviting. Guido is a farmer at heart; with him, you get what you see. He's dedicated to his vineyards and he makes wine to please himself. The quality of his grapes along with his passion equate to several lovely offerings, especially his Ripasso, his cru Amarone named "Bessole" and also his Recioto. Medium-sweet, this is a delicious wine with black raspberry, tar and licorice notes and a satisfying finish with sensations of bitter chocolate. This wine is best consumed seven to years after the harvest. **BRV**: 2008, 2007, 2006, 2004, 2001.

Guido Accordini, Proprietor, Igino Accordini winery,
Pedemonte, Valpolicella

BRIGALDARA RECIOTO DELLA VALPOLICELLA CLASSICO

At the Brigaldara estate in San Floriano in the heart of the Valpolicella Classico district, Stefano Cesari produces a magnificent lineup of local wines, products that are as refined as the man himself. I could have selected several of his wines, especially his "Casa Vecie" Amarone, a marvelous wine with outstanding complexity. I opted for his *recioto*, due not only to its purity and balance, but also its sheer pleasure. I love this type of wine, but sometimes producers can highlight the appealing fruit in favor of proper structure. Not so here, as the Brigaldara *recioto* with its big extract and concentration, also offers excellent persistence and a long, appealing finish with moderate sweetness. Enjoy this from five to ten years of age. **BRV**: 2008, 2007, 2006, 2004.

ROMANO DAL FORNO "VIGNA SERE´" (PASSITO ROSSO VINO DOLCE)

When is a Recioto della Valpolicella not a Recioto della Valpolicella? When the authorities say so! That is exactly the case with this gorgeous wine from Romano dal Forno, named for one of their best vineyards. This is a Recioto by every definition of the word, except for the fact that the tasting panel that regulates DOC quality told Dal Forno that they couldn't call this wine a Recioto; their reasoning was that it tasted "different." When I asked Romano's son Michele what that meant, he reponded, "I don't know!" The wine offers remarkable depth of fruit, as is typical for this producer, the mid-palate is layered and there is outstanding persistence with moderate sweetness. Tasted in early 2012, the current 2004 release showed beautifully, but it was clearly an infant of a wine; my estimate is that this wine will be at its best in some 12-15 years, thanks to its massive concentration as well as overall balance and acidity. **BRV**: 2004.

QUINTARELLI RECIOTO DELLA VALPOLICELLA CLASSICO

The Recioto made at Quintarelli is one of the best balanced, most graceful versions of this wine you could ever imagine. Made only in the best vintages - generally three or four times every ten years - the wine is given the utmost care in the cellar as the grapes are dried for a full five months and then matured in very small (3.5 liter) oak casks for seven to eight years! Cassis, black raspberry and purple iris aromas highlight the wine, which has excellent depth of fruit and an ultralong finish with cleansing acidity. The complexity of this wine is off the charts – I've never tasted a Recioto della Valpolicella that exhibits this sort of class, breeding and finesse. The current vintage I tasted at the winery in January 2012 was, believe it or not, the 1997 – talk about taking your time with releasing a wine! I noted that this wine will drink beautifully for another ten years or so. **BRV**: 1997 and 1995 (note that the next vintages to be released will be the 2001 and 2003).

ASTORIA REFRONTOLO PASSITO "FERVO"

Here's a neat dessert wine that you rarely hear anything about. At their vineyards in the hills of Conegliano, Prosecco producer Astoria grows Marzemino and produces a sweet red using the *appassimento* system, naturally drying the grapes on bamboo racks for three months; the result is pretty special. Inky purple, this displays aromas of myrtle, purple iris, black raspberry and tar. Medium-full with very good acidity and moderate tannins, there is a distinct bitter chocolate note that emerges in the finish. Lightly sweet, this develops a longer mid-palate and finish after an additional year in the bottle; it should drink beautifully for seven to ten years after the vintage. **BRV:** 2009, 2008, 2007.

Trentino

Principal Varieties

White:
Nosiola, Gewürztraminer (Traminer), Riesling Renano,
Moscato Giallo, Müller-Thurgau, Peveralla, Pinot Bianco,
Chardonnay, Sauvignon

Red:
Marzemino, Pinot Nero, Lagrein, Cabernet Sauvignon,
Cabernet Franc, Merlot, Syrah, Carmenere

———

FERRARI GIULIO FERRARI RESERVA DEL FONDATORE BRUT
Trentino is south of Alto Adige and while the region is officially
referred to as Trentino-Alto Adige, the two zones are generally dis-
cussed in different evaluations. A strong point of winemaking in Trentino is classically made sparkling wine and no one does it any better
here than the company of Ferrari. The firm produces several sparklers,
all excellent, but it is their Giulio Ferrari bottling, made from grapes
originating in a vineyard some 1700 to 1900 feet above sea level that
is their finest. 100% Chardonnay aged on its own yeasts for as long as
ten years, the wine has tremendous weight on the palate as well as an
extremely long finish with vibrant acidity. There are aromas of grapefruit, pear, caramel and biscuit, while the perlage is persistent with
very small bubbles. Offering outstanding complexity and character,
this can be enjoyed twelve to fifteen years after the vintage date.
BRV: 2001, 2000, 1999, 1998.

FERRARI ROSE´ "PERLE´"

While the Ferrari Giulio Ferrari Riserva impresses with its remarkable structure and breeding, the firm's Perlé Rosé dazzles you with its vivaciousness. First produced from the 1993 vintage, this is a blend of 80% Pinot Nero and 20% Chardonnay; the grapes are sourced from estate vineyards situated 985 to 1970 feet above sea level. The brilliant copper color is eye-catching and the aromas of fig and plum are lovely and quite focused. The perlage is very persistent and ultra fine – what a treat to just look at this wine in the glass! Medium-full with excellent concentration, this offers beautiful ripeness, lively acidity and a rich finish with excellent persistence. This is ultra delicious and quite simply one of the finest sparkling rosés I have tasted from anywhere. The wine spends at least five years on its own lees and is generally released at six years of age. Enjoy this up to seven to ten years after the vintage date. **BRV**: 2006, 2005, 2004.

LETRARI BRUT RISERVA

Another excellent sparkling wine from Trento is the Brut Riserva from Letrari. A blend of 60% Chardonnay and 40% Pinot Nero, the wine sports a deep yellow color along with an impressive perlage. Medium-full with a rich mid-palate, the wine displays aromas of golden apples, pears and cedar. Aged for 48 months on its yeasts, this is quite rich on the palate with excellent complexity, lively acidity and good backbone. Drinkable upon release, the wine is usually at its best within the first three to five years.

LETRARI BRUT RISERVA 976 "RISERVA DEL FONDATORE"

This cuvée, named for Leonello Letrari, "the young lion" who established his family winery in Rovereto in 1976, is the finest example of sparkling wine from this firm and is truly one of the best in all of Italy. A 50/50 blend of Chardonnay and Pinot Nero that is aged for the amazingly lengthy period of 96 months on its yeasts, this has very a bright yellow appearance with very fine bubbles and a very persistent perlage. Offering excellent complexity, this has aromas of apple peel and dried pear along with a light toastiness, while there is excellent acidity and outstanding depth of fruit on the palate an the finish. This current release in 2012 was the 2000 vintage, which displayed excellent freshness; it should be in peak form in another 3-5 years. While this can certainly stand up to rich seafood and some white meats, this is such a marvelous wine that I prefer enoying this with a simple plate of sautéed scallops.

SAN MICHELE NOSIOLA
Founded in 1874, the Istituto Agrario San Michele is an enological school, carrying out all sorts of research for the region and helping farmers with their work. They produce several lines of wine under their own label; I am impressed with the Nosiola, made from the local indigenous white variety. From pergola vineyards first planted in 1989, this is vinified in a traditional method, aged in stainless steel and given several months of lees aging. The aromas of chamomile, hawthorn and lemon zest are quite lovely, backed by a rich-mid palate, sleek finish and lively acidity; there is a light touch of minerality along with notes of white spice. Enjoy this from two to four years of age.

VALLARIUM "VADUM CAESARIS"
The name of this excellent white is translated from Latin as "the stream (or shallows) of Caesar," a reference to the fact the Julius Caesar crossed the Adige River not far from this estate. This area is the Vallagarina in southern Trentino not far from the border with Veneto. This is a blend of primarily Pinot Bianco with the remainder Chardonnay, Riesling and Sauvignon Blanc. Medium-bodied, this has pleasant apple and green tea aromas, but it is in the finish, with notes of saffron and dried oranges, where the wine takes on its own unique character. There is good acidity, very good persistence and complexity; slightly earthy, this is meant to be consumed from two to five years.

FORADORI GRANATO
Elisabetta Foradori, truly a beautiful individual, has accomplished much since her first vintage back in 1984 at her family winery in Mezzolombardo. While she crafts lovely white wines made from the indigenous

Nosiola variety, she is best known for her various offerings of Teroldego, a red variety indigenous to this area. This wine is made entirely from Teroldego, which has been aged for eighteen months in wood. Deep ruby red with aromas of black cherry, currant and hints of balsamic, the wine has excellent concentration and persistence with very good acidity. Foradori has transformed her estate over the years and now farms in a biodynamic method and has experimented with *amphorae* – clay pots – for aging her wines. Granato generally is at its best ten to twelve years after the vintage. **BRV:** 2007, 2004, 2003, 2001.

CONCILIO TEROLDEGO "BRAIDE"

Concilio is one of the oldest (founded in 1860) and largest (1500 planted acres) wineries in Trentino. There is a wide range of products; the Pinot Grigio "Giovanna Manci" and the Gewürztraminer "Conoidi" are very well made with excellent varietal character. My favorite is the "Braide" Teroldego, produced from grapes grown on alluvial soils near the Noce River. Fermented in steel and oak, this has excellent typicity, with plum, prune, tar and lavdender aromas, very good acidity and medium-weight tannins. This is a fruit-forward, elegant wine with subtle wood notes that is a pleasure to drink; peak consumption is from five to seven years.

MARCO DONATI MARZEMINO "ORME"

Marco Donati is the fifth generation to work the vines at the family estate in Mezzacorona; the company dates back to 1863. He is most famous for his Teroldego, but his Marzemino "Orme" is another of his notable red wines. Aged solely in steel tanks, this has Lambrusco-type aromas, with black raspberry and candied plum perfumes. Medium-bodied, this has good acidity, moderate tannins and a fruit-laden, elegant finish. This is the type of red that is ideal for lighter pastas or mild *salumi*; enjoy this in its youth (the wine is released within ten months of the harvest), from one to three years of age.

LA CADALORA "SAN VALENTINO"

The name of this medium-sized estate at San Margherita Di Ala near the Adige river, means "home of the ora" in local dialect; ora being the wind from Lake Garda that blows along this terrirory. Marzemino is a specialty and what a lovely version this firm has crafted with this San Valentino bottling. Offering inviting aromas of red plum, myrtle and raspberry jam along with a hint of rhubarb, this has delicious berry fruit on the palate, lively acidity, moderate tannins and beautiful varietal focus. This is a delicious version of this local variety with just a touch of wood; the focus is on the appealing varietal notes. I'd love to pair this with braised rabbit or roast chicken. Enjoy from three to five years of age. **BRV**: 2011, 2009.

ENDRIZZI GRAN MASSETO

While the label of this wine reads "Terlodego & Teroldego", don't worry, you're not seeing double. Rather this is the producer's way of letting you know this is a wine made entirely from Teroldego treated in two different fashions. One of the oldest wineries in Trentino (established in 1885), Endrizzi makes a wide range of very good varietal wines, but really sends a message with this red from vineyards planted in both the traditional pergola as well as the more modern Guyot systems. Half of the grapes are dried naturally for three months in the *appassimento* method (as in Amarone from the Veneto) and half are fermented as with a normal red wine. Deep ruby red in appearance, there are aromas of prune, ripe black cherry, *frutti di bosco* and tobacco. Medium-full to full-bodied (15% alcohol), there is excellent concentration, medium weight tannins that are fine tuned, good acidity and impressive persistence. I love the elegance for such a big wine and I'm also quite impressed by the first-rate complexity. While approachable after its release approximately four years after the vintage (the 2008 is marvelous now), this is meant for peak enjoyment seven to twelve years down the road. **BRV**: 2009, 2008, 2007, 2006, 2005.

ALBINO ARMANI CASETTA "FOJA TONDA"

While Albino Armani's winery is located in Veneto, he does produce a few wines from vineyards in Trentino. The most unique is the red made from the Casetta grape, an ancient variety that was headed for extinction before Armani rescued it; today there are a mere 35 acres in all of Italy, with Armani owning twelve, planted near the commune of Avio in the Vallagarina district, some 35 miles south of Trento. The term Foja Tonda, meaning "round leaf" refers to the variety's foliage; Armani trademarked the name and is the only producer that labels the wine in this fashion. Armani ages the wine in 45-hectoliter Slavonian oak casks, so as to let the variety's fruit notes emerge in the finished wine. Medium-full, this offers red cherry and currant aromas with a hint of cranberry; tannins are moderate, there is good natural acidity and a subtle spiciness. This wine improves over the course of a few years in the bottle (peak consumption comes around seven to ten years), but given the round tannins and bright fruit, this is a joy to drink upon release. **BRV**: 2008, 2007, 2006, 2005.

LETRARI ENANTIO

Enantio is an extremely rare variety found primarily in the southern Trentino; a few producers have combined their efforts in the Terra dei Forti wine zone. Of the approximately thirty hectares of this variety in all of Italy, Letrari has one hectare planted. Matured for one year in barriques, this has aromas of blackberry and cherry fruit along with notes of pepper, thyme and oregano. Medium-full, this has a very long, beautifully structured finish, polished tannins and balanced acidity. This is quite lovely and delicious; enjoy from five to ten years of age. **BRV**: 2008, 2007, 2006, 2005.

SAN LEONARDO "TERRE DI SAN LEONARDO"

Trentino is most often associated with cool climate varieties – white and red – yet Bordeaux varieties also perform well here, as evidenced by two reds produced at San Leonardo near Rovereto in the southern reaches of this territory. Carlo Guerreri Gonzaga has been producing Bordeaux blends from estate grapes since 1982; that was the first vintage for his San Leonardo red, which has become one of Italy's most renowned Cabernets. The "Terre di San Leonardo" is lighter, but no less stylish. This is a blend of Cabernet Sauvignon, Cabernet Franc, Merlot, Petit Verdot and Carmenere that offers complex aromas of pink peppercorn, currant and thyme, notable concentration and persistence along with very good acidity, as you would expect in this cool climate. If you didn't know, you'd swear you were tasting an actual Bordeaux instead of an Italian red wine; the style and structure are subdued, as this is not a powerhouse red, but a gracious one styled for several years in the cellar. This is at its best seven to ten years after the vintage. **BRV**: 2008, 2007, 2006.

Alto Adige
Principal Varieties

White:
Gewürztraminer, Sauvignon, Pinot Bianco, Pinot Grigio, Moscato Giallo, Riesling, Müller-Thurgau, Kerner, Sylvaner, Chardonnay

Red:
Pinot Nero, Lagrein, Schiava (Vernatsch), Moscato Rosa, Merlot, Cabernet Sauvignon

———

CANTINA TRAMIN GEWÜRZTRAMINER "NUSSBAUMER"

While Pinot Bianco is the most widely planted white variety in Alto Adige, it is Gewürztraminer, that in my opinon, which yields the finest wines. Especially notable are several bottlings from the town of Tramin (hence the name of the wine, *gewurz* or "spice" from Traminer, the town of Tramin). This cru bottling from the outstanding cooperative producer, Cantina Tramin, is my favorite and among the finest whites of Italy. The aromas are simply textbook with notes of lychee, pink roses and grapefuit and the wine has excellent depth of fruit and persistence along with outstanding complexity and harmony. While delicious upon release, this tends to show better after a year in the bottle and is generally at its best three to five years after the vintage.

J. HOFSTATTER GEWÜRZTRAMINER "KOLBENHOF"

This is another Gewürztraminer from Tramin; the Hofstätter estate, however, is not a cooperative, but a private firm, managed by the insightful and very personable Martin Foradori Hofstätter. Matured for eight months on its lees, this wine has similar perfumes to the Cantina Tramin, but it has a different mouthfeel, as there is a distinct oiliness on the palate. Quite rich, this needs a few years to come around and show its best, but when it does, it is among the finest examples of Gewürztraminer from anywhere. Enjoy this from two to five years after the vintage date.

ELENA WALCH GEWÜRZTRAMINER "KASTELAZ"
The third great Gewürztraminer from Tramin, the Elena Walch version is from a gorgeous vineyard near the winery and is ultra consistent. This is a touch lighter than the other two examples, but can generally be enjoyed a bit earlier than those wines. The aromatics however, are just as lovely, as there are notes of lychee, grapfruit and yellow roses with distinctive spice in the finish as well as lively acidity. The balance, as with all wines from this esteemed producer, is impeccable. Enjoy up to five years of age.

PETER SÖLVA GEWÜRZTRAMINER
While I adore Gewürztraminer, I must admit that some versions come off smelling more like perfume than wine. Given the striking aromatics of this variety, that's not surprising, but to be a excellent version, there has to be a solid structure behind the aromas. The regular Gewürztraminer from Peter Sölva, sourced from several vineyards near Tramin,

is an excellent example of this variety in which the aromatics are toned down, yet still unmistakably classic, with notes of lychee, yellow roses and even a hint of almond. Medium-full with impressive concentration, very good acidity and beautiful ripeness, this offers lovely complexity and is beautifully balanced. The finish and midpalate are epecially lush, making this a delicious wine! Enjoy this from one to five years of age, depending on the structure of the vintage.

CANTINA PRODUTTORI SAN PAOLO PINOT BIANCO "PASSION"
Named for the town in which the cellars are located, St. Pauls (or San Paolo, the Italian name), is located just west of Bolzano in far north-

ern Alto Adige. For this Pinot Bianco, the winery sources grapes from vineyards situated on limestone cliffs at 2200 feet of elevation; these were planted in the pergola system in 1920! Medium-full with rich texture, the wine is aged for six months in large casks, which adds a subtle touch of spice, while allowing the purity of the Pinot Bianco (also known as Weissburgunder in the region) to shine through. This is an ultra clean wine with delicious fruit and vibrant acidity; appealing upon release, the wine generally peaks at five to seven years of age.

CANTINA TERLANO PINOT BIANCO "VORBERG" RISERVA

Pinot Bianco is the everyday grape of Alto Adige, but there is nothing common about this version. From one of the region's finest cooperatives, this is a single vineyard Pinot Bianco aged for a short time in large oak casks. Displaying an array of aromas ranging from dried pea to tea leaf, the wine has marvelous texture, excellent depth of fruit and distinct minerality. This wine displays the potential and the promise of Pinot Bianco in this region and is at its best from five to seven years after the vintage. It is no exaggeration to say that this is one of finest white wines in all of Italy.

MANINCOR PINOT BIANCO "EICHHORN"

Manincor, near Lake Caldaro in the heart of Alto Adige, is a 400 year-old estate, but it is the work done by proprietor Count Michael Goëss-Enzenberg over the past fifteen years that has elevated this firm to one of this region's finest. Biodynamic agriculture – complete with a flock of sheep for natural manure – is a decision that has resulted in striking wines of great varietal intensity and power. The Eichhorn Pinot Bianco, given skin contact to derive more flavor and greater complexity, is a stunning example of how complex this wine can be; medium-full with excellent concentration, there are striking aromas of guava, quince, Bosc pear and lemon oil. There is outstanding persistence, lively acidity and marvelous harmony. This is a vibrant wine with amazing varietal focus, one that is among the very best examples of its type in this region. Enjoy from three to seven years of age.

NALS MAGREID PINOT BIANCO "SIRMIAN"

This cooperative in Nalles has been at the top of its game over recent years, producing a wide range of nicely focused whites and reds. Among their best wines each year is this single vineyard Pinot Bianco that offers enticing aromas of fresh pippin apple, pineapple and hyacinth. Medium-full with a lenghty, clean finish with very good acidity, this is nicely structured with excellent varietal focus; there's no mistaking this for anything else, as this is textbook Alto Adige Pinot Bianco. Enjoy up to three years of age.

ALOIS LAGEDER PINOT GRIGIO "PORER"

Unless you have spent the last few years traveling to another planet, you realize that Pinot Grigio from Italy has become an enormous success. As with other wine types that thrive in the marketplace, there are hundreds of inexpensive, poorly made versions of Pinot Grigio, so to combat this sea of dreariness, enter Alois Lageder with his "Porer" offering, a wine that shows the true potential of this variety. The secret is in the vineyard, some 750 feet above sea level; comprised of sand, gravel and limestone soils, the vines range from 12-35 years of age. Medium-full, this is a Pinot Grigio of richness on the palate and impressive length in the finish; the beautiful aromas of fresh apples, magnolia and cinnamon are pure and focused. Aged on its own lees, this is a Pinot Grigio with lovely texture and a lengthy mid-palate. If that wasn't enough to recommend this wine, note that this vineyard is farmed according to the Demeter biodynamic method, an approach that Lageder has been concentrating on to a greater degree over the past five to ten years. This tends to drink well up to five years of age, something not often seen with this variety.

CANTINA NALS MAGREID PINOT GRIGIO "PUNGGL"

It's clear that if a producer is going to be known for their Pinot Grigio, they need to work with the best source material. The "Punggl" offering from Nals Magreid is such a wine, as the vineyard, located 820 feet above sea level, is planted in the pergola system with vines ranging between 80-100 years of age. Matured half in steel tanks and half in *botti*, this features lovely aromas of golden apple, pineapple and hints of almond. This is a beautifully textured wine with a generous mid-palate and a lengthy, flavorful finish with very good acidity; enjoy this from three to five years of age.

KÖFERERHOF PINOT GRIGIO

Ask people throughout Alto Adige about the best wineries of the region and chances are that Köfererhof will be among their top five. That's quite a tribute to owner/winemaker Günther Kerschbaumer, who has been producing a wide variety of shimmering whites since 1995 at his estate in the Novacella in the Valle d'Isarco. The Pinot Grigio is a typically excellent wine from him with inviting aromas of ripe red apple, Anjou pear and geranium backed by impressive persistence. The acidity is quite good and the persistence is impressive as is the varietal focus. Enjoy this up to three years of age.

WEINGUT NIKLAS KERNER

A few producers in northern Alto Adige work with Kerner, a German variety that is a cross between a red (Schiava Grossa, known as Trollinger in Germany) and a white (Riesling). At Weingut Niklas in Kaltern (Caldaro), the Sölva family produces one of the most complex version in Südtirol, with Dieter making the wines from vineyards planted with cuttings his father imported some 35 years ago. The age of the vines combined with the limestone, gravelly soils yield a marvelous wine, one displaying perfumes of pear, green tea, white pepper and magnolia. Medium-full, this is very rich on the palate with a slight oiliness and a flavorful finish with notes of spearmint and ginger. Enjoy this unique offering from three to five years of age.

ABBAZIA DI NOVACELLA KERNER "PRAEPOSITUS"

The Abbazia di Novacella estate is situated in far northern Alto Adige, near the border with Austria. Their entire roster of wines – both the regular line as well as those under the Praepositus label - is very impressive, especially the Sylvaner, Müller-Thurgau, Riesling and Kerner, this last variety being a specialty of this region. The aromatic profile of the Praepositus Kerner is striking, offering perfumes of papaya, melon and orange rind; the mid-palate is very rich and the finish is long and satisfying with subtle notes of yellow spice and a delicate note of minerality. Instantly approachable, this is usually at its best three to five years after the vintage.

ELENA WALCH SAUVIGNON "CASTEL RINGBERG"

Elena Walch was trained as an architect, a profession that demands precision as well as an artistic vision and here is a Sauvignon Blanc that shares those same characteristics. Sourced from the winery's Castel Ringberg vineyards sited 1250 feet above sea level, the wine is partially barrel fermented; medium-full with beautiful aromas of pear, spearmint and rosemary, there is a long finish with a distinct herbal notes. As with all of her wines, the varietal character is first-rate! This is approachable upon release, but it is generally at its best three to five years after the vintage.

ST. MICHAEL-APPAN SAUVIGNON "SANCT VALENTIN"

While high quality wine depends most importantly on great vine-yards, a talented winemaker can also make a difference. That has cer-tainly been the case for the past decade at this cooperative where Hans Terzer has elevated this firm into one of the region's finest. This Sauvignon, made from several vineyards in Appiano at elevations ranging from 1000-1600 feet, is a flavorful and charming with aromas of white peach, figs and white flowers. Medium-full, the acidity is very good as is the overall balance and the wine is at its best three to five years after the vintage.

COLTERENZIO SAUVIGNON "LAFOA"

This cooperative is also known by its German name of Schreck-bichl, the hamlet in northern Alto Adige where it is located. The grapes are sourced from a site 1300 feet above sea level; the soils are sandy with some gravelly mineral deposits, which greatly adds to the character of this wine. Some of the grapes are fermented in steel tanks, with others fermented in large casks and barriques; the grapes that undergo wood fermentation are also similarly matured. This is a typically assertive Alto Adige Sauvignon offering excellent depth of fruit, ideal structure and vibrant acidity. Best seven to ten years after the vintage, this is an outstanding expression of Sauvignon.

MANINCOR SAUVIGNON "LIEBEN AICH"

This Sauvignon from a single vineyard of volcanic origins near Lake Caldaro, is one of Manincor's most striking wines. Fermented and matured in wood, this offers gorgeous aromas of Anjou pear, lemon rind, chamomile and grapefruit; there is impressive concentration and a rich mid-palate. There is outstanding persistence, vibrant acidity and a lengthy finish with notes of gooseberry. The herbal notes of the variety are quite subtle here; this is a delicious wine, one with great complexity and a marvelous vitality. Clearly one of the finest examples of Sauvignon in Italy, enjoy from two to seven years of age.

Vineyards at Cortaccia

ALOIS LAGEDER CHARDONNAY "LOWENGANG"

Alois Lageder can seem to do no wrong, as he weaves his magic with many varieties, be they indigenous or international. His "Lowengang" Chardonnay, produced from vineyards farmed according to biodynamic methods, is a powerful, yet graceful wine and certainly among the very best examples of this variety in the region. Fermented with natural yeasts in barriques and matured in these same small casks, this displays plush aromas of pear, grapefruit, almond and butter, while the finish is quite lengthy with excellent persistence. As with all of Lageder's wines, this ages gracefully; expect this to be at its best some five to seven years after the vintage.

KUENHOF RIESLING "KAITON"

Founded in 1990 by Peter and Brigitte Pliger, the Kuenhof estate is planted to twelve acres of varieties such as Riesling, Sylvaner and Grüner Veltliner; the location is the Valle d'Isarco – also known as Eisacktal – in far nothern Alto Adige, very near the border with Austria. The Pilgers have planted in high density fashion at their estate; the soils are compised of quartz, schist and crushed rock. The resulting wines are certainly a result of the local terroir as well as products that offer striking aromatics, thanks to the cool climes and slow ripening at these high plantings.

One smell of this Riesling and you might think you were in the Pfalz district of Germany, given the classic perfumes of apricot and petrol and even a note of green tea. Medium-full with steely acidity, this is quite dry, with a nicely structured finish with well-defined minerality. This has impressive texture and richness on the palate, yet it is quite subtle and gentle in its approach; the overall balance is exquisite. This is an outstanding wine! Enjoy this from two to as many as ten years after the harvest.

FALKENSTEIN RIESLING

One of the least known wine zones of Alto Adige is the Val Venosta, in the far northeastern reaches of the region, not far from the Swiss border. Once known only for its apples, there are now some brilliant wines emerging from this district. At Falkenstein, proprietor Franz Pratzner crafts a lovely dry Riesling that offers deeply concentrated aromas of apricot, yellow peach and a hint of saffron. Generally the aromas are a bit closed, as the wine needs time to open up and display its best qualities. Medium-full, this is quite rich on the palate with excellent persistence, lively acidity and a slight oiliness in the lengthy, well structured finish. This tends to be at peak at five to seven years of age.

STRASSERHOF SYLVANER

Given the German/Austrian influence in Alto Adige, it is no surprise that varieties from those lands, such as Riesling and Grüner Veltliner thrive in this region. Another is Sylvaner, a grape that plays second (or third) fiddle to Riesling in Germany. At Strasserhof, located at Novacella, in the extreme north of the region, winemaker Hannes Baumgartner crafts an earthy, very rich style of Sylvaner with aromas of apricot, Anjou pear and geranium; the mid-palate has layers of fruit and the earthy finish displays notes of white spice and a hint of minerality. Steel aged, this is a robust white meant for pork or veal preparations; enjoy from two to five years of age.

GARLIDER SYLVANER

At his tiny estate and cellars up a small, winding road in Velturno (Feldthurns) in the Valle d'Isarco, Christian Kerschbaumer practices organic farming, producing miniscule amounts of finely tuned wines from several local varieties, such as Pinot Grigio, Müller-Thurgau, Gewürztraminer, Grüner Veltliner and this marvelous version of Sylvaner. Displaying a bright, light yellow color and intriguing aromas of yellow peach, apricot and herbal tea, this is medium-full with very good concentration, impressive acidity, very good complexity and striking minerality. Aged only in steel tanks to preserve the delicate fruit, this is instantly appealing and quite delicious and may make you think again about the potential of Sylvaner. This has the richness and structure to drink well up to five years of age.

CANTINA TRAMIN "STOAN" (DOC Alto Adige Bianco)

This melange of Chardonnay, Sauvignon, Pinot Bianco and Gewürztraminer is a great representation of the allure of Alto Adige whites. Sourced from vineyards at elevations ranging from 1300 to 1800 feet that were planted in stages from 1984 to 2002, this is a fragrant, spice-driven white with gorgeous aromas of red apple, pear, grapefruit and kiwi. Offering a generous mid-palate, this has outstanding persistence and complexity with striking minerality in a finish that seems to go on forever. At its best five to seven years after the vintage, this is truly one of Italy's finest and most distinctive white wines! **BRV**: 2011, 2010, 2009, 2008 (outstanding), 2007.

CANTINA TERLANO "NOVA DOMUS"

This brilliant cooperative producer makes so many first-rate wines; their "Nova Domus" blend of Pinot Bianco, Chardonnay and Sauvignon is a stunner. Fermented in large barrels, the wine goes through partial malolactic fermentation and is then aged on its lees in both large and mid-sized casks. This is a lush, somewhat oily white with perfumes of dried pear, fig and yellow flowers; there is lively acidity and excellent persistence and hints of white spice in the finish. It's difficult to taste only one sip of this wine, as it's delicious and has such great complexity. The winery's regular bottling of Terlaner (this is a Terlano DOC) is legendary for its amazing aging potential; this wine drinks well from five to seven years of age, but even as long as ten to twelve years from the best vintages.

COLTERENZIO MOSCATO GIALLO "SAND"

Moscato Giallo or Goldmuskateller is a specialty of Alto Adige, a lovely aromatic white fermented to dryness. This version from Colterenzio is from twenty year-old pergola vines some 1300 feet above sea level, situated just south of Girlan, near the town of Cornaiano. The grapes are cold-soaked after pressing, which heightens the varietal perfumes and the wine is matured for six months in steel tanks on its lees. Offering enticing aromas of yellow peach, lemon zest, orange blossom and magnolias, this is medium-full with lively acidity and a clean, flavorful finish. This is best enjoyed in its youth, from two to three years of age; it is a natural with Oriental or Thai cuisine.

GEORG MUMELTER ST. MAGDALENER CLASSICO

I love how many "little" red wines that are produced throughout Italy. Tradition has something to do with the reason these wines exist, but I'd also like to think that this has much to do with the Italian way of slowing down and enjoying life; thus not every red wine has to be made to age for a decade or longer.

One of the most charming is St. Magdalener in Alto Adige (also known as Santa Maddalena, if you prefer the Italian name). The wine, named for the eponymous town just north of Bolzano, is made from a minimum of 90% Schiava, while Lagrein and/or Pinot Nero are also allowed in the blend. As Schiava has extremely light tannins, this is a red wine that is often served with a slight chill, making this a fine choice during the summer months. The wine also has high acidity, so it's a fine choice to start a meal, especially paired with *salumi*. The Mumelter version from his estate farm known as Griesbauerhof, is a lovely example of this wine, offering fresh morel cherry and wild strawberry fruit with a hint of clove. It's tasty, always delicate on the palate and quite refreshing; it's a wine to enjoy at one to three years of age, no more. You just have to love the simple charms of this wine!

GIRLAN VERNATSCH "GSCHLEIER"

Established in 1923, the Girlan cooperative winery, located in Cornaiano, just southwest of Bolzano, today has approximately 200 grower members in northern Alto Adige. One of their most alluring wines is this Vernatsch (a synonym for Schiava) from the Gschleier district near the winery. While most examples are meant for immediate consumption, this wine is much more concentrated, as it is sourced from vines some 80 to 100 years old. Pale garnet with aromas of myrtle, currant and cardamom, this has excellent persistence, very good acidity and typically delicate tannins. Beautifully balanced, this is a delight to drink upon release or it can be enjoyed after another two or three years.

PRANZEGG "CAMPILL"

This wine is proof that even a humble grape such as Schiava can be cultivated to produce an outstanding wine. Sourced from vineyards near Bolzano that range from 30 to 80 years of age (the average age of the vines are 45 years), this is primarily Schiava (about 95%) with small percentages of Lagrein and Barbera. Proprietor Martin Gojer tells me that this is his "most important wine," and it shows in the seductive aromas of strawberry, carnation and red roses along with the generous mid-palate and lengthy finish with lovely notes of Asian spice and nutmeg. The acidity is quite lively, wood notes are subdued and the tannins are round and lightweight. What a pleasure to enjoy this wine, one with amazing varietal character, finesse and breeding! Named for the place where the farm is located, Campill was given its moniker by the abbots who farmed this area some 1000 years ago. Perhaps this divine intervention is the reason, but it is clear that Martin Gojer was inspired when he created this singular wine! Enjoy from five to eight years of age.

J. HOFSTÄTTER PINOT NERO "BARTHENAU S. URBANO"

Few think much about Pinot Noir in Italy, yet the fact is that the variety performs beautifully in the cool climes of Alto Adige. There are two versions made at Hofstätter; the Mazzano, which is quite good and the Barthenau S. Urbano offering, which raises the bar. This offers lovely spice aromas (coriander, marjoram) along with notes of tart cherry and strawberry. Medium-full, this is a beautifully balanced wine with moderate tannins and excellent structure. The best bottlings show well for seven to ten years; the subtleties of this wine slowly emerge over that time. **BRV**: 2009, 2008, 2006, 2005, 2004.

FRANZ HAAS PINOT NERO "SCHWEIZER"

The Hass Pinot Nero is also one of Alto Adige's most notable versions of this variety. Medium-full, this has lovely floral aromas to go along with subtle spice notes as well as hints of red cherry, cola and currant. Although aged for at least a year in barriques, the oak is never obtrusive. Displaying excellent concentration, thanks in part to the use of low-yielding clones, this is a wine built for aging, thanks to very good acidity and notable structure; generally this is at its best seven to ten years after the vintage.

ABBAZIA DI NOVACELLA PINOT NERO RISERVA "PRAEPOSITUS"

Yes, white wines are the calling cards for this terrific producer, but this Pinot Nero is as accomplished a wine as any made at this estate. Sourced from vineyards more than 1100 feet above sea level, this is aged in French barriques for eighteen months, which adds complexity, yet the wood notes never get in the way of the lovely fruit. Offering aromas of bing cherry, thyme and turmeric, this is medium-full with precise acidity, medium-weight tannins and notable persistence. What I love about this wine is that while it is so instantly recognizable as Pinot Nero (or Blauburgunder, as it is also known in the region), it never shouts its intentions, as this is elegantly styled for food; power is never part of the approach here. Enjoy this from five to seven years of age. **BRV**: 2009, 2008, 2007.

CASTELFELDER PINOT NERO
"GLENER" / BURGUM NOVUM" RISERVA

Located in Kurtinig in the far southern reaches of Alto Adige, Castelfelder is managed by Günther Giovanett, who in 1989 took over operations as the winery from his father. These two examples of Pinot Noir are quite special; Both are elegantly styled; the Glener is the lighter of the two. Sourced from guyot and pergola vineyards (the latter as much as 50 years of age); the Glener has a delicate garnet color and aromas of bing cherry, strawberry and turmeric. Medium-bodied with moderate tannins and very good acidity, this is a charming wine with beautiful varietal character. The Burgum Novum Riserva, sporting bing cherry, thyme and cedar aromas, is richer on the palate with a touch more oak as well as slightly bigger tannins, yet it is not a powerful wine, but an elegant expression of this grape. One's preference of these wines may depend on the food each wine is paired with; the Glener is definitely for more delicate poultry and game birds, while the *riserva* can stand up to slightly heartier game as well as pork and veal. Peak drinking for the Glener is five to seven years, while one can expect the Burgum Novum to show its best from seven to ten years. **BRV** (both): 2009, 2008, 2007.

HARTMANN DONÀ PINOT NERO "DONÀ NOIR"

Hartman Donà, former enologist at Cantina Terlano, produces a sumptuous Pinot Nero from a vineyard planted in 1995, situated at Rungg a Cornaiano some 1600 feet above sea level. This site, combined with biodynamic farming, yields a marvelous wine, one with great complexity and structure as well as a meatiness that may remind you more of a Nuits-St. Georges Bourgogne than the typical Südtirol Pinot Nero. Offering bing cherry, red plum, cumin and coriander aromas, there is excellent concentration, a layered mid-palate, beautifully integrated wood notes and striking acidity. I've only tasted this wine once – the 2008 offering – for lunch at a restaurant in Bolzano, but was blown away by its varietal purity and delicious flavors. This 2008, the current vintage at this writing should drink well for another five to seven years. By the way, it was a perfect match with the suckling pig I enjoyed at that meal!

ALOIS LAGEDER CABERNET "LOWENGANG"

Here is one of Alto Adige's most ageworthy reds, a blend of Cabernet Sauvignon, Cabernet Franc and Merlot. The grapes, farmed according to biodynamic vineyards are from the Lowengang estate near the winery in Magré some 750-800 feet above sea level. Displaying intense fruit (black currant, black cherry) and spice (black pepper and oregano) aromas, this is a full-throttle Cabernet that has beautiful balance, very good acidity and ideal structure. Give this time to settle down, as the wine typically drinks well some seven to ten years following the vintage. **BRV**: 2008, 2007, 2005, 2004, 2001.

COLTERENZIO CABERNET SAUVIGNON "LAFOA"

This 100% Cabernet Sauvignon is made from grapes sourced from a 20-year old vineyard situated some 1300 feet above sea level. Fermented and matured in a combination of new and used French barriques, this is a rich, deeply fruity wine with black plum, black currant and chocolate aromas. Medium-full with excellent concentration and with very good acidity, this is generally at its best 10-15 years after the vintage. I love this wine's combination of varietal character and sense of place – you know right away that this is a northern Italian version of Cabernet Sauvignon. **BRV**: 2009, 2005, 2004, 2001.

CANTINA BOLZANO LAGREIN "TABER RISERVA"

Lagrein is a wonderful indigenous red variety of Alto Adige; the wines made from this grape are deeply colored (bright purple) with effusive plum and dark cherry-berry fruit, while the tannins are generally round and pleasant. This cooperative has a wide range of wines, a select few of which are single vineyard offerings. The Taber vineyard, from which this wine is made, has some vines that are more than 100 years old; these low-yielding plants ensure deeply concentrated wines. Matured in about one-third new French barriques, this is a vigorous, seductive, elegantly-made example of this variety. While appealing upon release, it is generally at its best some five to seven years after the vintage, although some of the best examples drink well a decade after the vintage.

CANTINA TERLANO LAGREIN "GRIES" RISERVA

This outstanding producer sources its best Lagrein grapes from vineyards in Gries, a suburb of Bolzano, where the alluvial soils are ideal for this variety. Matured in both large casks and small oak barrels, this offers appealing aromas of black raspberry and black plum along with notes of bitter chocolate in the finish. The oak is well integrated and the medium-weight tannins are nicely balanced. As is typical from this winery, there is excellent harmony of all components. This is generally at its best five to seven years after the vintage, though certain bottlings are in fine shape after a decade.

FRANZ GOJER LAGREIN "FURGGL"

Florian Gojer and his father Franz manage the family estate known as Glögglhof vineyard just below the church of St. Magdalena just north of Bolzano. At this farm, which has been in the family since the 14th century, Franz planted Lagrein on the plains of the Isarco River; these vineyards are set in the traditional pergola system. This Lagrein, aged in large oak casks, is bright purple with intriguing aromas of black cherry, blackberry, tar and roasted meat; there is impressive concentration. Displaying excellent ripeness and forward fruit, this needs one or two years after release to soften the youthful tannins; it is best consumed from five to seven years of age.

PRANZEGG "QUIREIN"
Here is a Lagrein given a helping hand with tiny percentages of Cabernet Franc and Teroldego. Deep purple with aromas of black raspberry, myrtle, black plum and dark chocolate, this is a seductive wine with excellent depth of fruit, good acidity, round tannins and notable persistence. This is a nicely structured wine, with beautiful varietal purity – the *frutti di bosco* flavors are wonderful - and while it's at its best at five to seven years of age, it's absolutely delicious upon release! **BRV:** 2009.

PRANZEGG LAGREIN ROSE´ "JACOB"
Given its rich fruit and deep color, it's no surprise that there are numerous Alto Adige vintners that make a *rosato* version of Lagrein. One of the most complex I've tasted is the "Jacob" bottling from Tenuta Pranzegg, owned by Martin Gojer, who crafts wines that are vibrant, complex and highly original. This is sourced from a vineyard in the commune of Bolzano with vines ranging from 15-40 years of age; the soils are predominantly sandy, ideal for enhanced aromatics and soft tannins. Displaying intense perfumes of black cherry, plum and currant, this has excellent ripeness, lively acidity, notable backbone and a very dry finish. It is appealing upon release and can improve with an extra year or two in the bottle.

ARUNDA SPUMANTE ROSE´ BRUT
There are a few hearty souls in Alto Adige that produce sparkling wine, none better than Joseph Reiterer. His cellars are located near Bolzano and are situated more than 3500 feet above sea level, the highest spar-

kling wine cellar in Europe. The Spumante Rosé Brut – made according to the classic (Champagne) method (as are all the sparkling wines here) is a 50/50 blend of Pinot Nero and Chardonnay with vibrant acidity and excellent depth of fruit. The wine features lovely floral aromas and has a rich mid-palate and good length in the finish. This wine generally drinks well for three to five years after the release.

FRANZ HAAS MOSCATO ROSA

Moscato Rosa is a variety found in Alto Adige and rarely anywhere else; Franz Haas crafts a routinely marvelous version. The wine has a lovely deep strawberry color and heavenly aromas of black raspberry, bing cherry and strawberry along with lovely floral perfumes (red and orange roses). Medium-full, the wine has a delicate sweetness with lively acidity. This is a seductive, sensual wine that is at its best five to seven years after the vintage. It's lovely on its own or paired with a berry tart or bitter chocolate.

CANTINA TRAMIN GEWURZTRAMINER "TERMINUM VENDEMMIA TARDIVA"

Cantina Tramin produces an amazing dry Gewürztraminer, so why not a sweeter version as well? This is a late harvest selection from a vineyard some 1200 feet above the village of Tramin where botrytis affects the berries. The wine is matured for a short time in wood and the result is a stunning dessert wine that is rich and lush, but quite well balanced with medium sweetness. The color is amber gold and the array of aromas is quite impressive: apricot, honey, mango and ginger. This wine ages beautifully, as it shows best some seven to ten years after the vintage, while some bottlings drink well on their 20th birthday.

J. HOFSTATTER GEWURZTRAMINER VENDEMMIA TARDIVA "JOSEPH"

Here is another impressive sweet Gewurztraminer from Alto Adige. Martin Hofstatter sources grapes from several vineyards around the village of Tramin and then crushes the grapes gently; the juice is left to clear by natural sedimentation; fermentation is in small oak casks followed by aging in small barrels for 12 months. The aromas are of lemon oil, apricot, mandarin orange and a touch of vanilla; medium sweet (the wine is labeled as a "Spätlese" for the German market), this has a long, rich finish with excellent persistence and ideal balance. What a delicious, memorable wine! This generally at its best 7-10 years after the vintage.

MANNI NÖSSING KERNER VENDEMMIA TARDIVA

This tiny estate (less than 2000 cases per year), located in the Valle d'Isarco zone of Alto Adige, is a specialist with Kerner. The dry version is routinely excellent, while this late harvest offering is outstanding. Displaying a light, bright yellow color and tempting perfumes of apricots, yellow peaches, papaya and honey, this is a marvelous wine! Medium-full with excellent concentration, this is ultra clean in the finish with lively acidity and excellent persistence. Enjoy this on its own or with a simple lemon, peach or apricot cake from five to seven years after the vintage.

Friuli Venezia Giulia
Principal Varieties

White:
Friulano, Sauvignon, Ribolla Gialla, Malvasia, Vitovska, Pinot Bianco, Pinot Grigio, Verduzzo, Picolit

Red:
Refosco, Schioppetino, Tazzelenghe, Terrano, Cabernet Franc, Merlot, Cabernet Sauvignon

———

LIVIO FELLUGA "TERRE ALTE"

Located in Brazzano di Cormons in the province of Gorizia (Colli Orientali del Friuli DOC), the Livio Felluga estate is known for their striking white wines, from the basic Pinot Grigio to several memorable blends. Terre Alte ("high lands") is the most famous and iconic from this firm. Sourced from estate vineyards in the small Rosazzo zone, this is a blend of Friulano, Pinot Bianco and Sauvignon. Each year's blend is deeply concentrated and has marvelous aromas, ranging from Bosc pear to kiwi to elderflowers with hints of saffron and chamomile emerging as well. The wine offers lovely texture and ideal structure and is one of Italy's longest-lived white wines, often in prime shape anywhere from 10-15 years of age. **BRV**: 2009, 2008 (exceptional), 2007, 2006, 2004, 2001.

LIVON "BRAIDE ALTE"

This intriguing blend of Chardonnay, Sauvignon, Picolit and Moscato Giallo from vineyards in the Collio and Colli Orientali del Friuli is a bit more forceful in its use of oak than other white blends from Friuli, but the balance on this wine is no less impeccable. Offering lovely texture and plenty of spice, this is a rich white wine that also ages extremely well, as evidenced by the 1996 vintage I tasted at VinItaly in 2010. The winemaking here is superb, as each version expresses the special characteristics of that particular vintage. **BRV**: 2009, 2008, 2007, 2005, 2004, 2001.

BASTIANICH "VESPA BIANCO"

This is a blend of Chardonnay, Sauvignon and Picolit; the first two varieties are partially fermented in large oak casks and partly in stainless steel, while the Picolit ferments in mid-size *tonneaux*. Offering tantalizing golden apple and pineapple perfumes, this has a rich, almost fat mid-palate and is always beautifully balanced with vibrant acidity; the wine increases in complexity as it ages and drink well after five to seven years in the bottle and often is at its best some seven to ten years after the vintage. This is the flagship offering of the Bastianich winery, owned by New York restaurateur Joseph Bastianich and his mother Lidia. **BRV**: 2010, 2009, 2008 (especially lovely and complex), 2007, 2006, 2004, 2001 (these last two vintages both outstanding).

ZUANI "VIGNE"

The Felluga family produces two blended whites from their vineyards in Collio; the "Zuani" bottling is aged in barrique, while the "Vigne" bottling is aged solely in stainless steel. Both are beautiful wines and of the two, I prefer the "Vigne," a blend of 25% each of Friulano, Chardonnay, Pinot Grigio and Sauvignon. Medium-full with a generous mid-palate and excellent persistence, this has lovely texture, vibrant acidity and outstanding complexity. The wine is so appealing upon release, but it ages beautifully for anywhere from five to ten years in the bottle. This has become one of Collio's signature whites. **BRV**: 2011, 2010, 2009 (outstanding), 2008, 2007, 2006, 2004.

EDI KEBER COLLIO

Edi Keber labels his white merely as Collio, as he feels the Bianco terminology is needless, given the outstanding quality of the whites in Collio; indeed this is his only white wine. A blend of Friulano, Malvasia and Ribolla Gialla, the wine spends a small time in wood before bottling. Offering excellent concentration and outstanding complexity with vibrant acidity, this is a marvelous white wine, combining power and finesse; this is, in a word, sublime! Enjoy this anywhere from two to ten years of age. **BRV**: 2010, 2009 (exceptional), 2008, 2007, 2006.

PRIMOSIC "KLIN"
Here is a gorgeous blend from Collio that should be better known. This is a melange of Sauvignon, Chardonnay, Ribolla, Friulano and Picolit that is aged for one year in barriques. Like the other examples of Collio Bianco listed here, this is quite rich with gorgeous complexity, while the oak aging here takes this wine in another direction, making it more comparable to a white Burgundy. Just great! This is at peak drinking from five to seven years of age. **BRV**: 2008, 2007, 2006.

GRADIS'CIUTTA "BRÀTINIS"
Tall, youthful and bighearted, Robert Princic has been making quite a name for himself over the past half-dozen years with his vibrant white wines at Gradis'ciutta. Named for a local hamlet near San Floriano del Collio on the border with Slovenia, this estate is best known for its Collio Bianco known as "Bràtinis," a blend of Chardonnay, Sauvignon and Ribolla Gialla. Aged only in stainless steel, the featured aromas of ripe red apples, Bosc pear and ginger are very appealing; there is lively acidity and excellent harmony throughout. This is in the style of many famous Collio whites, but the price tag is one-half to one-third of those illustrious wines; enjoy this from three to five years of age.

MARCO FELLUGA "MOLAMATTA"
I've loved this Collio Bianco for years, if for no other reason than sheer pleasure. This is a blend of Friulano, Pinot Bianco and Ribolla Gialla with lovely aromas of cranshaw melon, apple, pear and peony. Winemaker

Roberto Felluga has a very particular approach with this wine, fermenting and maturing the Pinot Bianco in wood, while treating the other varieties in steel tanks only. Medium-full with lively acidity, beautiful texture and great length, this is complex and rich, yet always delicate on the palate. It's very enjoyable upon release, but can be consumed for up to five years of age.

SCHIOPETTO BLANC DE ROSIS
Mario Schiopetto was one of the producers that moved Friulian whites into the modern era, emphasizing intense varietal fruit as a key to the success of his wines. The Blanc de Rosis is a great example of this; a blend of Friulano, Sauvignon, Ribolla Gialla, Pinot Grigio and Malvasia, this is a powerful white wine of marvelous complexity. There are aromas of pineapple and melon along with sage and a hint of caramel (especially after a few years in the bottle). Beautifully structured, this has impeccable balance; enjoy from three to seven years of age **BRV**: 2009, 2008, 2007.

JERMANN VINTAGE TUNINA
Silvio Jermann is an original, producing wines in his own uniquely singular way. He's given wine lovers a barrique-fermented Chardonnay from Friuli called "Were Dreams" as well as a Pinot Nero he labels as "Red Angel on the Moonlight." But it was with Vintage Tunina that he shook up the world of Friulian white wines, producing a bold blend of indigenous and local varieties. A melange of Chardonnay, Sauvignon, Ribolla Gialla, Malvasia and Picolit, a small part of the wine is fermented and aged in very large casks. My notes on a recent vintage I tasted will give you an idea of how distinct this wine really is, as I mention the aromas of "beeswax, dried pear, cauliflower and pink grapefruit." There is a graceful entry on the palate, good but not vibrant acidity, excellent persistence and an earthy finish. This improves after five to seven years in the bottle and is often enjoyable at ten to fifteen years. **BRV**: 2009, 2008 (exceptional), 2006, 2005, 2004.

RONC SORELI "UIS" BLANC

Ronc Soreli is an impressive new estate located just south of Prepotto in the Colli Orientali zone; Fabio Schiratti manages the property, of which a little more than 100 acres are planted to local varieties. His newest wine, "Uis" blanc, is one of the more unique blends from Friuli, an assemblage of Friulano, Sauvignon, Ribolla Gialla and Riesling; the wine is aged on its lees in steel tanks for four months. Medium-full with impressive concentration, there are aromas of dried pear, honey and chervil along with well-defined notes of lime and green tea in the well-structured finish. Though quite rich, this is a wine of great subtlety, one that should display greater complexities after a few years in the bottle. **BRV**: 2010.

RUSSIZ SUPERIORE SAUVIGNON RISERVA

Not every great white from Collio is a blend. This Sauvignon from the Russiz Superiore estate of Marco Felluga is an excellent version of this variety, offering powerful aromas of spearmint, freshly cut hay and even a touch of incense. Fermented in both oak and steel (primarily the latter), this is quite rich on the palate with a long, flavorful finish and is a textbook example of what an assertive Sauvignon from Collio is all about. This demands time in the bottle, so enjoy this from five to seven years of age. **BRV**: 2008, 2006.

VENICA SAUVIGNON "RONCO DELLE MELE"

There are two versions of Sauvignon produced by this great Collio estate: the "Ronco del Cero" bottling is a typical herbal style of Sauvignon, while the "Ronco delle Mele" bottling is more fruit driven and less aggressive. Both are first-rate wines; I generally rate the "Ronco delle Mele" a bit higher. The wine has lovely aromas of pears and apples, is medium-full with beautiful texture and a long finish with excellent persistence and lively acidity. This tends to age well; five to seven years after the vintage is generally the best time to drink this wine. **BRV**: 2010, 2009, 2008, 2007, 2006, 2004.

VILLA RUSSIZ SAUVIGNON "DE LA TOUR"

This great estate in Capriva del Friuli, founded in 1869 by Theodore La Tour, a French count, has risen to the ranks of the finest Collio producers under the leadership of Silvano Stefanutti and enologist Gianni Menotti over the past two decades. One of the most celebrated wines is the "De La Tour" Sauvignon, a *selezione* of their best grapes from hillside vineyards. As the work in the cellar is rather typical for a wine such as this (steel tank maturation, lees aging), the *anima* of this wine emerges from the vineyards themselves, as evidenced by the intense varietal aromas of freshly cut hay, gooseberry, sage and spearmint. Full-bodied, this is a powerful Sauvignon that is not for everyone, but is a great example of what this variety can be in the cool climate of Collio. This ages well; given the outstanding concentration and powerful structure, five to seven years is typical for this wine – a bit longer for the best vintages. **BRV**: 2010, 2009, 2008, 2005.

VIE DI ROMANS SAUVIGNON "PIERE"

Vie di Romans, managed by the Gallo family since 1900 – the labels feature a drawing of a rooster (*gallo*) – is situated in Mariano in the Isonzo zone in southern Friuli. Their wines are marvelous examples of varietal purity; a prime example is the "Piere" Sauvignon, named for the source vineyard that is planted to Italian and French clones of Sauvignon. The must undergoes cold maceration; there is no malolactic fermentation and the wine is aged for eight months on its lees. This is an intense, powerful Sauvignon with alcohol often reaching 14% or slightly more. The aromas are of pippin apple, pine and eucalyptus, there is excellent concentration, vibrant acidity and excellent structure; notes of white pepper and herbal tea deepen the wine's sense of place. This is a highly unique wine, one that will have lovers of Sauvignon from Friuli savoring every drop! This ages marvelously and can be enjoyed from three to as much as twelve years of age.

LA VIARTE SAUVIGNON

La Viarte has quietly been crafting extremely well made white and red wines from their cellars near Prepotto since their first releases in

1984. Giuseppe Ceschin purchased the property in 1973; today his son Giulio manages the sixty-seven acres of hillside vines. Their Sauvignon is a marvelous wine, refreshing and very delicious, with expressive aromas of chervil, spearmint, lemon rind and chamomile perfumes – this grabs you right from the first smell! Medium-full, there is lively acidity and excellent persistence along with marvelous varietal purity; the wine received no wood aging, as it was matured on its less in steel tanks for seven months. This is not as herbaceous in nature as many examples of Sauvignon from Friuli; just enjoy this with most seafood or even some risotto dishes upon release at one year, with peak drinking at three to five years of age.

RONC SORELI SAUVIGNON "VIGNA DEI PESCHI"
This Sauvignon from the "vineyard of the peaches," is an excellent example of the deeply concentrated, yet elegant wines produced by Fabio Schiratti at this estate. Aged on its lees for seven months, this offers inviting aromas of spearmint, chamomile, fig and lilacs; medium-full, this has an explosive finish with lively acidity and a light note of minerality. This is a vibrant wine of marvelous complexity, impeccably varietal focus and outstanding balance. This will only improve for five to seven years after the harvest.

GRAVNER ANFORA
Josko Gravner has become one of the artists of the Italian wine industry thanks to this wine as well as his other bottling known as Breg, as both wines are matured in *anforae*, clay pots that rest underground. In this manner, he replicates to some degree how the ancients made their wines thousands of years ago. This wine is 100% Ribolla with a deep orange color and marvelous texture; there is lively acidity and the finish is extremely long. The complexity is amazing and there are strong herbal notes to go along with the mature fruit. This is an original, as today there are several producers in Friuli that craft "orange" wines; these products are almost always compared to this wine of Gravner. The current vintage as of this writing is 2006 - the wine is not released for five years after the vintage. Other recommended vintages include the 2005 and 2004.

VODOPIVEC VITOVSKA ANFORA

Vitovska, a white variety, is one of the principal white grapes of the Carso zone, located in the far southeastern reaches of Friuli. Paolo Vodopivec produces two versions, the most famous of which is matured in *anforae*. The wine displays a bright orange color and has flavors of mandarin orange, squash and pekoe tea and has a long, seductive finish with lively acidity. As the wine approaches six or seven years of age, more dried fruit and herbal notes come to the forefront, while the finish lengthens and becomes even more rounded. Given that there have only been a few releases of this wine to date, it's impossible to say how long the best vintages will age, but it's safe to say that ten to twelve years is probably a safe bet. **BRV**: 2006, 2005.

EDI KANTE VITOVSKA

Edi Kante has a truly remarkable winery, one built on three levels underground the limestone soils of Prepotto in Carso. His wines are marvelous, combining local terroir with dazzling complexity and beautiful varietal purity. For his tiny production of Vitovska, he ages the wine in used barriques for twelve months, not adding any sulfur. The aromas unfurl very slowly on this wine- this is definitely a white wine that needs to breathe – while at first, the nose is rather closed, it opens over the course of forty to sixty minutes to reveal perfumes of grapfruit rind, orange peel and even a note of talc powder. Medium-full with excellent concentration and lively acidity, this has layers of fruit on the mid-palate and a lengthy, very rich, almost oily finish with great persistence. A vintage such as the 2009, tasted in early 2012 has another five to seven years of improvement ahead of it, but I wouldn't be surprised if this wine is in fine shape for another few years after that. **BRV**: 2009, 2008, 2006.

ZIDARICH MALVASIA

Benjamin Zidarich crafts some of the freshest, most multi-dimensional wines in Friuli at his winery in Prepotto in the Carso district. This Malvasia is a striking example; displaying a light yellow tint with strong hues of light orange, there are sensual perfumes of tangerine, mango and orange blossom. There is remarkable richness on the palate and in the finish, along with vibrant acidity. This is ultra clean with amazing varietal purity and focus, but above all, this is a wine of remarkable texture as well as delicacy and harmony, as every component is seamlessly woven together. Last but not least, this is delicious! This is as singular a Malvasia as I have tasted from Italy; enjoy this from three to seven years of age, although I would not be surprised if some bottles are in great shape on their tenth birthday. **BRV**: 2009, 2008, 2007, 2006.

SKERK "OGRADE"

The Carso district, the small section of Friuli at the extreme south-eastern reaches of the region near the Adriatic Sea is home to some of the most individualistic producers in all of Italy. Boris Skerk and his winemaker son Sandi are among those vintners, embodying the rugged nature of this land in all of their remarkable wines. For their "Ograde," a blend of Vitovska, Malvasia, Sauvignon and Pinot Grigio, they have crafted a stunning wine, a pleasure to the eyes, nose and taste buds. This has a light copper/burnt orange color and a cloudy appearance; the back label reads *"non chiarificato e non filtrato"* (not clarified or filtered). The aromas are quite stunning, with notes of persimmon, lychee and bing cherry; medium-full, this is a wine of remarkable texture as well as very good acidity and a long, beauti-fully structured finish. The complexity is outstanding and there are so many flavors in this wine, presented with such a delicate wine-making hand. This is not a powerful wine, but one with great finesse and subtlety and one crafted to reveal a little bit more character as it opens up after a while in the glass as well as a few years in the bottle. Just marvelous! Enjoy from three to seven years of age, perhaps lon-ger from the finest growing seasons. **BRV**: 2009, 2008, 2007.

ZIDARICH "PRULKE"

Along with producing sublime versions of Malvasia and Vitovska, Benjamin Zidarich also crafts a remarkable blend of these two variet-ies – along with Sauvignon – in a wine he labels as Prulke. Displaying a beautiful medium-deep orange color, there are sensual aromas of orange blossom, yellow peach and Anjou pear. Matured for eighteen months in small conical shaped wooden casks, this has a generous mid-palate, excellent persistence and lively acidity. There is a nice sensation of orange custard in the finish and overall the balance is superb. This is an orange wine that offers appealing freshness as well as an exceptional distinctiveness – to me, this is an ethereal wine, one that offers pleasure to the senses on so many levels. This is a wine of exceptional character and subtlety that is like few others; it is an original to be savored and treasured. Enjoy this from three to ten or twelve years of age. **BRV**: 2009, 2008, 2006, 2004.

JACUSS FRIULANO
Friulano, formerly known as Tocai Friulano, is a variety that many estates in Friuli are judged on; to me this is a chameleon grape, as aromas and flavors vary from zone to zone. A favorite of mine is the version produced at Jacuss, also known as Iacuzzi, for the owners Sandro and Andrea Iacuzzi. Their Friulano offers lovely aromas of grapefruit, pear and kiwi along with vibrant acidity and a lengthy finish. Steel aged with lees contact, there is excellent varietal focus with this release, which is generally at its best five to seven years after the vintage.

ISIDORO POLENCIC FRIULANO / FRIULANO "FISC"
This family estate in Plessiva in the Collio zone produces a wide range of local white and red wines; clearly their finest efforts are with Friulano. There are two versions: the regular bottling, aged partially in large oak casks, offers shimmering aromas of ripe pear, sweet pea and yellow pepper, the acidity is very good and there is a lengthy, well-structured finish. The "Fisc," named for the area where the vines are planted, is 100% fermented and matured in Slavonian casks; there are notes of Bosc pear and almond on the nose, while there is a bit more richness on the palate and slightly lower acidity than the regular offering. Both wines drink well from two to five years of age.

SKOK FRIULANO "ZABURA"

Giuseppe Skok founded this small estate at Giasbana in San Floriano del Collio; since 1991, his children Edi and Orietta have continued to craft some of the area's most complex and intense whites. The "Zabura" Friulano is typical of the house style with marvelous perfumes of quince, Bosc pear and marjoram that leads to a flavorful mid-palate and a finish with excellent persistence and lively acidity. As with the finest examples of Friulano, this has lovely texture and notable structure; it is also one of the most delicious I've tasted. Enjoy this from two to five years of age, perhaps longer from a great vintage such as 2009.

Vineyards at Giasbana, looking from the Skok estate

CARLO DI PRADIS FRIULANO "SCUSSE"

David and Boris Buzzinelli produce wines from both the Collio and Isonzo zones of Friuli; this Friulano is from the former. "Scusse" means "skins" in local dialect; the juice of this Friulano was in contact with the skins for eighteen days, resulting in a deep golden yellow color and aromas of beeswax, golden apples and dried pear. Medium-full with very good acidity and persistence, this offers lovely complexity from the winemaking process (this was matured for one year in large casks) and is very rich on the palate and in the finish. Enjoy this from three to seven years of age.

LE VIGNE DI ZAMO FRIULANO "VIGNE CINQUANTANNI"
Located in the superb growing area of Rosazzo in the heart of the Colli Orientali del Friuli zone, this wine estate is among Italy's finest. This special bottling of Friulano labeled as "Vigne Cinquantanni" (50-year old vines) is from marvelously situated vines that are actually now 60 years of age. Displaying a deep yellow-light golden color, the wine has intense aromas of Anjou pear, mango and almond along with notes of white flowers and spice. Full-bodied with outstanding persistence and complexity, this has vibrant acidity and tremendous structure with prominent minerality in the finish. The best vintages of this wine drink well upon their 10th or 12th birthday. This is an outstanding wine! **BRV**: 2008, 2007, 2006, 2005, 2004.

I CLIVI FRIULANO "CLIVI GALEA"
At the I Clivi estate, Ferdinando Zanusso and his son Mario produce wines from vineyards in both the Collio and Colli Orientali del Friuli zones. While they make excellent examples of Malvasia as well as a dry version of Verduzzo Friulano, it is their offerings of Friulano that excel. There are two distinct releases: Clivi Brazan and Clivi Galea; I slightly prefer the latter. Medium-full, the wine is from old vineyards and displays intense aromas of dried pear, lemon oil and magnolias; there is tremendous complexity and a powerful, earthy finish. This wine can age for many years, as evidenced by the 1999 bottling I tasted at VinItaly in 2010. **BRV**: 2006, 2005, 2004, 2001, 1999.

RADIKON "JAKOT"
At his tiny estate in Oslavia, just across the border from Slovenia, Stanko Radikon produces some of Italy's most distinct wines. Everything here is quite special, be it the Merlot, which spends two and one-half months on the skins or any of the whites. I could have

selected any one of three whites from Radikon, which include Oslave, a blend of Pinot Grigio, Chardonnay and Sauvignon or the sumptuous Ribolla Gialla, which is released after five years. However, I went with the Jakot, which is Tokaj spelled backwards (Tokaj – or Tocai, if you will – is the former name of Friulano, the variety used in this wine). Released after five years in the cellar, the color is bright orange and the aromas are quite complex, with notes of burnt orange, crème caramel and toffee. The mid-palate is quite rich and there is a long finish with notes of dried pear and orange peel. Here is a wine of tremendous complexity, one that is a pleasure to drink and one that enlightens your senses as well as your appreciation of wine. This is a wine that ages for ten to twelve years with no problems. **BRV**: 2005, 2004, 2001.

LA TUNELLA "RJGIALLA"

Massimo and Marco Zorzettig, members of a family that has been involved in local viticulture for several decades, established La Tunella in 1986 in the hamlet of Ipplis di Premariacco, east of the city of Udine. At this state-of-the art-facility in the Colli Orientali del Friuli zone, the brothers have focused on fruit-driven whites and reds crafted from indigenous varieties; especially notable is the RJGialla, a *selezione* of their finest Ribolla Gialla grapes. While this variety is often thought of as secondary to Friulano in this area, the La Tunella version is first-rate. Fermented and aged in stainless steel to emphasize the striking Bosc pear, chamomile and magnolia blossom aromas, this is lees-aged to ensure ideal texture. There is very good acidity and persistence, while the varietal purity and focus are quite impressive. This is a delicious wine, one of my favorite examples of Ribolla Gialla; enjoy this upon release and up to five years of age.

LA CASTELLADA RIBOLLA GIALLA

While many producers in Friuli make a fresh, delicate style of Ribolla Gialla meant for short term consumption, there are a handful of individuals who aim for a truly unique example of this variety. One of the best is that of La Castellada, situated in Oslavia in Collio; the Bensa family is involved in every aspect, from grape growing to cellar work. The grapes are from 20-35 year-old vines, situated at an elevation of 575 feet. Matured for two years in large Slavonian oak casks, the wine has an orange/amber color, aromas of dried pineapple, caraway and caramel, along with layers of fruit on the mid-palate leading to an extremely long finish. Generally the current vintage in many markets for this wine is at least six or seven years old; at this stage the wine has secondary and tertiary aromas of dried flowers and even notes of thyme and sage. The fruit flavors are mature, but there is precise acidity that maintains freshness; overall, this is a wine to be savored when its is between eight to twelve years of age. **BRV**: 2007, 2006, 2005, 2004, 2003.

RENATO KEBER RIBOLLA GIALLA "EXTREME"
Renato Keber produces a range of striking white wines (as well as a bit of red) from his estate vineyards in Cormons in the Collio zone. This Ribolla Gialla, named "Extreme" – 35 days of skin contact helps explain the name – is a highly original wine, one with a deep golden yellow color, distinctive aromas of dried apricot, dried pear, mandarin orange and dried pekoe tea. Offering excellent concentration, vibrant acidity and a long, long finish, this has amazing complexity and harmony; enjoy this from three to seven years of age. **BRV**: 2007, 2006, 2005.

MARCO FELLUGA PINOT GRIGIO RISERVA "MONGRIS"
Dozens of Friulian producers make Pinot Grigio, but few craft as special a version as Marco Felluga. The vintner likes to point out that Pinot Grigio is not a trend in this area, but rather a variety that dates back to the 19th century. His *riserva* "Mongris" offering – "mon" for mono-varietal and "gris" the local name for the variety - is partially fermented in steel (about two-thirds) with the remainder fermented in large oak casks. Medium-bodied with apple and cinnamon aromas, supple texture and notes of pear and yeast in the finish, this has marvelous complexity and tends to improve for a few years in the bottle; it generally peaks around five years of age.

LIS NERIS PINOT GRIGIO "GRIS"

Established in 1879, Lis Neris – "the blacks" – is currently managed by the fifth generation of the Pecorari family involved in this winery; their vineyards are in the Isonzo zone in southern Friuli. Their "Gris" offering of Pinot Grigio is a strikingly original version of this variety; sourced from 25 year-old vines and fermented in *tonneaux*, this has unique aromas of dried pear along with notes of almond and biscuit. Medium-full, with very good acidity and persistence, this offers distinct white spice notes in the finish. This tends to drink better a year after release; enjoy from two to five years of age.

VALTER SCARBOLO PINOT GRIGIO RAMATO "XL"

Valter Scarbolo, like numerous producers in Friuli, makes a Ramato Pinot Grigio; the term means "copper" or "coppery colored" and refers to the hue of the skins of the Pinot Grigio grape. His version is quite special, as the grapes are sourced from a fourteen year-old vineyard; half the fruit is destemmed and left on the skins for four days; part of the Pinot Grigio juice is fermented in *tonneaux* and half in stainless steel tanks. This has unique aromas of ripe Bosc pear, mandarin orange and radishes; medium-bodied, this has lovely texture, very good acidity and a light earthiness in the finish with a hint of currant. What a stylish wine and what a nice change from the unassuming Pinot Grigio too often made in Italy! Enjoy up four or five years after the harvest.

STURM CHARDONNAY "ANDRITZ"

Given the wonderful wines produced from varieties such as Friulano, Sauvignon and Ribolla Gialla in Friuli, I don't pay much attention to Chardonnay from this region; in fact, I find most examples a touch boring. So how nice to find a beautifully made Chardonnay from an excellent Collio producer. Sourced from thirty-five year-old vines, this offers fragrant aromas of hibiscus, golden apple, melon and Bosc pear. Only 20% was aged in wood, giving this impressive varietal character; there is very good acidity and persistence. Overall, this is a clean, beautifully balanced wine that is a pleasure to drink as the winemaking avoids the obvious clichés of modern Chardonnay (toasted almond, vanilla aromas) and focuses instead on just letting a Chardonnay be a Chardonnay! Enjoy this from three to five years after the vintage date.

LA RONCAIA REFOSCO DEL PEDUNCOLO ROSSO

Refosco, or more formally Refosco del Peduncolo Rosso – the name refers to the red stalk of the vine – is an indigenous variety planted in various zones of Friuli. This version is from vineyards in the commune of Nimis in the Colli Orientali district. This is deeply colored with a bright purple rim and the aromas are quite distinct, with notes of mulberry, bitter chocolate and anise. Medium-full, this is an expressive version, aged in new and used barriques for one year; there is excellent persistence with notes of black plum and tar in the finish. Give this time to settle down, as it drinks best at seven to ten years of age. La Roncaia is a winery owned by the Fantinel family, who also produce more value-oriented wines from other zones of Friuli. **BRV**: 2008, 2007, 2006, 2005, 2004.

VENICA REFOSCO DEL PEDUNCOLO ROSSO "BOTTAZ"

Being a red variety from Friuli means Refosco will never be a wine sought by the masses, which in the case of the Venica "Bottaz" is a good thing, as there's more available for those of us that truly love it! Deeply colored and fruit-driven with perfumes of black plum, licorice and myrtle, this is appealing on so many levels, especially given the elegant tannins, very good natural acidity and subtle black spice notes. Aged in large casks, this is sleek and delicious and extremely well balanced. This is appealing upon release and drinks best at five to seven years of age. **BRV**: 2009, 2008, 2007, 2006.

SKERK TERAN

Terrano – or Teran, if you will – is the predominant red variety of Carso; it is thought to be a strain of Refosco, grown elsewhere in Friuli. I find that Terrano tends to have more of a *frutti di bosco* quality along with soft tannins, as compared to the black fruits and firmer tannins of Refosco. The Skerk version of Terrano is a beauty and a real charmer with effusive notes of ripe red plum, cranberry and tar; medium-bodied with a rich mid-palate, this has remarkable focus and varietal purity and is a sheer delight to drink. I'd love to pair this with the classic duck breast with cherry sauce; it would also work well with lighter game or a meaty style of *prosciutto*. Consume from three to five years of age, perhaps longer from the best years. **BRV**: 2009, 2008, 2006.

ERMACORA SCHIOPPETTINO
Dario and Luciano Ermacora produce a wide range of white and red wines at their estate in Ipplis, a bit north of Udine in the Colli Orientali del Friuli zone. Their Schioppettino, a low-yielding indigenous variety yields a striking wine with black cherry and black currant flavors alongside notes of licorice and bitter chocolate. There are firm tannins – typical for this variety – lively acidity and a distinct note of black pepper in the finish. This is not as powerful as some examples of this wine, but the overall roundness makes this a pleasure to enjoy from three to five years of age. **BRV**: 2009, 2008, 2007, 2006.

JERMANN PIGNACOLUSSE
Silvio Jermann has certainly made a name for himself with his whites, but his reds are also first-rate, especially this 100% Pignolo. The grape, named for its pine-cone shaped bunches, delivers wines with savory flavors and perfumes, such as black plum, black raspberry and confectionary sugar as in this version. The tannins are moderate, acidity is quite juicy and the wood notes are nicely integrated, despite maturation in new oak for as much as two years. Given the aromas as well as notes of anise and coriander in the finish, this is a wine that needs a spicy cuisine for food pairings (Indian food would be ideal). The wine is at its best five to seven years after the harvest. **BRV**: 2005, 2004, 2001.

EMILIO BULFON PICULIT NERI
Lovers of singular wines made from indigenous varieties in Italy owe a great deal of thanks to Emilio Bulfon, a vintner fascinated in varieties

that were thought to be lost. At his winery in Valeriano in the province of Pordenone in western Friuli, Bulfon has been working with rare varieties such as Cividìn, Sciaglin and Ucelùt (white) and Cordenossa, Forgiarìn and Piculit Neri (red). He crafts so many lovely wines; I have selected his Piculit Neri for its overall charms and seductiveness. Displaying marvelous aromas of Queen Anne cherry, raspberry and hints of toffee and a touch of smoked meat, this is medium-bodied with impressive depth of fruit, very good acidity, lovely varital purity and an appealing finish with notes of cinnamon and nutmeg. It's a sensual wine with great finesse and it is definitely meant for the dinner table; I'd love to try this with a lighter pasta or perhaps quail or hare. Enjoy this from two to five years of age. The striking labels are a reproduction of a medieval fresco depicting The Last Supper; this work can be seen in a nearby church. **BRV**: 2010, 2009, 2008.

RUSSIZ SUPERIORE CABERNET FRANC
The cool climes and naturally low-yielding hillside vines of Collio combine to deliver high acid, aromatic wines; this is true for reds as well as whites. This Cabenet Franc from Roberto Felluga is a great example of how edgy and vibrant Collio reds can be; currant, myrtle and plum flavors are the highlights, while there is a strong note of pink peppercorn in the finish, a trademark of this variety in a cool climate. As you might imagine, acidity levels are very good; dark chocolate notes add to the complexity of this wine, one that is at its most enjoyable at five to seven years of age. **BRV**: 2009, 2008, 2007, 2006.

STURM CABERNET FRANC
There is a lovely focus on varietal character in all of Oscar Sturm's wines; this Cabernet Franc is prime evidence. Sourced from 25 year-old vines in Cormons, this has textbook aromas of pink peppercorn and bing cherry along with a hint of mince. Matured for twenty months in oak, this has very good acidity, round, medium-weight tannins, notable persistence and notes of tar and black chocolate in the finish. This pairs beautifully with *salumi* and lighter red meats and game; enjoy from three to seven years of age. **BRV**: 2010, 2009.

LA VIARTE TAZZELENGHE

As you study indigenous varieties from all over Italy, you can't help but be charmed by how many of these grapes were named. This red Friulian variety may be my favorite in all of the country! Tazzelenghe literally translates as "tongue cutter," a reference to the wine's aggressive, firm tannins. The version from La Viarte is typical with aromas of roast coffee, dried cherry and cumin; there is balanced acidity and explosion of fruit on the palate and in the finish, along with those tannins you can't dismiss! This is certainly not a wine that one would label as subdued, but if you're looking for a hearty red to pair with rich game, stews and very strong, aged cheeses, this is for you. Give this time upon release, as the tannins need to settle down; this is at its best from five to ten years of age. **BRV**: 2007, 2006.

RADIKON MERLOT

Stanko Radikon is so famous for his "orange" wines from Collio that one forgets how good his other wines are. His Merlot is a great example, one that is made with an amazing attention to detail. The grapes are macerated for more than two months on its skins and then matured for five years in used barriques! Yet the wine has great freshness upon release; produced from low-yielding vines, there is also excellent concentration and roundness. Dried cherry, oregano and paprika aromas lead to a rich mid-palate and a lengthy, beautifully structured finish with very good acidity and a light herbal edge. The wine slowly reveals greater complexities as it ages; I tried the 1997 version in 2010 and noted that it would improve for another five to seven years; the 2002 is now the current vintage. Clearly Radikon is in no hurry to share this wine with the world! **BRV**: 2002, 2000, 1998, 1997.

LIVIO FELLUGA "VERTIGO"

There are several notable reds produced by at the Livio Felluga estate that are nice counterparts to their more famous white wines; my favorite is "Vertigo," a blend of Merlot and Cabernet Sauvignon. While both cultivars are so-called international varieties, Merlot actually has a long history in Friuli, so the winery sees this blend as a bridge between Old and New World. I love the elegance and polish of this wine, as this is a wine that represents a classically-oriented style; it is meant for the dinner table, as it's not forced or pushed toward super ripeness. The aromas are of black cherry, bitter chocolate and licorice and the wood notes are subtle, while there is very good acidity. This is a delicious red with excellent complexity; it drinks best between five and seven years of age. **BRV**: 2009, 2008, 2007, 2006.

BASTIANICH "CALABRONE"

Anyone familiar with the wines of Friuli knows about the fabulous white blends; here is a blended red made with the same attention to detail. This is a cuvée of 70% Refosco, with 10% each of Schioppetino, Pignolo and Merlot. What makes this wine special is the fact that a percentage of the Refosco and all of the Schioppetino undergo a natural drying process known as *appassimento*, a procedure used in Veneto to make Amarone. Medium-full with excellent depth of fruit, this has invigorating aromas of dark chocolate, black plum, black cherry and mince that lead to a powerful finish with outstanding persistence, round tannins, good acidity and flavors of bitter chocolate. This is a robust red meant for strong aged cheeses in its youth, but one that would be ideal with venison or most game a few years after its release and up to seven to ten years of age. **BRV**: 2007, 2003, 1999.

DARIO COOS ROMANDUS

The Dario Coos estate in Colli Orientali del Friuli specializes in Ramandolo, a DOCG dessert wine made from the Verduzzo Friulano grape indigenous to Friuli. The grapes are hand harvested and then dried on mats for a few months in the *appassimento* method. The resulting wine is golden amber in color with aromas of apricot, butterscotch, dried tea leaves and candied fruit. Quite rich on the palate and with very good persistence, this is medium-sweet with a rich, nutty finish. Coos produces a Ramandolo and this wine named Romandus, which is a bit richer with a touch more oak influence. These wines are meant for long-term aging; 15-20 years would not be out of the question for the best vintages. **BRV**: 2008, 2007, 2006.

LA TUNELLA VERDUZZO FRIULANO

La Tunella's version of this famed Friulian dessert wine is something special! The Verduzzo grapes are harvested late, so as to accumulate as much natural sugar as possible; it is fermented and aged in barriques. Offering a deep amber, almost butterscotch color, there are seductive aromas of dried apricot and honey with just a note of oak. Medium-full, this is very lush and layered on the palate with a rich, medium sweet finish; good acidity levels prevent this from ever being cloying. The 2004, tasted in mid-2012, was drinking beautifully, as this wine will have no problem being enjoyed at age ten or twelve. I'd pair it with a simple pound cake or almond torte; the winery also recommends it with pumpkin gnocchi – does that sound great or what? **BRV**: 2009, 2008, 2006, 2004.

LIVIO FELLUGA PICOLIT

Picolit is a variety found primarily in the Colli Orientali del Friuli district; its most distinctive characteristic is that is does not bloom like other varieties. This condition, known as floral abortion, means that there are far fewer berries per cluster of Picolit than any other variety. Given this condition, the wine is, of course, not inexpensive to make.

Several local producers craft a lovely dessert wine from Picolit; the finest I have tasted is from Livio Felluga. Golden yellow in appearance, the heavenly aromas are of dried peach, lemon peel, caramel, golden raisins, almond and hazelnut! Medium-full, the wine is quite lush on the palate and has a long, delicate finish with a light sweetness balanced by ideal acidity. This can age anywhere from 10-15 years after the vintage. **BRV**: 2006, 2004, 2001.

JACUSS PICOLIT

To say that Picolit is rare is an understatement; I was told by Sandro Iacuzzi that he produced 450 bottles of this wine from the 2006 vintage! Deep golden, this has enticing aromas of butterscotch, crème caramel and orange peel; medium-full, this has a long, long finish with cleansing acidity and a light nuttiness. This is a gem – enjoy for anywhere from five to ten or twelve years, if you can find a bottle, that is! **BRV**: 2007, 2006, 2005, 2004.

LA VIARTE "SIÙM"

Here is a classy dessert wine, a blend of Picolit and Verduzzo Friulano grapes that have been naturally dried in temperature-controlled rooms for several months. Deep amber gold with powerful aromas of crème caramel, pecan, honey and butterscotch, this is lush and medium sweet with good acidity and a rich finish with excellent persistence and notes of caramel, cinnamon and honey. This is a wine that would be called a "sticky" in Australia; that is a compliment to this wine, a real original. This is at its best from seven to ten years of age. **BRV**: 2007, 2006, 2005.

Liguria

Principal Varieties

White:
Vermentino, Pigato, Rossese Bianco, Bosco, Albarola

Red:
Rossese, Ormeasco, Sangiovese, Canaiolo, Vermentino Nero,
Massaretta, Pollera Nera, Merlot

———

CANTINE LUNAE VERMENTINO "ETICHETTA NERA"

There are few white wines that enliven one's sense of smell and taste as Vermentino when it is done right. The Bosoni brothers, Diego and winemaker Paolo, produce several versions of Vermentino from the Colli di Luni zone not far from Tuscany and the sea. The Etichetta Nera is a dazzling wine and perhaps the finest Vermentino I have ever tasted. The aromas are room-filling, with notes of mango, lime, golden apple and orange zest. The texture is marvelous, as this mid-palate is quite lush and the finish is sleek and long, as there is vibrant acidity. As you might imagine, this was aged solely in steel tanks preceeded by a short maceration with the skins. As lovely a food wine as this is, I think I almost prefer it by itself, just to enjoy the amazing varietal purity. If you must pair it with food, try it with a simple preparation of crab legs. Enjoy this anytime between its release and three years after the harvest.

COLLE DEI BARDELLINI VERMENTINO "U MUNTE"

While the Lunae Vermentino is sleek, clean and outright delicious, the Colle dei Bardellini version is a bit more angular, or in street terms, more down and dirty. This is a single vineyard wine from a vineyard near Monte Rosa (*u munte* is local dialect for "mountain") in western Liguria. Sporting aromas of green apple, kiwi, lemon peel and saffron, this has a strong salty nose in the finish, so strong that is may turn some drinkers away from this wine. But if you can get by that note – a direct by-product of this variety when grown near the sea – this has impressive balance and structure. As strongly flavored a wine as this is, do pair with rich shellfish or seafood preparations and consume it over its first two to three years.

BIO VIO PIGATO DI ALBENGA "MARENE"

Giobatta Vio founded this winery in 1980, plating vineyards in the Albenga zone in south central Liguria; he emphasizes biological practices (bio) in the vineyards, opting not to use pesticides, fertilizers or chemicals. His "Marene" bottling of Pigato, one of Liguria's most distinct indigenous varieties, is a lovely subtle and complex white with golden apple, saffron, jasmine and dried pear aromas backed by impressive depth, lively acidity and notes of thyme, fennel and salted almonds in the finish. This is a restrained wine that grows on you; enjoy it within three to five years of the harvest.

LUPI PIGATO / VERMENTINO

Founded in the 1960s, Lupi is today operated by Massimo and Fabio Lupi, the second generation who have helped to make this one of the premier producers of white wines from the Riviera Ligure di Ponente zone. Their Pigato and Vermentino are excellent wines, both displaying wonderful harmony and varietal purity. The Pigato displays distinct aromas of sea breeze, guava and green tea; medium-full, there is good acidity, impressive complexity and a light touch of minerality. The Vermentino offers lovely aromas of melon, kiwi, Bosc pear and a hint of sea breeze; a bit richer on the palate than the Pigato, this has lively acidity, very good persistence, pleasing minerality and is ultraclean with great varietal focus. Both wines drink beautifully from three to five years, with the Vermentino sometimes lasting an extra year or two.

TERENZOULA CINQUE TERRE BIANCO

Cinque Terre is not only one of Italy's most famous attractions, it's also an excellent white wine from Liguria. The Ternzuola winery is actually located in far northwestern Toscana, on the border with Liguria, but they produce this delightful Ligurian white, a blend of Bosco (one of the region's most widely planted varieties), Vermentino and Albarola (also known as Bianchetta). The vineyards, near the coastal towns of Monterosso, Riomaggiore and Vernazza in southeastern Liguria, are largely comprised of sandy soils; owner Ivan Giuliani and his friend Marco Nicoloini have gone with high density plantings. This is an intriguing white, aged on its lees in steel tanks, offering aromas of apricot pit, melon and Bosc pear. But it is in the finish of this medium-bodied white where things get interesting, as there is are striking notes of a chalky, resiny minerality. Acidity, as you might expect is lively and this has beautiful focus and clarity; it's a delicious wine that's not all about pretty fruit, but also about the special flavors derived from the seaside locale. Enjoy this with a variety of shellfish or even artichokes or eggplant from one to three years of age.

BIO VIO ROSSESE DI ALBEGNA "U BASTIO"

Rossese is an indigenous variety planted primarily along the western reaches of Liguria; this version is from the Riviera Ligure di Ponente DOC near the town of Imperia. This is a red that has a lot in common with a rosé, given its pale garnet color and mild tannins; in fact, a slight chill would be just fine when serving this wine. The aromas are slightly wild with notes of rhubarb mixing with red cherry, currant and dried strawberry. The finish has a slightly rustic edge to it and there is tangy acidity, which adds some unique character to the wine. This is a delightful red meant for consumption upon release and for another year or so; there's really no need to lay it away.

LUPI ORMEASCO DI PORNASSIO

Ormeasco is the name of the Dolcetto grape in Liguria; this version from Lupi is from the Pornassio zone in far western Liguria not far from the border with Piemonte. Steel aged, this has aromas of tar, maraschino cherry and a hint of oregano; medium-bodied, this has moderate tannins, good acidity and nice varietal focus along with a slight earthiness in the finish. This has lovely balance and is quite approachable upon release; this graceful and elegantly styled wine should be consumed by its third or fourth year.

Emilia Romagna

Principal Varieties

White:
Pignoletto, Albana, Moscato, Riesling Italico,
Chardonnay, Sauvignon

Red:
Sangiovese, Barbera, Bonarda, Lambrusco Grasparossa,
Lambrusco Salamino, Lambrusco di Sorbara,
Cabernet Sauvignon, Merlot

———

CLETO CHIARLI LAMBRUSCO "ENRICO CIALDINI"
LAMBRUSCO "MODENA PREMIUM"

Lambrusco, a *frizzante* (slightly effervescent) red, is arguably Emilia Romagna's most famous wine. While there are some sticky sweet versions that resemble soda pop more than wine, thankfully, there are a good number of producers that treat Lambrusco with great respect. One of the best of these houses is Cleto Chiarli, founded in 1860 in Modena, the same town also known for its wonderful balsamic vinegars. Two of Chiarli's Lambruscos are worth mentioning: the "Enrico Cialdini" and the "Modena Premium." The former is made with the Grasparossa strain of Lambrusco from a single vineyard. Offering tasty red plum and black raspberry fruit, this is medium-bodied with a delicate finish with a trace of sweetness. The latter is produced from Lambrusco Sorbrara and is a bit fuller and drier. Both wines are meant to be enjoyed within two to three years of the vintage date; generally the fresher the better.

CAVICCHIOLI LAMBRUSCO DI SORBARA "VIGNA DEL CRISTO" LAMBRUSCO GRASPAROSSA DI CASTELVETRO "ROBANERA"

Founded in 1928 in San Prospero in the province of Modena, Cavicchioli is one of the largest vineyard owners of Lambrusco, with some 230 acres planted. Two wines from different DOC zones – based on the particular strain of Lambrusco – are stellar. The "Vigna del Cristo" from Sorbara has tasty strawberry fruit and an off-dry finish; this is a wonderful introduction to Lambrusco. The "Robanera" – literally "dark robe" based on its bright crimson, purple color – is produced from the Grasparossa strain and offers more floral aromatics (iris and violet) to accompany the ripe black plum fruit; it is also more weighty on the palate and has lovely complexity. This is a lovely Lambrusco, one that is more serious than most versions (there are noticeable tannins, though they are modest); it can drink well for up to five years.

PAOLA RINALDINI LAMBRUSCO "PRONTO"

Pronto Lambrusco is the wonderful effort of Paola Rinaldini, one of the most dedicated artisanal producers of this famous *frizzante* wine. This is a blend of 70% Salamino, 15% Marani and 15% Ancellotta that is non-stabilized and non-pasteurized. Displaying a deep crimson purple color and a lively mousse, the aromas are quite rich, with notes of myrtle, purple iris, clove and licorice. Medium-bodied with excellent concentration, this has a rich finish with abundant fruit and a light bitterness; this is a *dry* Lambrusco. This offers so much more complexity and richness on the palate than many other competing products; with a slight bitter chocolate note at the end, it's also tantalizing. This is a non-vintage product, enjoy within one to two years of release; it may change the way you think about Lambrusco!

GIOVANNA MADONIA "NEBLINA"

The Giovanna Madonia winery is situated in Bertinoro in eastern Emilia Romagna; Giovanna took over management of this estate from her father in the early 1990s. Her dry white "Neblia" is 100% Albana di Romagna from *albarello* vines that displays the unique qualities of this indigenous variety, with its copper color and intriguing aromas of musk oil and pippin apple. Medium-full with excellent concentration, this has lively acidity and notes of white spice in the finish. If one were to assemble a list of "tannic whites," this would definitely be included; this is best enjoyed from three to seven years of age. The art work on the label was designed by Giovanna herself.

GIOVANNA MADONIA "TENENTINO"
"FERMAVENTO"

Here are two very different treatments of Sangiovese from this wonderful producer. The "Tenentino," from vineyards in the modern cordon spur system, is aged in steel tanks only and has a light peppery note to accompany the dried cherry and dried flower aromas. Medium-bodied, this has an earthy, herbal finish with moderate tannins and good acidity. The "Fermavento" sourced from older *albarello* vineyards, is more typical fruit-driven Sangiovese matured primarily in steel with about a third aged in barriques. The red cherry fruit is riper and there are also notes of tar and thyme on the nose; medium-full, this is a nicely balanced Sangiovese for medium-term enjoyment (three to five years). **BRV** (for both): 2009, 2008, 2007.

SAN PATRIGNANO "AVI"

The story of wine at San Patrignano is one of the most unusual and heartwarming found anywhere in the world. Situated in Coriano, not far from the Adriatic Sea in southeastern Emilia Romagna, San Patrignano is a rehabilitation facility for drug addicts and other troubled individuals; they are offered a home and a job at no charge. Founded by Vincenzo Muccioli in 1978, his son Andrea assumed control in 1995 upon his father's death; Andrea has expanded the wine and food operations. The top wine is a 100% Sangiovese called "Avi", which refers to one's ancestors; it is also a tribute to Vincenzo – "a Vi". Aged in large casks, there are aromas of black cherry, cacao and balsamic; there is excellent persistence, good acidity and the oak notes stay in the background. This is at its best some five to twelve years of age. Incidentally, the wines at San Patrignano are made by renowned enologist Riccardo Cottarella, who in keeping with the spirit of this venture, donates his time. **BRV**: 2008, 2007, 2006, 2005, 2004, 2001.

SAN PATRIGNANO "MONTEPIROLO"

While "Avi" is a premier Sangiovese from San Patrignano, the "Montepirolo" is a sumptuous Bordeaux blend that is primarily Cabernet Sauvignon along with Merlot and Cabernet Franc. Matured in barriques, this is medium-full with expressive black cherry, black plum, myrtle and black pepper aromas. There are layers of fruit on the mid-palate that leads to a powerful finish with excellent persistence; acidity is nicely tuned and there are balanced tannins and subdued oak notes. This needs some time to settle down, generally it is at its best from five to twelve years of age. **BRV**: 2006, 2004, 2003, 2001.

FATTORIA ZERBINA ALBAGNA DI ROMAGNA PASSITO "ARROCCO"

If you haven't tasted an Albagna di Romagna *passito*, you are missing one of Italy's most distinctive dessert wines. This great estate was established in 1966 when Vincenzo Geminiani puchased property in Faenza, near Forli, and planted Albana and Sangiovese. His niece Maria Cristina Geminiani began her work here in 1987 and has made this into one of the region's finest, especially with her *passsito* versions of Albana di Romagna. There is an offering known as Scaccomatto as well as this Arrocco bottling, both of which are affected by botrytis, known as *muffa nobile* in Italy. Deep yellow with copper tones, the aromas are of fig, date, apricot, almond and hazelnut; this has a particularly rich mid-palate, very good acidity and a lengthy finish with notes of herbal tea and mint.

Fermented and matured partially in barriques and partially in small steel tanks, this is a rich, nutty dessert wine with marvelous complexity and amazing depth of fruit. This is truly a *vino da meditazione*, a wine to be savored on its own, although I would love to pair this with *foie gras*! This has the structure and concentration to age gracefully for 12-15 years. **BRV**: 2008, 2007, 2001.

Toscana

Principal Varieties

White:
Vermentino, Vernaccia, Sauvignon, Trebbiano Toscano, Malvasia

Red:
Sangiovese, Canaiolo, Colorino, Ciliegiolo, Cabernet Sauvignon, Merlot, Syrah, Cabernet Franc

———

GUADO AL MELO BIANCO

This small estate in Bolgheri makes some value oriented reds from the local DOC zone, but it is this intriguing white that really caught my attention during my initial visit. This is a blend of 90% Vermentino – the typical white variety of this area – along with 10% Petit Manseng, a grape most widely planted in France's Jurancon area. Light yellow, the aromas are of pine and spearmint (classic Vermentino), the acidity is vibrant and there is a distinct chalkiness. Proprietor Michele Scienza, son of famed Italian wine grape authority Attilio Scienza, tasted out six vintages of this wine with me at dinner; the 2002, six years old at the time, had taken on aromas of tea leaves and hazelnut and was nearing peak. This may be an unusual blend from Bolgheri, but when you realize that Scienza also produces a red called Jassarte made from at least 30 different varieties, well, maybe it's not so surprising after all.

GRATTAMACCO BOLGHERI BIANCO

In Bolgheri, there are generally two white varieties of choice. One is Sauvignon, which tends to deliver a rather aggressive, herbal-oriented wine;

only a few local producers deal with this variety. The more preferred white of choice is Vermentino, which is ideally suited to the climes of this small zone along the Tuscan coast near Livorno. The moderate temperatures here are perfect for this high acid variety and the long growing season allows for intense aromas. At Grattamacco, the wine is given subtle oak treatment (50% is aged in used barriques), to ensure greater texture. Brilliant straw in color with some hints of gold and green, the aromas offer notes of pine, grapefruit and a touch of apricot. Medium-full, this has a very rich finish with vibrant acidity and a light saltiness. This is best consumed within three to five years of the harvest, while a few exceptional bottles are at peak at age seven.

ENRICO SANTINI BOLGHERI BIANCO "CAMPO ALLA CASA"

Enrico Santini is a true "garagiste," a producer whose cellars are in his small garage just outside the city of Castagneto Carducci in the Bolgheri DOC. His Campo Alla Casa, named for the road on which his house is located, is a blend of the two leading white varieties of the area: Vermentino (60%) and Sauvignon Blanc (40%); the aromas are quite lovely with notes of pine, Bosc pear and spearmint. This has a lovely texure, excellent persistence and lively acidity with just a touch of seaside minerality. Instantly appealing, this generally is at its best at three to five years of age.

TENUTA DELL'ORNELLAIA "POGGIO ALLE GAZZE"

While several producers in Bolgheri and nearby towns along the Tuscan coast work with Vermentino as their white variety, only a few make a Sauvignon. At this date, arguably the finest version of this variety from the Livorno province is the "Poggio alle Gazze" (hill of the magpies) from Tenuta dell'Ornellaia. The winery made this wine back in the 1980s, but stopped production after a few years; they have started to make this wine again, starting with the 2009 vintage. Lovers of great white wines can be thankful, as this is a marvelous offering! Partially fermented in steel and partly in new and used barriques and then aged for six months on its lees, this is an expressive Sauvignon with aromas of dried pear, saffron, fig and almond. Medium-full to full-bodied, this is a powerful wine with excellent persistence, a layered mid-palate, very good acidity and subtle herbal notes in the finish. Though assertive in nature, this is a wine of lovely harmony; it is at its best from three to seven years of age.

FATTORIA DI MAGLIANO VERMENTINO

There are many producers in the Tuscan provinces of Grosseto and Livorno near the Tyrrhenian Sea that grow Vermentino, a high acid variety. While many of their offerings are quite pleasant, too many examples are rather simple in nature. Clearly the version from Fattoria di Magliano, an estate near Scansano, is much more complex with fascinating kiwi, magnolia and guava perfumes. Medium-full with textbook acidity, a lengthy finish and pleasant minerality, this is a first-rate example of what Tuscan Vermentino can offer. Enjoy this wine upon release and up to five years after the vintage date.

COLLE MASSARI VERMENTINO "MELACCE"

There has been a lot of attention given to the Montecucco reds at this estate, owned by Claudio Tipa, but I also love the "Melacce" Vermentino, one of two versions of this variety produced by this firm. Medium-full, this is aged in steel tanks, so as to highlight the beautiful melon, pear and kiwi aromas that lead to a lengthy finish with notes of white spice. There is typical lively acidity and the wine is as refreshing as a cool rainfall on a hot summer's day. Enjoy this within two to three years of the harvest.

TENUTA ROCCACIA BIANCO DI PITIGLIANO SUPERIORE "OROLUNA"

Pitigliano is an ancient town built on a bedrock of tufa soil, located southeast of Scansano in the province of Grosseto, not far from the border with Lazio. Near the town, the Bianco di Pitigliano wine zone focuses on several white varieties, primarily Trebbiano Toscano. While this variety too often delivers thin, acidic wines, there are a few vintners that take the care to limit yields and produce a notable wine, one that is usually blended with other varieties that add some weight on the palate. Tenuta Roccacia, established over a century ago, makes one of the loveliest examples of this wine with its Superiore offering named "Oroluna," first produced from the 2006 vintage. Incorporating Vermentino, Chardonnay and Sauvignon Blanc with the mandated Trebbiano Toscano, this is a delightful wine with Bosc pear, red apple and tea leaf aromas; medium-bodied, this has delicious fresh fruit, notable acidity and nice complexity. What a lovely wine for lunchtime seafood pasta! Enjoy within two to three years of the harvest.

LA PARRINA "POGGIO DELLA FATA"

There are more than 30 different DOC wine zones in Tuscany, many of them quite small and a few of them relatively unknown. The Parrina DOC is definitely one of the least recognized; certainly the fact that there is currently only one producer in this zone – fittingly La Parrina – is a major reason why. The zone is located in Grosseto province, south of Scansano and very close to the sea. Both the reds and whites have lovely character, with my favorite wine being the Sauvignon (Blanc)/Vermentino blend called "Poggio della Fata," an IGT wine. Aged solely in stainless steel, this displays lovely aromas of pear and fig along with yellow flowers and spices. There is excellent persistence, lively acidity and distinct minerality; the wine is at its best five to seven years old.

POGGIO ARGENTIERA "ANSONICA BUCCE"

At Poggio Argentiera, proprietor Gianpaolo Paglia has been one of the most influential producers of Morellino di Scansano. Yet Paglia realizes the potential of other varieties in this area and other local zones. His Ansonica, an indigenous Tuscan variety planted near the sea, is a dazzling example of what he can acccomplish. Given skin contact during fermentation (*bucce* in Italian means "skins"), the wine is aged in both cement tanks and old *tonneaux* on its lees for 18 months, resulting in a wine of lovely texture. Light yellow with golden tints, the aromas of yellow peach, chamomile and green pepper are quite striking. Medium-full with excellent persistence and very good acidity, this is a wine for medium-term enjoyment, some three to five years after the harvest; it is also one of the most distinct examples of this variety in the Maremma.

BIBI GRAETZ BIANCO "BUGIA"

Bibi Graetz produces a varied lineup of wines, ranging from value whites, reds and rosé to one of Tuscany's most famous cult reds known as Testamatta. His most distinctive wines however are his whites coming from the island of Giglio, just off the coastline of Grosseto province. His "Bugia" white is produced entirely from the Ansonica variety, a typical grape found along the Tuscan coast; the vineyards average 80 years of age and donkeys are used to transport the fruit. Graetz ferments a small part in barriques, with the rest in steel; for maturation, 5% is aged in barriques, while 95% is matured in cement tanks. This is a sensual white with aromas of apricot, melon and a hint of nuttiness; medium-full, this has lovely texture and a long finish with very good acidity and distinct minerality. This is a very rich white that can stand up to any type of seafood. Impressive in its first two to three years, this is at its best from five to seven years of age.

PANIZZI VERNACCIA DI SAN GIMIGNANO

Vernaccia di San Gimignano is Tuscany's most famous dry white; produced entirely from the Vernaccia grape grown near this touristy town of the towers. Giovanni Panizzi is one of the leading producers here and makes about as good a "regular" – read stainless steel aged – version you will find. Medium-bodied with lovely aromas of pine, apple peel and dried flowers, this has zippy acidity, excellent freshness and always, beautiful balance. Panizzi also produces two wood-aged Vernaccia, a *riserva* and a cru named Santa Margherita. I love the clever label design of all this producer's examples of Vernaccia.

MONTENIDOLI VERNACCIA DI SAN GIMIGNANO "CARATO"

Elisabetta Fagiuoli is the first lady of San Gimignano, a truly delightful person who is always excited to have you taste her wines. She makes several versions of Vernaccia di San Gimignano and has for many years shown the world the potential of this Tuscan white. While I admire the regular "Fiore" bottling with its pine and resin oil aromas, the "Carato" is my favorite version of Vernaccia that she produces. Produced from estate vineyards farmed organically – her labels read *Solo Montenidoli* to let the buyer know that she uses only her own fruit – this is made from late harvested Vernaccia grapes. Entirely first run must, this is aged for one year in barriques. Sporting dried pear and yellow flower aromas, this has lovely texture, very good acidity, excellent persistence and complexity. This is a rare achievement for Vernaccia di San Gimignano and one that should be celebrated! **BRV**: 2008, 2007, 2006, 2005 (exceptional), 2004.

TERUZZI & PUTHOD "TERRE DI TUFI"

Husband and wife Enrico Teruzzi and Carmen Puthod established their winery in 1974 with the intent of being one of the finest producers in San Gimignano, home of Italy's most famous dry white, Vernaccia di San Gimignano. Their regular bottling has always been one of the most typical of its type with an appealing freshness, but it is the Terre di Tufi wine that has been their calling card. Although this is primarily made from Vernaccia (about 80%), this is not a DOCG wine, but an IGT, due to the blending regulations of this area; the remaining 20% is a mix of Malvasia, Trebbiano and Chardonnay. The other aspect that makes this wine different is its oak aging, as most examples of Vernaccia here are aged solely in stainless steel; this is matured in 30% new and 70% used barriques for a period of four to six months. Medium-full, there is a light toastiness to this wine from the wood along with aromas of lemon zest, quince and a light nuttiness. This is at its best at three to five years of age. The packaging, feauring a postage stamp-sized square label on a long, Bordeaux-type bottle, is quite striking.

ISOLE E OLENA CHIANTI CLASSICO

Chianti Classico, produced primarily from Sangiovese in vineyards located between Florence and Siena, may be the world's most loved red wine. There are hundreds of producers in the Classico zone and styles vary from very simple, short-term wines to those that will reward the patient drinker with seven to ten years of cellaring. At Isole e Olena, Paolo de Marchi crafts a stylish Chianti Classico *normale* that is on the short list of my favorites of this type each vintage. There are lovely red cherry, thyme and red rose aromas along with very good acidity and delicate tannins and wood notes. This is a Chianti Classico that has great typicity, but above all it's very agreeable and it's delicious! Enjoy this over the first three to five years after the harvest, although the best bottlings age for a few additional years. **BRV:** 2009, 2008, 2007, 2006, 2004.

QUERCIABELLA CHIANTI CLASSICO

Located in a remote corner in Greve, Querciabella is one of the most modern and innovative cellars in Chianti Classico, thanks to the leadership of proprietor Sebastiano Cossia Castiglioni. Along with his viticultural team, Castiglioni has sought to make the most authentic and typical wines; to that end, he first changed over to organic farming in 1988 and then to biodynamic agriculture in 2000. The results have been spectacular as his Chianti Classico is one of impressive weight and balance, yet the wines are cleanly made with great varietal purity. Here is a Chianti Classico that will drink well for a minimum of seven years and often up to a decade or more from great vintages such as 2004 and 2001. **BRV:** 2009, 2008, 2007, 2006, 2005, 2004, 2001.

LILLIANO CHIANTI CLASSICO

If you are looking for a traditionally made Chianti Classico with varietal purity, exquisite balance and excellent typicity, look no further than Lilliano. The Ruspoli family has owned this beautiful estate in Castellina since 1920 and began bottling wine under its own label in 1958. There is nothing magical about these wines; just a realization of superbly sited vineyards some 800-1000 feet above sea level that are between 20 and 25-year of age, yielding marvelous fruit that is handled with great care in the cellar. The regular Chianti Classico at Lilliano is always distinguished by its appealing perfumes of cherry and currant with touches of rose and carnation. This is an elegant Chianti

Classico that emphasizes grace over power; consume within five to seven years of the vintage. **BRV**: 2010, 2009 (outstanding), 2008, 2007, 2006, 2005, 2004.

CASTELLARE DI CASTELLINA CHIANTI CLASSICO

This renowned estate, ideally located in Castellina, has been recognized from its beginnings in 1978 as one of Chianti Classico's finest wine firms. The amiable Alessandro Cellai is the winemaker here and with his sure and steady hand in the cellar, he has succeeded with several wine types, including so-called Super Tuscans, including Poggio ai Merli, a 100% Merlot; Coniale, a wine made exclusively from Cabernet Sauvignon and I Sodi di San Niccolo, a blend of Sangiovese and Malvasia Nera. His regular Chianti Classico, generally 95% Sangiovese and 5% Canaiolo, a traditional blending variety in the area, is a harmonious wine with perfect balance of fruit, acidity and tannins. Produced from 20 year-old vines, the wine is aged in older barriques for seven months, so as not to overwhelm the fruit. This wine always displays impressive weight on the palate along with a fine sense of the local terroir. Enjoy upon release and for its first five to seven years. **BRV**: 2010, 2009, 2008, 2007, 2006, 2004.

LA PORTA DI VERTINE CHIANTI CLASSICO

Today in a market where many wines begin to show great similarity, it's always a pleasure to taste products that are truly distinct. This is certainly the case with the Chianti Classico at La Porta di Vertina in Gaiole in the southern reaches of Chianti Classico. Dan and Ellen Lugosch, an American couple, purchased this property in 2006 and have succeeded brilliantly in producing wines that reflect the local terroir as well as honoring the heritage of Chianti Classico. Produced from a blend of Sangiovese (much of that from 40 year-old vineyards) along with small amounts of local varieties Canaiolo, Colorino and Pugnitello, the aromas give a clue to the complexities of this wine as cherry and currant perfumes intermingle with notes of rosemary and thyme. The depth of fruit is impressive – this is a bit of a muscular style of Chianti Classico – yet there is a delicacy as well, thanks to ideal acidity and overall balance. Structured to drink well for five to seven years, the best offerings may be in fine shape for up to a decade. What impressive results for such a new producer! **BRV**: 2009, 2008, 2007.

PANZANELLO CHIANTI CLASSICO

Panzanello, owned by Andrea and Iole Sommaruga is a pretty-as-a-postcard estate situated amidst the rolling hills of Panzano in Chianti Classico. There is some remarkable wine that originates from this sector and the Panzanello Chianti Classico is no exception. Produced solely from estate grapes, this is aged partially in steel and partially in used barriques; medium-full, there are aromas of ripe red cherry, currant and thyme followed by an elegant entry on the palate. Offering very good acidity, properly balanced tannins and wonderful harmony, this has a touch of modernity, as there is about 5% Merlot in the blend, but this displays its Panzano roots admirably. Enjoy this from two to five years of age; it is especially fine paired with lighter game birds. **BRV**: 2009, 2008, 2007.

Vineyard at Panzano in the heart of the Chianti Classico zone

BADIA A COLTIBUONO CHIANTI CLASSICO RISERVA

Emanuela Stucchi Prinetti is one of the great ladies of Chianti Classico for her vision and leadership qualities; indeed, she was the first woman to be president of the Chianti Classico consorzio. The wines produced at her estate in Gaiole are textbook examples of traditional Chianti Classico; wines that combine varietal character with very good acidity, graceful tannins and a sense of place. Aged for two years in *grandi botti* of 15 and 25hl, this is a wine of marvelous complexity and drinkablility. Points and ratings are the last things on the mind of enologist Maurizio Castelli when he crafts this wine, but they inevitably follow, given the wonderful track record with this *riserva*. While approachable upon release (three to four years after the harvest), the wine improves for another six to seven years in the bottle and in some instances is ideal on its 15th birthday. **BRV**: 2008, 2007 (outstanding), 2006, 2005, 2004, 2001.

CASTELLO DI VOLPAIA CHIANTI CLASSICO
RISERVA (BLACK LABEL)
CHIANTI CLASSICO RISERVA "COLTASALLA"

Another of Tuscany's great wine women is Giovanella Stianti, who received the Volpaia estate as a wedding gift from her husband Carlo. The estate itself is something to see, situated on a hilltop outside the town of Radda, with just over 100 acres of vineyards some 1300 to 2100 feet above sea level. Stianti is a perfectionist and over the past two decades, has separated the vineyards into distinct plots whose grapes are destined for special bottlings; she also hired renowned enologist Riccardo Cotarella as winemaker. At Volpaia, there are two *riserva* Chianti Classicos: the black label, a more traditional wine aged in *botti* and barrique and Coltasalla, a single vineyard wine made from 35 year-old Sangiovese vines and aged in barrique. The Black Label is a sumptuous, elegant wine with lovely acidity and finesse, while the Coltasalla is slightly more powerful with richer tannins. Both wines drink well after five to seven years with the Coltasalla tending to peak after a decade. **BRV** (both wines): 2009, 2008, 2007, 2006, 2004.

CASTELLO DI MONSANTO CHIANTI CLASSICO RISERVA "IL POGGIO"

Way back in 1962 – how long ago that seems today! – Fabrizio Bianchi produced the first single vineyard Chianti Classico from this planting at his estate at Barberino Val d'Elsa. Over the years, the cellar practices have changed, as today the wine is aged in barriques as opposed to the first several vintages in which the wine was aged in botti, but the notable quality and fame of this wine remains unchanged. The wine is a blend of traditional local varieties – 90% Sangiovese with 10% a mix of Colorino and Canaiolo – from extremely small yields, some 60-65 quintals per hectare or 2.7 to 2.9 tons per acre. Medium-full, this wine is typified by ripe cherry fruit, nicely integrated oak (both new and used barriques are used) and healthy acidity. Always displaying backbone and impressive structure, this is a wine that drinks well for 12-15 years. The regular Monsanto Chianti Classico *riserva* is also a notable success, but to experience one of the finest wines from this zone, opt for Il Poggio. **BRV**: 2007, 2006, 2004, 2001.

VILLA CALCINAIA CHIANTI CLASSICO RISERVA "VIGNA BASTIGNANO"

When you've been around since 1524, you can talk about experience as well as tradition! That's the situation at this unassuming estate in Greve, currently managed by Count Sebastiano Capponi, the latest in a long line of family members to operate this property. Sebastiano has made numerous changes over the past decade, introducing barriques in the cellar as well as creating new blends, albeit with an eye on local heritage. His latest creation, the "Vigna Bastignano" Chianti Classico Riserva, made solely from Sangiovese, is a brilliant example of his ongoing refinements at Calcinaia. To create this wine, Capponi took Sangiovese cuttings from his estate that date back to 1910 and propogated them in this vineyard. As this site is terraced – vineyard rows are supported by rock walls – the stones reflect the sun's heat on the vines, resulting in more even ripening.

Given this combination of unique plant material and a meticulously farmed vineyard, the wine is as special as you might imagine. Displaying a beautiful garnet color and lovely aromas of red cherry, strawberry and thyme, this has excellent depth of fruit, very good acidity, nicely integrated wood notes along with youthful, refined tannins. The finish, which has a subtle note of tar, is quite long with notable persistence; overall, this is a wine that brilliantly represents its origins in an understated manner. The ancestors of Sebastiano Capponi would be proud! This was first produced from the 2008 vintage, so judging this wine's aging potential is an educated guess, but seven to ten years of age seems like it will be the ideal period in which to enjoy this wine. **BRV**: 2009, 2008.

CASTELLO DI BOSSI CHIANTI CLASSICO RISERVA "BERARDO"
Maurizio and Marco Bossi established their winery at Castelnuovo Beradenga at the far southern end of the Chianti Classico zone in 1983. This is a huge estate, encompassing 1600 acres of which 300 are planted to vines; there are also buildings on the property that are centuries old. Alberto Anonini, one of Tuscany's finest enologists crafts a modern style of Chianti Classico here as the Berardo is aged in barrique for two years. There are tar and vanilla notes from the small oak barrels, but also pure cherry fruit as well as inviting truffle notes. Medium-full, this wine requires time to settle down after release and is at its best 7-10 years after the harvest. **BRV**: 2009, 2008, 2007, 2006, 2004.

TERRABIANCA CHIANTI CLASSICO RISERVA "CROCE"
The Terrabianca estate is situated in a lovely spot in Radda in Chianti, a bit northeast of Siena; the name, meaning "white earth" refers to the chalk and limestone strata found at this location. While the Baron de Ladoucette of France purchased the estate a few years ago, it was the vision of founder Roberto Guldener, a Swiss native, that elevated this firm to its heights. Guldener would produce wines from indigenous as well as international varieties, but he believed they were different and should be kept separate. This Chianti Classico Riserva, a blend of 97%

Sangiovese and 3% Canaiolo, is evidence of that; but more so, it is the gentle winemaking style that makes this wine what it is, a beautifully made, traditional (matured in *botti*) Chianti Classico with textbook notes of cherry, thyme, menthol and cedar. It's a true *riserva*, meaning that it's not about intensity, but elegance and greater complexity. This is a lovely, understated wine that should be better known! Enjoy from five to twelve years of age. **BRV**: 2007, 2006, 2004, 2001.

VILLA CERNA CHIANTI CLASSICO RISERVA

The wines at Villa Cerna in Castellina in Chianti are made by the Cecchi family, who produce a lot of Tuscan wine! I say that as you see their basic Chianti in markets throughout Italy; this humble wine is inexpensive, but pleasant and has certainly made the Cecchi name known in many households in the country.

But they also produce several limited Tuscan reds, including an elegant Morellino di Scansano under the Val de Rose label that offers lovely typicity. I admire their Chianti Classico Riserva a great deal, as this is a wine that really speaks of its origins. It's a blend of 90% Sangiovese and 10% Colorino that is aged in large and small barrels; there is very good acidity with proper tannins, nicely integrated wood notes and notable persistence. What I like about the wine is its style, as it doesn't announce itself as being special; that is, it isn't made to win big points or prestigious awards from famous magazines. Instead this is a wine that is all about simply being a representative, well-made, beautifully balanced bottle of Chianti Classico that just happens to be delicious! Enjoy this with foods such as veal and pork over the course of five to seven years of age. **BRV**: 2009, 2008, 2007, 2006.

FÈLSINA CHIANTI CLASSICO "VIGNETO RANCIA"

Established in 1966 by Dominic Poggiali Fèlsina, this estate has become one of the unmistakable reference points for Chianti Classico. Situated in Castelnuovo Beradenga at the southern reaches of the Chianti Classico wine zone, this is a property where every wine is treated with the utmost care and attention to detail. While there is an excellent, if admittedly showy Chardonnay named "I Sistri" that has gained a great deal of attention for the firm, the various forms of Chianti Classico are the wines that Fèlsina is best known for. I absolutely love the Chianti Classico *normale*, a Slavonian oak-aged wine that displays lovely red cherry and red rose aromas. The *riserva* is another lovely wine, offering a bit more depth on the palate with fragrant perfumes of red cherry and marmalade; medium-full, this has beautiful varietal character and balance and is meant for peak enjoyment in seven to ten years.

It is with the single vineyard "Rancia" Chianti Classico that Fèlsina displays its best winemaking. First produced from the 1983 vintage, this is 100% Sangiovese (as are the *normale* and *riserva*), with the grapes sourced from a vineyard 1200 feet above sea level in Castelnuovo Beradenga. This is matured in new and used small barrels, so this is a more modern style of wine from the producer, but it is a lovely bottling of Chianti Classico that displays red cherry, myrtle, cassis and vanilla aromas. Medium-full with very good acidity, medium-weight tannins and substantial persistence, this is a wine of outstanding complexity and breeding. When you find a young vintage, lay it away for a few years in the cellar, as peak consumption is generally at age 10-12. **BRV**: 2009, 2008, 2007, 2006.

ROCCA DI MONTEGROSSI CHIANTI CLASSICO "SAN MARCELLINO"
Marco Ricasoli-Firidolfi is an gentleman farmer, one who produces graceful wines that speak of their locale. At his certified organic estate in Gaiole in Chianti, he produces a striking Chianti Classico from the San Marcellino vineyard, a portion of which contains Sangiovese vines more than 40 years old. To add some spice, he blends in 5% Pugnitello and then ages the wine in medium-toast barriques for 24 months. Medium-full with excellent ripeness, this has a lengthy finish with excellent persistence and round tannins. This tends to age gracefully, with 10 and 12 year-old bottlings showing extremely well. **BRV**: 2008, 2007, 2004.

CASTELLO DI CACCHIANO CHIANTI CLASSICO RISERVA

Giovanni Ricasoli-Firidolfi, brother of Marco at Rocca di Montegrossi, heads this estate, located in Monti, only a few minutes away. The Chianti Classico Riserva made here is a graceful wine, one with very good acidity and structure. This is a traditional – you might call it old-fashioned – style of Chianti Classico, a wine that is not forward and ripe, but one that only shows its best qualities after a few years in the bottle, as the textbook cherry and currant fruit flavors start to emerge amidst its distinctive earthy and dried herb characteristics. Heritage is a big part of this wine, but so too is balance and finesse. Best some seven to ten years after the harvest, this is a wine for those who respect a producer who seeks to represent the local terroir in his products. **BRV**: 2007, 2005, 2004.

CASTELLO DI BROLIO CHIANTI CLASSICO

Don't be fooled by the simple Chianti Classico designation on the label, for this is one of the finest wines produced anywhere in the area. Proprietor Francesco Ricasoli – cousin of Marco and Giovanni Ricasoli-Firidolfi – manages this historic estate, a winery that has been continuously producing Tuscan wines since 1141! Ricasoli does not believe in using the *riserva* term for Chianti Classico, so even though this wine could be called that, he prefers the basic denomination. What he is saying here is that this is his finest wine and that he wants consumers to remember his estate and the type of wine he is capable of producing; he bases this decision on the great *chateaux* of Bordeaux, as with Lafite, Latour and Mouton. For Ricasoli then, his philosophy is "I make Chianti Classico and here is my best wine." This is a modern style wine with a small percentage of Merlot and/or Cabernet Sauvignon (usually less than 10%) and the wine is aged in barriques, but it is unmistakably Tuscan. Ripe and rich, yet very delicate in nature with round tannins and a great deal of finesse, this is outstanding virutally every vintage and often stands out in the so-called lesser vintages. First produced in 1997, this drinks well for at least 10-12 years and perhaps even longer

– we will have to wait a few more years to know! **BRV**: 2009, 2008 (exceptional), 2007, 2006, 2005, 2004.

SAN FELICE VIGORELLO

Way back in 1968, San Felice produced this wine for the first time as a 100% Sangiovese product, but as Chianti Classico regulations required some white varieties in the blend, it had to be designated differently. This was in reality, one of the first – if not the first – examples of what would soon become known as a Super Tuscan. Today the wine contains about 50% Sangiovese with the remainder Cabernet Sauvignon and Merlot and is aged in French barriques, so the wine bears little resemblance to that initial bottling. Yet this is still one of the more notable Super Tuscans, quite full and rich with good spice and acidity as well as the structure and enough stuffing to ensure as much as two decades of potential enjoyment. Every wine from this great producer from Castelnuovo Beradenga is beautifully made and the Vigorello remains one of their most singular as well as classiest. **BRV**: 2008, 2007, 2006, 2004.

ANTINORI TIGNANELLO

Piero Antinori has been at the forefront of changes for Chianti Classico for much of the past four decades; this wine is primary evidence. First produced from the 1970 vintage when Antinori labeled it as a Chianti Classico Riserva, he made subtle changes over the next few years, omitting the required white varieties in 1975 and then adding Cabernet Sauvignon in the wine a few years later. Over the years, the blending has changed – today the wine is generally 75% Sangiovese with 20% Cabernet Sauvignon and 5% Cabernet Franc – but the influence this wine has had in Toscana may be unmatched. Today there are dozens of Super Tuscans such as this, wines that have a Chianti thumbprint along with the modern influences of Bordeaux varieties and small French oak aging, yet Tignanello remains one of the best-known and most critically praised. The wine needs a few years after release to show its best; 20-25 year old bottles are still in fine shape. **BRV:** 2009, 2008, 2007, 2006, 2005, 2004, 2001 (exceptional).

FONTODI FLACCIANELLO DELLE PIAVE

Giovanni Manetti has made Fontodi into one of the most celebrated wine estates in all of Italy. There are many reasons, as he has a state of the art cellar that is employed by his brilliant enologist Franco Bernabei. But above all, the strength of his wines lay in the vineyards. His estate is located in Panzano in Chianti, in the heart of the Classico zone, in a small area known as the "Conca d'Oro" ("the golden ampitheater"); Manetti has 170 acres planted to vine. While he works with international varieties such as Pinot Noir and Syrah, it is of course, Sangiovese that represents his finest wines. His regular Chianti Classico is one of the priciest of its type, yet given the quality of the wine, the cost of this wine seems fair; medium-full with excellent concentration and balance, this is a Chianti Classico of great style.

Manetti's superstar wine however is Flaccianello delle Piave, a 100% Sangiovese that is sold as a Toscana Rosso IGT, though it could clearly be labeled as a Chianti Classico. A selection of the best Sangiovese from the estate and aged in French barriques for 18 months, this is a powerful offering of Sangiovese that combines varietal purity, outstanding concentration and persistence with breeding and a sense of place. This is a wine that has stood the test of time and is recognized as one of Tuscany's finest offerings; in fact, it challenges many examples of Brunello di Montalcino for superiority as a wine made entirely from Sangiovese. Flaccianello ages beautifully; the 1999 I tasted in early 2012 was still quite fresh and promised another decade (at least) of enjoyment. A solid estimate would be that most vintages of Flaccianello will peak in 20 years plus. **BRV**: 2008, 2007 (exceptional), 2005, 2004, 2001, 1999 (exceptional).

IL MOLINO DI GRACE "GRATIUS"

The windmill of Grace, refers to the Panzano estate of American-born Frank Grace, who purchased this property in 1995. An art lover as well as a passionate wine drinker, Grace has placed several striking statues at various locales on the estate. His versions of Chianti Classico are rich, ripe and deeply concentrated and to capture the essence of the local terroir, he wisely hired Franco Bernabei as enologist. "Gratius" is his top estate wine, a 100% Sangiovese from very old vines (between 55 and 70 years of age), situated 1300 feet above sea level. Sporting a deep ruby red appearance with aromas of myrtle, currant and tobacco leaf, this has a generous mid-palate and excellent persistence, with a beauitfully structured finish with notes of dark chocolate and dried brown herbs that emerge after a few years in the bottle. While this is aged in small and mid-size oak casks, the wood notes are in the background; as always Bernabei lets the terroir shine through. This is a marvelous wine that should be better known; it is at is best from ten to twelve years of age. **BRV**: 2006, 2005, 2004.

COLOGNOLE CHIANTI RUFINA
Not including Chianti Classico, there are seven sub-zones that make up the overall Chianti territory; arguably the finest is Chianti Rufina (*rue-fee-na*), located east of Florence. The vineyards here, situated around 1800 feet above sea level, are among the highest in all of Chianti and yield wines that have excellent aging potential. At this attractive, yet humble estate, Cesare Coda Nunziante is interested more in producing wines of typicity than flash; scores are not important to this man.

Maybe that's why I like him as well as his wines so much, as they're honest versions of what this small Chianti zone does so well. Medium-bodied, this has lovely red cherry aromas along with tart acidity and subtle wood notes; this is a wine that instantly transports you to Chianti with its earthiness and light herbal notes. I love the simple charms of this wine, which drinks well from three to seven years of age. **BRV**: 2009, 2008, 2007, 2006.

FATTORIA DI VETRICE CHIANTI RUFINA RISERVA
This gem of an estate is producing some of the most elegant, precise examples of *riserva* from anywhere in the Chianti zone. Tradition is the keyword here for the Grati family that runs this estate; only local varieties such as Canaiolo and Colorino are used to complement Sangiovese in the blend, while aging is strictly in *botti*. Too often a *riserva* Chianti is all about oak being used to add a little more punch to the

wine, but not here, as the wood notes are quite subdued. This wine is for me, one of the most honest and typical of any Chianti Riserva; it drinks well immediately upon release and tends to offer optimum enjoyment at around ten years of age. **BRV**: 2008, 2007, 2006, 2004.

SELVAPIANA CHIANTI RUFINA RISERVA "VIGNETO BUCERCHIALE"

Among the most renowned producers in the Chianti Rufina sub-zone is Selvapiana, headed by Federico Giuntini Antinori, who has been refining his wines with great precision over the last twenty years. Along with a very good Chianti Rufina *normale*, the single vineyard Bucerchiale is typical of the elegance and varietal character from this estate. 100% Sangiovese from vines that were planted in 1968, the wine matures for fifteen months in large casks. This is Sangiovese personified with delicious cherry fruit along with tobacco and subtle spice notes. Everything about this wine is so graceful, from the tannins to the use of wood as well as the elegance in the finish. It's a safe bet to say that the Vigneto Bucerchiale is not just one of the most accomplished examples of Chianti Rufina, it's simply one of the best possible realizations of any Chianti. This wine tends to show its complexities at five to seven years and can age for 15-20 years after the harvest. **BRV**: 2007, 2006, 2004, 2001, 1999.

FRESCOBALDI CHIANTI RUFINA RISERVA "MONTESODI"

The Frescobaldi family, one of Tuscany's most recognized wine producers, makes wines from several areas of the region. For me, their most successful red wines come from their estate in Chianti Rufina; this includes the elegant and delicious Nipozzano *riserva*, a wine with an excellent price/quality ratio. However, it is the Montesodi, a *riserva* made only in optimum vintages from a single vineyard that truly displays the quality of this estate. The grapes are sourced from a beautifully situated vineyard 1300 feet above sea level; the vines have an average age of 13 years. Aged in one-year old barriques for two years, this 100% Sangiovese is medium-full with expressive cherry and strawberry fruit along with subtle thyme and tobacco notes. Packed with layers of fruit, one could mistake it for a Brunello di Montalcino in certain years. All in all, this is a sleek, sublime example of Tuscan Sangiovese at its most refined. This has a great track record for aging, as bottles from the mid-1980s are still in fine condition. **BRV:** 2008, 2007, 2006, 2005, 2004, 2001.

LA LASTRA CHIANTI COLLI SENESI

Chianti Colli Senesi – "the hills of Siena" – is one of the seven sub-zones for Chianti; it encompasses a fairly large area in the province of Siena. This is the common red wine for producers who also make Vernaccia di San Gimignano; for some vintners, this is somewhat of a basic red, for others, their version has a bit more character. One of my favorite examples of Chianti Colli Senesi is the La Lastra, from a winery established in 1994 and today managed by Renato Spanu. Comprised of 90% Sangiovese, 5% Canaiolo and 5% white varieties Trebbiano and Malvasia (these traditional white grapes are still allowed in Chianti Colli Senesi, but not in Chianti Classico), this harkens back to a simpler time when a Chianti was meant for drinking and not for maximum points in a review in a wine magazine. This has attractive fresh red cherry and strawberry fruit along with tangy acidity and notes of dried brown herbs; while it's a wine to be consumed by its fourth birthday, the La Lastra has a surprisingly big finish. This is a pleasant surprise and a wine with an excellent price/quality ratio. **BRV:** 2010, 2009, 2008.

TENUTA DE CAPEZZANA CARMIGNANO "VILLA DI CAPEZZANA"

Carmignano is a red wine produced in a small section in the province of Prato, a bit north and almost straight west of Florence. This is arguably the oldest wine zone in Tuscany, with documents showing that wine was produced here as far back as 800 AD. Today, there are approximately a dozen producers of Carmignano, with several of them having been established more than 150 years ago. One of the most prestigious of the area is Tenuta de Capezzana, owned by the Bonacossi family, who was instrumental in Carmignano obtaining its

DOC designation in 1975 and then DOCG status in 1990. While Sangiovese is the principal variety used in this wine (as with most reds from Tuscany), Cabernet Sauvignon must be part of the blend. There are various styles of Carmignano produced, from simple quaffing reds to more full-bodied versions meant for a decade of cellaring. The Villa de Capezzana offering is 80% Sangiovese with 20% Cabernet Sauvignon that is matured for 15 months in *tonneaux* and barriques. Deep ruby red, this is quite ripe and generally a bit tightly wound upon release; the flavors on the palate are of black fruits, tar and coffee. There are noticeable tannins, but they are nicely balanced as are the wood notes. This needs time after release to settle down, at is is structured for peak enjoyment some 12-15 years after the harvest in the finest growing seasons. **BRV**: 2008, 2007, 2006, 2004, 2001.

AMBRA CARMIGNANO RISERVA "MONTALBIOLO"

The Ambra estate has been owned by the Romei Rigoli family since 1870; the estate takes its name from a 15th century poem of the same name written by Lorenzo Il Magnifico. Over the past decade, this producer has clearly become one of the most consistent in the area, giving great attention to all their wines, from the simple rosato Vin Ruspo to their top examples of Carmignano. This *riserva* is a blend of 70% Sangiovese, 10% Cabernet and 20% Canaiolo; the fruit is sourced from a vineyard 800 feet above sea level comprised of loose clay and sandstone. The aromas offer typical cherry varietal fruit along with tobacco and brown herbs; medium-full, this has excellent persistence, with a bit more tannins than the examples of Chianti Montalbano produced locally. This is a bit rustic and wild, but never too much; peak consumption is a decade after the vintage, sometimes longer in exceptional vintages. **BRV**: 2008, 2007, 2006, 2004, 2001.

CAPEZZANA GHIAIE DELLA FURBA

At Tenuta di Capezzana, the Bonacossi family is most famous for their various bottlings of Carmignano, a blend of Sangiovese and Cabernet Sauvignon. In 1979, they decided to craft a local wine made solely of Bordeaux varietals, calling it Ghaie della Furba, meaning "pebbles of the Furba," the name of a local river. This first blend was Cabernet Sauvignon, Cabernet Franc and Merlot and was widely praised. A few years later, Syrah was added to the blend and the standard cuvée today is 60% Cabernet Sauvignon, 30% Merlot and 10% Syrah. Bright ruby red with aromas of black cherry, black currant and tar, this offers impressive concentration, notable, but not overdone oak and a finish with ample fruit as well as firm tannins. The sweetness of the fruit is a primary reason for the charm of this wine, that as well as the excellent structure and balance. This drinks well at seven to ten years of age and is usually at peak condition at 12-15 years of age. **BRV**: 2007, 2006, 2004, 2001 (exceptional), 2000, 1998.

FATTORIA CASTELLINA "IL POGEO"

Here is an example of a blended Tuscan red (Super-Tuscan if you must, but I prefer not to think of this wine in that fashion) that is an elegantly made wine crafted for balance and suppleness and not power or high media ratings. This is a blend of Sangiovese, Cabernet and Syrah from this organically-farmed estate in the Chianti Montalbano district, a bit west of Florence. There are aromas of cherry, black currant and rhubarb with medium weight tannins, subtle wood notes and tart acidity. While it's got a touch of modernity, this harkens back to the day of field blends in Toscana, which is not a bad thing and almost refreshing in today's wine environment. Enjoy this from five to seven years of age. **BRV**: 2009, 2008, 2007.

SESTA DI SOPRA BRUNELLO DI MONTALCINO

About an hour's drive south of Siena, the fortress town of Montalcino is home to Tuscany's longest-lived red wine, Brunello di Montalcino. The word Brunello is the local term for Sangiovese, the only variety used in the production of this wine. This area is warmer than Chianti Classico and receives less rain, so the wines here tend to be more full-bodied with slightly bigger tannins, with the final result being wines that have the capacity to age for 20-25 years and even longer in the best offerings. Brunello di Montalcino is aged for a minimum of two years in wood, although most estates keep the wine in barrels longer than that, as the wine is not released until it is five years old. They type of wood is left up to the individual producer; traditional aging is done in *grandi botti*, while some winemakers have opted for barriques and others, the mid-size *tonneaux* (some even go with a combination of two of these vessels).

Sesta di Sopra, situated in Castelnuovo dell'Abate, is an ultratraditional producer, aging only in large Slavonian oak (30hl) for two years. This is a tiny estate, as only 400 cases of Brunello are produced in a typical vintage; in fact, each vintage is contained in one large oak cask in the cellar! Owner Ettore Spina has in just a few short years established this wine as one of the most elegantly styled in Montalcino; this is a Brunello that focuses on purity of fruit as well as floral aromas. There is impressive weight on the palate along with excellent persistence in the finish, but the emphasis is always on finesse as well as expressing local terroir. While it is impossible to predict the aging potential of this wine as only a handful of vintages have been produced, 15-20 years should not be a problem, given the overall balance of this wine. **BRV**: 2007, 2006 (outstanding), 2005, 2004 (outstanding).

EREDI FULIGNI BRUNELLO DI MONTALCINO
If you had to select the best examples of traditional Brunello among all those produced, it's a safe bet that Fuligni would be at or near the top of the list. Maria Flora Fuligni and her nephew Roberto manage the estate, producing about 2500 cases of Brunello in a typical year. Most of the wine is aged in large Slavonian oak casks with a small percentage in *tonneaux*; clearly the wood notes are subtle, allowing the exquisite perfumes of red cherry and strawberry preserves to emerge clearly. Medium-full, this is a seamless wine with every component in harmony; the tannins are remarkably silky. This is a Brunello of great complexity, displaying both strength (thanks to very low yields) and grace. While this is appealing upon release, the wine improves over the course of 15-20 years and from time to time can drink well at 30 years of age. Clearly, this is one of Tuscany's finest red wines! **BRV**:

2007, 2006 (both exceptional), 2005, 2004, 2001 and 1999 (the last three vintages all of exceptional quality).

POGGIO DI SOTTO BRUNELLO DI MONTALCINO

True Brunello advocates speak in hushed tones when they refer to Poggio di Sotto. From day one in 1989 when Piero Palmucci established this estate on a hill in Castelnuovo dell'Abate, the goal has been uncompromising – to craft the finest version of Brunello di Montalcino possible. For Palmucci, this does not mean the biggest wine, but rather the most complex, most elegant offering possible. The work starts in the vineyard, as yields are incredibly low, averaging 30-35 quintals per hectare, some 1.4 to 1.6 tons per acre, a remarkably low figure. The other factor in the wine's style is the long aging in Slavonian oak casks, some 48 months, or two years longer than is required by law. This lengthy period in wood greatly rounds out the tannins and also helps achieve a generous mid-palate with layers of fruit. The resulting wine is one of those that when you taste it, a light goes on, for you realize that greatness in wine is not about intensity or power, but instead elegance, grace and finesse. The Poggio di Sotto Brunello is as light as a feather on the palate, yet this is still a wine of outstanding depth of fruit and persistence. One would expect the regular bottling of this estate's Brunello to peak in 20-25 years; the Riserva, which is aged for five years in wood, even longer. As a side note, even the humble Rosso di Montalcino, which is aged for two years – again, much longer than the requirements for this wine – is a stunning wine, one that matches the complexity of some versions of other producers' Brunello.

As Palmucci has no descendants, he decided to sell the estate in 2011, requiring that the new owner would continue with a traditional philosophy of winemaking. That new proprietor is Claudio Tipa, the owner of two great Tuscan estates: Colle Massari in Montecucco and Grattamacco in Bolgheri. Tipa, a brilliant vintner and marketer, has agreed to stay the course, great news for lovers of the wines from this brilliant Brunello di Montalcino estate! **BRV:** 2007, 2006 (both exceptional), 2005, 2004, 2001 and 1999 (the last two also of exceptional quality).

IL PARADISO DI MANFREDI BRUNELLO DI MONTALCINO

If you were to select the best qualities of a Brunello di Montalcino, structure would be at the top of the list. Brunello can age for a quarter of a century or longer, thanks to proper structure, which comes from the ideal harmony of acidity, fruit and tannins. At his small estate a bit northwest of the town of Montalcino, Florio Guerrini carries on his father's work of producing ultratraditional bottlings of Brunello. These are wines that display great subtleties throughout, from the morel cherry and orange peel aromas to the pinpoint acidity and subdued wood notes (aging is only in large casks). No chemicals are used in the vineyards, giving these wines a remarkable purity. These are wines structured for the long haul and are at their best anywhere from a dozen to twenty-five years after the harvest. How nice to see wines such as these made today, as these are products that buck modern trends and rely on tradition and varietal character. **BRV:** 2007, 2006, 2004, 2001, 1999 (these last four vintages all outstanding.)

CIACCI PICCOLOMINI BRUNELLO DI MONTALCINO "PIANROSSO"

This estate is located in the southwestern reaches of the Montalcino zone, just across the road from the Montecucco DOC area. Paolo and Lucia Bianchini have been carrying on the work of their father Giuseppe, who passed away in 2004. Produced entirely from the eponymous vineyard, the Pianrosso Brunello is aged for 36 months in various sized *grandi botti*, ranging from 20 to 62hl, resulting in a wine that has subtle wood notes. Rich and ripe, there are distinct notes of tobacco along with dried cherry and cumin. Combining outstanding complexity with a distinct sense of place, this is a Brunello that has individual style, yet is unmistakably a wine of great varietal purity. Give this a bit of time, as it shows its best qualities down the road, peaking at 15-20 years. There is also a Pianrossso

Brunello Riserva produced here that is also quite impressive. **BRV**: 2007, 2006, 2004, 2001, 1999.

POGGIO ANTICO BRUNELLO DI MONTALCINO
BRUNELLO DI MONTALCINO "ALTERO"

Today there are more than 135 producers of Brunello di Montalcino, but many of them have only been established over the past decade. This makes Poggio Antico, purchased by Giancarlo and Nuccia Gloder in 1984, a true veteran among this area's estates. Today their daughter Paola and her husband Alberto Montefiori manage the winery on an everyday basis and have made it into one of the area's most consistent in terms of quality. There are two regular bottlings of Brunello di Montalcino made most years. The white label is more of a traditional wine, aged for three years (one year above the minimum required time) in large Slavonian casks, while the Altero ("other") is aged in mid-sized French *tonneax*, also for three years. Both wines are impeccably made, offering lovely aromatics, a beatifully full mid-palate and exceptional structure. Think about the sensual aspect of cherry and strawberry fruit with notes of cedar, backed by subtle wood notes and silky tannins and you've got a pretty good sense of what the Brunellos from Poggio Antico are all about. Both wines are released at the same time; generally the Altero (easy to recognize with its brown label), tends to need an extra two or three years before it opens up, while the white label bottling tends to be more approachable upon release; both wines however, are built for the long haul, as in 20 years plus. **BRV:** 2007, 2006 (both exceptional), 2005, 2004, 2001 and 1999 (these last two vintages also exceptional).

CAPARZO BRUNELLO DI MONTALCINO "LA CASA"

The Caparzo estate has been the source of some of the area's finest wines since its founding in 1968. Located at the far northern reaches of the Montalcino district, the property is situated in a small valley, ensuring ideal ripeness as well as cool temperatures at night that help preserve acidity. Current proprietor Elisabetta Gnudi has carried on the work of previous owners by producing a Brunello *normale*, *riserva* and a special bottling called La Casa, appropriately named as it is made entirely from a vineyard next to the main house on the property. First produced in 1977, La Casa is the richest of the Brunellos produced at Caparzo; it is also the one that best expresses the local terroir, given its rugged earthiness and mineral streak in the finish. This is a modern updating of Brunello, as it is intially aged in barriques and then in larger casks of French oak (30hl). The color is a bit darker than many examples of Brunello, the cherry aromas are a bit riper and the tannins are quite firm. This is a tightly packed wine that needs several years after release to open up; generally the wine peaks at 15-20 years after the harvest. **BRV**: 2006, 2004, 2001, 1999.

COL D'ORCIA BRUNELLO DI MONTALCINO RISERVA "POGGIO AL VENTO"

Col d'Orcia represents a great deal of history in Montalcino, dating back to 1933, when it was called Fattoria Sant'Angelo in Colle, referring to its ideal location just below that hillside town. The company has changed hands a few times since then and today Francesco Marone Cinzano, a native of Piemonte from the famed vermouth firm of Torino, is the proprietor. The property, at an elevation of 1475 feet above sea level at its highest point, is ideally situated so that fog and strong winds are rarely a problem. The Poggio al Vento Riserva, made only in the finest vintages from the eponymous vineyard planted in 1974, is a great example of what a Riserva Brunello is all about. Full bodied, with an elegant entry on the palate, the wine has outstanding concentration, rich, refined tannins and very good acidity. The winemaking team has decided to age this wine at their cellars for a longer period of time than most producers - four years in large casks and then two additional years in the bottle. Thus in 2012, when many producers were releasing their 2006 Riserva Brunello, the current release for the Poggio al Vento was the 2004. Traditional in every sense of the word, this is a wine that you remember for many reasons - its elegance, varietal purity, finesse, class and breeding. How nice that Col d'Orcia continues to lead the way in Montalcino with wines as magnficent as this! As this is made only in the finest years, aging potential depends on the particular year, but it is certain that twenty years after the harvest, this wine will be drinking beautifully, several years from its peak. **BRV**: 2004, 2001, 1999, 1998.

IL POGGIONE BRUNELLO DI MONTALCINO RISERVA

Il Poggione has been one of the flag bearers for Brunello di Montalcino since the 1950s. Through the combined forces of owner Leopoldo Franceschi along with winemaker Fabrizio Bindocci, Il Poggione has maintained a consistent vision of Brunello di Montalcino as a traditional wine. While a few changes have been made along the way – several years ago Bindocci changed the oak from Slavonian to French – maturation for the Brunello and Brunello Riserva has always been in large casks. The regular bottling is excellent every year, offering layers of fruit and a long, graceful finish, but the *riserva* is a standout. Produced entirely from the estate Paganelli vineyard, which was planted in 1964, the wine is a touch riper than the regular bottling with more weight on the palate and greater persistence and grip in the finish. A key to this wine is that there is always very good acidity, which helps maintain both beautiful freshness in the wine along with ideal structure; the finest examples of this wine age for 25-30 years. The "Vigna Paganelli" designation has been on the label since the 2003 bottling. **BRV**: 2006, 2004, 2003, 2001, 1999 (exceptional).

LISINI BRUNELLO DI MONTALCINO RISERVA "UGOLAIA"

Since the mid 1800s, the Lisini family has owned this splendid estate in Sant'Angelo in Colle and has an admirable track record of producing Brunello that is slow to open, but displays excellent aging ability. For years, noted Tuscan enologist Franco Bernabei was the winemaker, but today those duties belong to Filippo Paoletti and Giulio Gambelli. The Ugolaia, from a single vineyard of Sangiovese vines chosen according to a massal selection (some of the original plants are pre-phylloxera), is aged for a period of between 36 and 42 months in large Slavonian oak casks. Cherry and tobacco notes highlight the aromas and there is an elegant entry on the palate, excellent persistence, subtle wood influence and very good acidity; this is a beauti-fully structured wine that often peaks at 20-25 years. Over the past few years, the quality of each bottling of Brunello at Lisini has been on the increase- the regular 2007 is one of their best of the last decade; the Ugolaia is slowly moving into the rarified atmosphere of one of Montalcino's finest wines. **BRV**: 2006 (exceptional), 2004, 2003, 2001, 1999.

TALENTI BRUNELLO DI MONTALCINO RISERVA

I have selected the riserva bottling from Talenti, but the truth is that I could have opted for the regular bottling as well, as each of this company's wines is routinely outstanding virtually every vintage. Established in 1980 by Pierluigi Talenti, the estate is situ-ated in Pian di Conte, a *frazione* of Sant'Angelo in Colle. The Talenti Brunellos are made in a traditional manner by Carlo Ferrini, who has become a household name in Montalcino, ironically for his more modern style of Brunello for other estates. Aging here is in a combination of large and mid-size casks for the regular Brunello and only *botti* for the Riserva. This wine is notable for its spot-on fruit aromas of cherry and strawberry preserves with restrained notes of cedar. The mid palate is generous and there is excellent persistence along with precise acidity and silky tannins. This is not a Brunello that attacks, but rather charms the palate and the com-plexity and structure are ideal. All in all, this is a seamless wine that has great typicity, wonderful varietal purity and prominent class and breeding. Thanks to its outstanding overall balance, the wine is quite attractive upon release, some six years after the harvest, but like the best examples of Brunello, this offers more character after a few years in the bottle. Peak development for this wine is generally somewhere between 20 and 25 years. **BRV**: 2006, 2005, 2004, 2001 (exceptional), 1999.

BANFI BRUNELLO DI MONTALCINO RISERVA "POGGIO ALL'ORO"

John Mariani and his brother Harry established Banfi in 1978 when they purchased the existing Poggio alle Mura ("hill surrounded

by a wall") estate near Montalcino. As they were Americans getting established in this ancient Tuscan countryside, they naturally
attracted attention, both positive and negative. Today Cristina
Mariani-May is the face of Banfi and the winery has achieved many
great strides, not the least of which is that they have become one
of the best-known of all Brunello producers. The Mariani family has
always believed in the big picture, working all the time to promote
not only their wines, but Brunello as a wine type in general. One of
the primary ways they have accomplished this is a lengthy study
in Sangiovese clones suitable for the area; they have shared their
results with their neighbors and have helped the overall development of Brunello di Montalcino the past 15-20 years. The top wine
for Banfi is the Riserva Poggio all'Oro ("hill of gold"), from a single
vineyard at their estate in Tavernelle. This is a very modern style
of Brunello, aged for 30 months in barriques, displaying aromas of
cherry, tar and vanilla; there is always excellent concentration and
the finish is complete with big tannins and impressive persistence.
This demands several years after release to soften; optimum consumption time is 15-25 years of age. **BRV**: 2006, 2004, 2001, 1999,
1998.

VAL DI SUGA BRUNELLO DI MONTALCINO RISERVA "VIGNA SPUNTALI"

Tenimenti Angelini began with the purchase of three Tuscan estates,
including Val di Suga in Montalcino in 1994; the Angelini family has
since also purchased a winery in Friuli and they have been grape
growers in Marche for several decades. Val di Suga is a large estate,
with more than 135 acres of Sangiovese wines in several locations.
Their Brunello is a modern, forward style; while the regular bottling
can be a bit oaky in some years, that is not a problem with the Riserva
Vigna Spuntali. Produced only in the best vintages, this is matured for
twenty-four months in slightly larger than normal barriques; this has
dried cherry and tobacco notes in the aromas and finish, the tannins
are medium-weight and nicely balanced and there is excellent persistence and structure. This definitely needs time to settle down and

round out, especially in a vintage such as 2006, which will be at its best somewhere between 2026 and 2032 – let's hope we're all around to enjoy it! **BRV**: 2006, 2004, 2001, 1999.

UCCELLIERA BRUNELLO DI MONTALCINO RISERVA

Proprietor Andrea Cortonesi has quietly been going about his work at his estate in Castelnuovo dell'Abate in the shadow of Sant'Antimo, realizing beautiful fruit-driven, polished bottlings of Brunello di Montalcino. His style is largely traditional with a slight modern updating, as he does use barriques to some degree. His regular Brunello is simply delicious with appealing cherry and strawberry fruit and subdued oak notes and has become one of the most consistent over the past decade. But his *riserva* Brunello takes things up a few notches both in terms of aromatics as well as depth of fruit. Here the perfumes are of cherry, strawberry preserves and even a touch of cranberry; medium-full, this has outstanding persistence and displays silky tannins and precise acidity. Aging here begins in French barriques and the continues in large Slavonian oak casks; total time in wood is approximately 42 months, yet the wood notes are barely noticeable on this wine. This is so tantalizing upon release, yet the real class of this wine does not emerge for seven or eight years, with the wine at optimum drinking condition at 20-25 years of age. **BRV**: 2006, 2004, 2001, 1999.

LE CHIUSE BRUNELLO DI MONTALCINO RISERVA

It should come as no surprise that the wines of Le Chiuse would rank among the finest in Montalcino; after all, the vineyards at this estate were once owned by Biondi-Santi, who would use them in their *riserva* Brunello – talk about the high rent district! This small estate, situated at Montosoli just northeast of the town of Montalcino, is comprised of fifteen acres of Sangiovese vineyards, all organically-farmed to miniscule yields. The *riserva*, produced only in the finest vintages, is aged for 46 months in large Slavonian oak casks of 20 and 30hl. This is Brunello that combines excellent concentration with a lightness on the palate along with an extremely long finish. This is a seamless wine that has pinpoint acidity, outstanding varietal purity and heavenly complexity. This wine has great longevity and while it improves over the years with time in the bottle, it is graceful enough to enjoy upon release, some six years after the harvest. Only about 4000 bottles of the *riserva* are produced, so this is admittedly a difficult wine to locate. If that is the case, you will certainly not be disappointed by the regular bottling of Brunello from Le Chiuse either; this has the same grace and typicity of the *riserva*, albeit a touch (just a touch) lighter; the regular is among the very best Brunello produced every year. **BRV** (for the *riserva*): 2006, 2004, 2001, 1999.

CAPANNA BRUNELLO DI MONTALCINO RISERVA

The Cencioni family has owned this estate, situated north of Montalcino in Montosoli, since 1957. Today Patrizio Cencioni oversees production of traditionally made wines from 50 acres of vineyards, farmed to very small yields. The Riserva Brunello is aged for four years in large Slavonian oak casks and is among the most authentic of the traditional Brunellos, especially as the wine is subdued and refined, offering an authentic sense of place. The wine has a lovely aromatic profile, offering perfumes of red cherry, strawberry preserves and red roses; there is impressive concentration and a lengthy finish with excellent persistence. The acidity is beautfully tuned, maintaining balance and freshness, while offering ideal structure for long term aging. This is not a powerhouse wine, but rather one of subtle charms; this tends to peak some 12-20 years after the harvest. **BRV**: 2006 (exceptional), 2004, 2001.

TERRALSOLE BRUNELLO DI MONTALCINO RISERVA

Mario Bollag can clearly be defined as a modern day Renaissance man, having been involved with activities as varied as operating a mountain bike company in Nepal to working with Haitian artists to help them become better known throughout the world. A Swiss native, Bollag first ventured into Montalcino by establishing Il Palazzone, where he crafted small lots of traditional Brunello throughout the 1980s before selling the estate in the late 1990s. He then inaugurated Terralsole in a beautifully situated spot at the end of a long road high above the countryside just south of the town of Montalcino. The view from his estate is breathtaking, especially the panorama looking towards Castelnuovo del'Abate. His vineyards at the winery are some 1350 feet above sea level and are perfectly exposed for the late afternoon sun; he also has some vineyards planted in lower areas a few miles away. His Riserva offerings are clearly his finest wines, made in a style that have some modern touches (aging in *tonneaux*), yet are classically crafted with impressive depth of ripe fruit coupled with ideal structure and very good harmony of wood and acidity. Best consumed some 12-15 years after harvest, the Terralsole Brunello Riservas can be easily identified, given their striking original art labels from some of Mario's friends in Haiti. Mario always plans on keeping this a hand-crafted estate, so the wines will never be easy to find outside of Europe, but they are worth a search. **BRV**: 2006, 2005, 2004, 2001.

CAMIGLIANO BRUNELLO DI MONTALCINO RISERVA "GUALTO"

Established in 1956, the Camigliano estate is named for the charming little town in the southeastern reaches of the Montalcino district in which it is located. The wines here are traditionally made, with each release displaying a light touch on the palate backed by precise acidity. The regular Brunello is medium-full with excellent persistence, admirable balance and round tannins; often approachable upon release (as with the 2007), it is at its best from 12-15 years of age. But it is the "Gualto" Brunello Riserva – Gualto is the nickname for owner Gualtiero Ghezzi – that is the shining star from this producer. Displaying a lovely youthful garnet color, the aromas of ripe red cherry, myrtle, plum and cedar are just ideal; medium-full with excellent concentration, there are silky tannins and subtle wood notes. Look for this to be in peak form at 15-25 years of age. **BRV**: 2006, 2004 (outstanding), 2001.

IL PALAZZONE BRUNELLO DI MONTALCINO RISERVA

Richard Parsons, an American businessman, purchased this estate, just outside the town of Montalcino, from the original owner Mario Bollag in 1990 (Bollag would go on to establish another Brunello estate, Terralsole – see entry). Parsons loves the traditional style of Brunello, matured in large casks, which allows the wine to display a lovely sense of place. These wines tend to be a bit closed when released, needing a few years to open, but this also allows them a long life, as the *risevrva* bottlings drink well some 12-20 years after the vintage date. The wines routinely have very good acidity as well as subdued wood notes. These are classically styled Brunellos of great breeding and class! **BRV**: 2006, 2004, 2001, 1999 (these two vintages outstanding), 1998, 1995.

CITILLE DI SOPRA BRUNELLO DI MONTALCINO RISERVA
Fabio Innocenti started his production of Brunello di Montalcino in 2000 with a release of only 800 bottles; today that total is 35,000 bottles. His wines originate from estate vineyards in Torrenieri, in the far northeastern reaches of the Brunello zone; here the rich soils yield very powerful wines. The style is traditional; his wines offer excellent ripeness as well as a touch of minerality. The Brunello Riserva offers very good acidity, nicely integrated wood and big, but balanced tannins. Tightly wound upon release, this is a wine meant for peak consumption in 20 years' time. **BRV**: 2006, 2005, 2004.

PIAN DELL'ORINO BRUNELLO DI MONTALCINO RISERVA
Husband and wife Jan Hendrik Erbach and Caroline Pobitzer own this attractive estate, located adjacent to the vineyards of Biondi-Santi. They tend to their vineyards in a true organic fashion, shying away from using chemical pesticides, herbicides or mineral fertilizers. They also plant clover and legumes in between the rows, as these plants produce nitrogen which are in turn absorbed by the vines. It is this attention to detail and careful planning of the best ways in which to treat the soils that make the Pian dell'Orino wines so remarkable. The varietal purity is just that much more focused in all of their wines and the *riserva* especially displays lovely finesse as well as excellent length in the finish. Structured for optimimum enjoyment at 20-25 years of age, this is among

the most singular examples of Brunello di Montalcino. **BRV:** 2006, 2004 (outstanding), 2001.

BIONDI-SANTI BRUNELLO DI MONTALCINO RISERVA

What more can I say about this magnificent Brunello estate, one that was established in 1825 and credited as the birthplace of this great wine? Happily I can say that this most traditional of Brunello producers is still relevant in this day and continues to produce splendid wines under the leadership of Franco Biondi-Santi. The 5000 or so cases of Brunello are produced entirely from estate vineyards, located just outside the town of Montalcino. Aging is traditional as its gets, as the Brunello matures for 36 months in large Slavonian casks, ranging in size from 30 to 140 hectoliters-these latter among the largest in use in the area. Another point to note in terms of tradition is the fact that a few of these barrels in use today are more than 100 years old!

The Biondi-Santi Brunello Riserva features amazing aromas that combine many characteristics, from dried cherry and rhubarb to menthol, tobacco and hints of truffle. Yet these perfumes are only one integral part of this wine, as subtle wood notes, earthy tannins and a distinct herbal character are also important components. The final analysis of this wine is all about length on the mid-palate and in the finish with outstanding balance and finesse. Clearly with the precision work being done in the vineyards as well as in the cellar, the Biondi-Santi Brunello Riserva is a wine that is structured for long-term aging, as 40 years is normal, while superb vintages such as 1961 and 1955 are still drinking well. The *riserva* is limited and somewhat expensive, yet the owners have earned the price they charge, not only for creating history, but also for continuing to refine their wines and remain as one of the textbook producers of Brunello di Montalcino. This is one of the few wines from Montalcino – or really anywhere in the world – that I would call ethereal. It is a wine you must try at least once in your life. **BRV:** 2006, 2004, 2001, 1999, 1997 (all exceptional.)

POLIZIANO VINO NOBILE DI MONTEPULCIANO "ASINONE"

The "Noble Wine of Montepulciano" has had quite a remarkable roller coaster ride over the past several hundred years. In the 1800s, this wine was the most renowned from Tuscany, regarded as longer-lived than Chianti; it also enjoyed a lenghtier history than Brunello di Montalcino, which was not realized until the 1850s. But during the 20th century, Vino Nobile lost much of its luster, as Brunello became much more renowned, while Chianti Classico had become much more famous throughout the world. Not only had Vino Nobile become something of a less important wine, the quality began to suffer, as most examples lacked focus.

However over the past twenty-five years, a few dozen vintners in this southwestern Tuscan wine zone have begun a renaissance with Vino Nobile. One of the most celebrated producers in Montepulciano today is Federico Carletti, who studied agriculture at the University of Florence in the 1970s. It was his father Dino who years before had purchased 50 acres in the Montepulciano area with the hope of making superior wine to what had become the norm in the 1950s and '60s. In 1980, Federico decided to produce wine on his own and teamed up with Carlo Ferrini, a famed local enologist, who just happened to have been a colleague of Federico at the university. Their wines, deeper in color with riper black fruit and more aging time in small oak barrels, received great attention not only from other local vintners, but also from international wine journalists; here were new, exciting wines from Montepulciano!

The finest version of Vino Nobile di Montepulciano produced at Poliziano is labeled Asinone, from vineyards at an elevation of 1250 to 1300 feet above sea level; the soils here are a mix of clay, tufo and crushed red stone. The name Asinone incidentally, refers to the fact that the vineyards have a shape similar to a donkey's back (*asino* is Italian for donkey). The first bottling was from the 1983 vintage and was aged in large oak; soon though small oak barrels were used, as is the practice today. This is produced only from the finest vintages; the best of the best versions contain 100% Sangiovese, which is known as Prugnolo Gentile in Montepulciano; in some years, small percentages of Colorino and Merlot are included in the blend. Packed with black fruit, tar and licorice flavors and offering remarkable concentration, this has a round, fruit-filled finish with young, firm tannins. Enjoy between seven and ten years of age. **BRV:** 2007, 2006, 2005, 2004 (exceptional), 2003, 2001, 1999 (these last two vintages both exceptional).

RUFFINO VINO NOBILE DI MONTEPULCIANO "LODOLA NUOVA"

While Ruffino is famous for its Chianti Classico Riserva Ducale and honored for its Romitorio di Santedame (a Colorino/Merlot) blend, it is this Vino Nobile that deserves much more attention. What I love about this wine is the varietal purity of Sangiovese (Prugnolo Gentile) and the traditional approach taken with this wine, as it is aged solely in large casks. The tannins are gentle, the flavors are spot on and there is admirable acidity. In other words, a wine that is a pleasure to drink and a lovely representation of its type. Both the regular as well as the Riserva bottlings of this wine are recommended; the Riserva tending to age for 7-10 years, while the *normale* is at its best at five to seven years of age. **BRV:** 2009, 2008, 2007, 2006, 2004.

BOSCARELLI VINO NOBILE DI MONTEPULCIANO "NOCIO"

It may be hard to believe, but it's been fifty years since the De Ferrari family established their estate in Cervognano in the eastern reaches of the Vino Nobile di Montepulciano zone. All of the products here display lovely ripeness and admirable structure, from the entry level Rosso di Montepulciano to the regular bottling, *riserva* and finally this cru offering, produced entirely from Sangiovese. Aged for two years in large casks, this is a wine that offers a beautiful array of spices and herbs to accompany fruit flavors of red cherry and myrtle. There is excellent concentration and a rich mid-palate with youthful, but graceful tannins and very good acidity. Depending on the strength of the vintage, this wine can drink well from 7-15 years of age. **BRV:** 2009, 2008, 2007, 2006, 2004, 2001.

CARPINETO VINO NOBILE DI MONTEPULCIANO

I've known Antonio Zaccheo, owner of this estate, for more than a decade and I always look forward to meeting with him again, whether at his estate in Italy or on one of his visits to America. He's a soft-spoken man with a great sense of humor who almost always has a smile on his face. It also great seeing him, as I love his wines! The regular Vino Nobile is meant for lovers of this famous wine type, as it respects the traditions of this area. Aged solely in large casks, this is a blend of Sangiovese along with Canaiolo, an indigenous Tuscan variety, that rounds out the wine and adds to its drinkability, especially when young. I love the fact that Zaccheo lets the wine take its time in the cellar, as his current release is often one vintage behind that of other local producers. Medium-full with great typicity, this is a wine that is enjoyable from three to ten years of age and even longer from the best vintages. **BRV:** 2008, 2007, 2006, 2005, 2004, 2001.

LE TRE BERTE VINO NOBILE DI MONTEPULCIANO "POGGIO TOCCO"

Le Tre Berte is a tiny estate situated in the eastern portion of the Montepulciano wine zone; it is today owned by the Montefoschi family. They produce this Vino Nobile, named for the hill where the vineyards are located; there is also a *selezione*. I prefer the regular bottling, as the oak influence is less invasive, as this is matured solely in large Slavonian casks, while the *selezione* is aged in both these vessels as well as in barriques. This is a lovely traditional Vino Nobile with 95% Sangiovese (or Prugnolo Gentile, if you will) with the inclusion of 5% Colorino. The aromas of dried morel cherry, cedar, thyme and tobacco are simply textbook, there is very good acidity, nicely integrated wood notes and a complex, well structured finish. This is Sangiovese displaying its more subdued, classic side. Enjoy this from three to seven years of age. **BRV:** 2007, 2006.

VALDIPIATTA VINO NOBILE DI MONTEPULCIANO RISERVA

Giulio and Miriam Caporali established this estate in the late 1980s; a dream of Giulio's, he thinks of this as paradise. There are several wines produced here, including an impressive Super Tuscan known as Trincerone, a Colorino/Merlot blend, but it is the Riserva Vino Nobile that I believe best represents the Caporali's philosophy. 100% Sangiovese, the wine is aged both in small and large casks and offers beautifully ripe red cherry and plum fruit along with the precise acidity so typical of Sangiovese. This has outstanding complexity as well as typicity and truly is a terroir-driven wine. This is at its best 10-12 years after the vintage. **BRV:** 2008, 2007, 2006, 2004, 2001.

TENUTA SAN GUIDO SASSICAIA

What Italian wine lover, what wine lover period, has not heard of Sassicaia? This is certainly one of the two or three most famous wines in all of Italy (Gaja and Biondi-Santi being the others) and one of the most celebrated in all the world. "Airline stewardesses have heard of Sassicaia," winemaker Sebastiano Rosa told me during a recent visit. Yes, eveyone knows Sassicaia!

This wine actually dates back to the 1940s when Mario Incisa della Rocchetta decided to plant Cabernet Sauvignon at his estate near Livorno not far from the Tuscan coast. This was met with doubts from just about everyone he knew, as they were certain this cool territory was ideal for planting olive trees, but not grape vines. Yet Mario succeeded and continued to produce small anounts of Cabernet Sauvignon each year, primarily for himself and a few friends. Given the fact that he aged the wines in French barriques rather than the large Slavonian oak casks that were prevalent throughout Tuscany at the time, the wines were rather tannic upon release; praise for these wines would have to wait a bit. But in the mid-1960s, older wines that had been resting in the cellar were rounding out nicely and began to show the wisdom of Mario's decision. It was in 1968 that he finally decided to produce the wine for the international market and the praise for this wine has not stopped since.

Today, Sassicaia, literally "the place of stones" - named for a second vineyard della Rocchetta planted that was comprised of rocky soil - is a blend of 85% Cabernet Sauvignon and 15% Cabernet Franc and is the only wine in Italy with its own denomination – Sassicaia DOC. Some will tell you that the wine also has a small percentage of Petit Verdot – this adds to the depth of the color – but the official word is Cabernet Sauvignon and Cabernet Franc only, the blend put together by legendary winemaker Giacomo Tachis. The wine is aged in French barriques of Tronçais and Allier oak for 18 to 22 months; this may seem like a long time to mature in barriques, but the extraordinary concentration can support this amount of wood.

This is a Bolgheri Superiore; today there are about two dozen estates in Bolgheri and almost every red wine is based upon Bordeaux varieties instead of Sangiovese. Much of this has to do with the local soils, as Sangiovese prefers the clay of inland Toscana to the rocky soils of Bolgheri. Temperatures are warm enough to ripen Cabernet Sauvignon and other varieties, such as Merlot and Cabernet Franc, but the cool breezes from the sea help moderate conditions, ensuring healthy natural acidity and excellent structure. Sassicaia is not a very approachable wine upon release; but it is a product that rewards the patient, as most versions are in fine form some 25-30 years after the vintage.

Sassicaia is a benchmark wine not only in Bolgheri, but also throughout Italy. Try a bottle from any vintage and you will not only be impressed, but also instantly transported to the small growing area of Bolgheri, where you can sense the pride of Nicolo Incisa della Rocchetta over the trailblazing work of his father Mario, who took a gamble back in the 1940s that has worked amazingly well. **BRV**: 2009, 2008 (exceptional), 2007, 2006, 2005, 2004 (exceptional), 2003, 2001 (exceptional), 2000, 1999 and 1998 (these last two vintages also exceptional).

TENUTA DELL'ORNELLAIA BOLGHERI SUPERIORE ORNELLAIA

Many observers of Italian wine believe that the Bolgheri Superiore Ornellaia is on equal par with Sassicaia, at least in terms of quality; as far as name recognition, it's almost a dead heat. This marvelous estate was founded in 1981 by Lodovico Antinori, brother of Piero, who wanted to produce the best Tuscan red possible. The first vintage was in 1985; this wine, along with Sassicaia and Grattamacco, helped define the Bolgheri style of red wine – full-bodied, with excellent ripeness and structure, a wine meant for two or more decades of aging in one's cellar, much like a top Bordeaux.

Today, some thirty years later, Ornellaia has indeed become one of Italy's most famous and well-respected wines and the cellars here are among the most beautiful in the world; it strikes me as sort of a immaculate chapel of wood and glass. Lodovico Antinori built this estate into what it is today and then sold it to the Frescobaldi family, who have continued Antinori's vision. The top wine of the estate is a blend of Cabernet Sauvignon, Merlot, Cabernet Franc and Petit Verdot; unlike Sassicaia where the blend pretty much stays the same each year, the percentage of each variety differs slightly from one vintage to another. For example, the 2007 contained 55% Cabernet Sauvignon, while that number decreased to 54% for the 2008 and then 52% for the 2009. Displaying a deep ruby red color and explosive aromas of blackcurrant, blackberry, cassis, violet and fresh herbs, this is a wine of power and intensity with tremendous richness on the palate as well as outstanding persistence. While this often tends to be slightly more subdued than Sassicaia – this is always a powerful wine, so this is a relative comparison – in some years, such as 2008, Ornellaia is more intense than its famous counterpart. No matter the style, this is a wine that demands time in the bottle and is often not approachable until seven to ten years after release. Older wines are showing brilliantly, so 25 years plus is a typical time frame for peak enjoyment of this wine, while the best of the best offerings may be in great shape at 40 years of age – only time will tell. **BRV**: 2009, 2008, 2007 (exceptional), 2006, 2005, 2004 (exceptional), 2003, 2001 (exceptional), 2000, 1999 (exceptional).

GRATTAMACCO BOLGHERI SUPERIORE GRATTAMACCO

Founded in 1977, Grattamacco became the first great estate from Bolgheri after Tenuta San Guido. Yet, despite its impressive history, the wines of Grattamacco have never quite achieved the media praises of Sassicaia and Ornellaia. This is truly a shame, as the top wine here, named simply Grattamacco, is every bit the equal of those two wines. The vineyards are situated on one of the area's most splendid panoramas, on a hill between Castagneto Carducci and Bolgheri; viewed looking at the nearby hills, the vineyards seem to stretch forever.

Today, Claudio Tipa, the owner of Colle Massari in Montecucco and Poggio di Sotto in Montalcino, manages this estate, producing several Bolgheri wines (one white) as well as a great estate olive oil. The leading statement of what he is doing here is found in the Bolgheri Superiore Grattamacco, primarily Cabernet Sauvignon (normally about 65%) with Merlot and Cabernet Franc completing the blend. The aromas are, in a word, seductive, drawing you in with a mix of black cherry, black currant, tar and licorice; the depth of fruit is amazing in most years and the finish has outstanding persistence. The consistency of this wine is quite something, as it is never less than excellent; however in years where the acidity is a bit higher, as in 1999 and 2008, the wine has remarkable structure. This is ripe and quite delicious, even upon release, as it is generally a touch more approachable than Sassicaia or Ornellaia. Yet, make no mistake- this is a wine to be enjoyed 20-25 years down the road. **BRV**: 2009, 2008 (exceptional), 2007, 2006, 2004, 2003, 2001, 1999 (exceptional).

PODERE SAPAIO BOLGHERI SUPERIORE "SAPAIO"

Massimo Piccin established his Bolgheri estate in 1999; the name comes from *sapais*, the word for an old Tuscan vine. There are two reds made at this 100-acre estate, a Bolgheri Rosso named Volpolo and a Bolgheri Superiore with the estate name. While the former tends to be a bit dominated by small oak, that is clearly not the case with the top estate red; a blend of Cabernet Sauvignon, Cabernet Franc, Merlot and Petit Verdot, this is a ripe, instantly appealing red that shows off the qualities of this seaside zone. While this is aged for eighteen months in barriques, the oak is nicely integrated and never dominates as there is more than enough fruit concentration to balance out the wood notes. The acidity is very good (especially in a year such as 2008) and the final result is a very flavorful, beautifully balanced streamlined modern red that is at peak enjoyment from ten to fifteen years of age. **BRV**: 2008, 2007, 2006, 2005, 2004.

BATZELLA BOLGHERI ROSSO SUPERIORE "TAM"

While Sassicaia and Ornellaia have become the most famous ambassadors for the great red wines of Bolgheri, it's important to note the smaller producers in this zone that craft very fine wines that offer excellent quality/price ratio. At Batzella, established in 2000, Franco Batzella and his Vietnamese-born wife Khanh Nguyen focus on white and red wines from Bolgheri that are a bit more humble in nature than their famous counterparts. Their finest wine is Tam – a Vietnamese word meaning "passion" – that is a blend of 60% Cabernet Sauvignon and 40% Cabernet Franc aged for two years in French barriques. What's notable about this wine is the series of engaging plum and bitter chocolate flavors on the palate, which are nicely supported by the oak. While this has some traits of a classified Bordeaux, this clearly has Bolgheri roots, given its very good acidity. This is not meant for the long haul, but is a pleasure to consume at five to seven years of age. **BRV**: 2008, 2007, 2006, 2004.

LE MACCHIOLE PALEO ROSSO

Le Macchiole is one of the key estates in Bolgheri, both for the outstanding quality of their wines, but also the diversity of their products. Founded in 1983, today the estate is run by Cinzia Merli, who took over when her husband Eugenio Campolmi passed away in the early 1990s. Their vision was to produce not only a blended wine of the estate, much like Sassicaia and Ornellaia, but also to craft single variety wines. The results of this included Scrio, which is 100% Syrah, Messorio, a powerful 100% Merlot and Paleo, made exclusively from Cabernet Franc. Each of these wines are impressive; my favorite is the Paleo, as Merli and her winemaker Luca d'Attoma have done a brilliant job capturing the essence of this variety. While Cabernet Franc would not work well in clay soils found in other areas in Tuscany, it thrives in the gravelly and alluvial soils of Bolgheri. The mid-day heat is ideal for this variety, which can be overly herbaceous when underripe. The aromas are of blackberry, myrtle, bitter chocolate and lavender. Full-bodied, this has layers of fruit and plenty of spice as well as notes of balsamic. Even in a year that is not overly warm such as 2005, this has beautiful ripeness and richness; this is as complete a Cabernet Franc as you can find outside of Bordeaux! Though appealing and sexy upon release, this is at optimum drinking some 15-20 years after the harvest. **BRV:** 2009, 2008 (exceptional), 2007, 2006, 2005 (exceptional), 2004, 2001.

TENUTA DELL'ORNELLAIA MASSETO
Here we have one of the most spectacular red wines produced in all of Italy and really in all of the world. Masseto is 100% Merlot from a 16-acre vineyard siuated on the Tenuta dell'Ornellaia estate. The soils here – predominantly clay with some loose pebbles – are ideal for Merlot; the vineyard was planted in 1984. Winemaker Axel Heinz makes several base wines and then determines which of these are used in the final blend, meaning that Masseto is truly a "best of the best" selection from this vineyard. The wine undergoes malolactic fermentation in new French barriques and matures in these barrels for 24 months; it is then bottled and stored in the cellars for an additional 12 months before it is introduced to the market. The resulting wine naturally has intense varietal aromas, but it is the massive depth of fruit that truly sets this wine apart. While there is notable ripeness, the wine has impeccable balance, so that

the wine is never out of step; outstanding persistence and structure ensure at least 25 years or so of enjoyment for this wine; as the first vintage was from 1986, I can't go beyond that time frame, but let's come back to this discussion in another decade; perhaps then, I'll be pointing out the fact that the best bottles of Masseto can age for 35-40 years. **BRV**: 2009, 2008 (exceptional), 2007, 2006 (exceptional), 2005, 2004 (exceptional), 2001, 1999, 1998 (these last three all exceptional).

M.L.A. BISERNO

M.L.A. stands for Marchese Lodovico Antinori, the founder of the famed Tenuta dell'Ornellaia estate in Bolgheri. After 25 years of managing this property and making it one of the most critically acclaimed and financially successful wineries in all of Italy, he sold it to the Frescobaldi family in 2005. As he told me in an interview a few years back, his "creative energies had been exhausted" and he "wanted to find an area that had many small surprises." That area would be not far away in the small countryside town of Bibbona, where he would focus on Bordeaux varieties, just as he had at Ornellaia.

He named the property Tenuta di Biserno (though now the M.L.A. moniker is the preferred title) and worked with famed French enologist Michel Rolland as well as winemaker Helena Lindberg to create the ideal blend from this area. The Biserno wine, first made from the 2006 vintage, is a marvelous product, a Super Tuscan that is truly super, as it is a wine of great breeding as well as superb structure. Primarily Cabernet Franc with small amounts of Merlot, Cabernet Sauvignon and Petit Verdot to complete the blend, this is a full-bodied wine always under control. Displaying succulent aromas of fresh cranberry, raspberry, black cherry and a note of tobacco seed, there is tremendous concentration, very good acidity (especially with the 2008), polished tannins and outstanding persistence. What I love about this wine is its gracefulness and harmony; here is a marvelously rich wine that never announces itself, but rather glides across the palate. All the components are beautifully woven together, e.g., even with 15 months of aging in new French barriques, this is not a wine in which the wood notes dominate. The winery estimates 12-15 years of aging potential, but I think that may be a bit conservative. Antinori is off to a great start with this wine and this new property; I can't wait to try future releases! **BRV**: 2008, 2007, 2006.

CASTIGLION DEL BOSCO "PRIMA PIETRA"
The Castiglion del Bosco estate that dates back to Etruscan times has had many revisions over the centuries; today, this property, situated in the northwest corner of the Brunello di Montalcino zone, is owned by the well-known Ferragamo family of the fashion industry. While their offerings of Brunello are weighty and quite ripe with ample oak, it is their Prima Pietra wine that I am singling out for its quality. Sourced from high-density vineyards near Bolgheri, this is a blend of 50% Merlot, 30% Cabernet Sauvignon, 10% Cabernet Franc and 10% Petit Verdot. Offering aromas of black cherry, thyme, currant and vanilla (the wine is matured in new and old barriques), this has excellent concentration in most years with impressive persistence, balanced youthful tannins and good acidity and complexity. This is a modern style Tuscan red structured for seven to ten years of cellaring before reaching peak. **BRV**: 2009, 2008, 2007.

SADA "INTEGOLO"
There are four Sada wines made from vines in the Bolgheri area, although each is labeled as IGT Toscana. Along with a pleasant Vermentino, their best wine is a moderately priced red blend called "Integolo," a cuvée of 60% Cabernet Sauvignon and 40% Montepulciano. Medium-bodied with appealing aromas of black cherry, black plum and violets, this has light wood notes, moderate tannins and good acidity. This is not a wine that will receive much press, yet its balance, drinkability and notable varietal character make it very worthwhile; enjoy this from three to five years of age. **BRV**: 2010

CASTELLO DEL TERRICCIO "TASSINAIA" / "LUPICAIA"

Castello del Terriccio has quitely been producing some very impress-sive reds – so called Super Tuscans – from their estate vineyards in western Tuscany since the late 1980s. Before that, the estate sold grapes and produced some of their own wine in bulk, but once the decision was made to bottle their own wines, the specialization pro-cess began. Given the location of the estate in Castellina Marittima in the province of Pisa – about eighteen miles from the town of Pisa and some twelve miles from Bolgheri – Bordeaux varieties would be the focus, with cuttings of Cabernet Sauvignon and Merlot coming from France.

Carlo Ferrini, who consults at several of Toscana's finest properties, is the red wine enologist and he has crafted two lovely wines with the Tassinaia and the Lupicaia. The former has 20% Sangiovese in the blend that accompanies the Cabernet Sauvignon and Merlot; offer-ing aromas of cocoa powder, red cherry and red plum, this has a gen-erous mid-palate, nicely integrated wood notes, very good acidity and a beautiful freshness in the finish. This drinks well from five to ten years of age. The Lupicaia – "the place of the wolves" – has a small dol-lop of Petit Verdot in the blend along with Cabernet Sauvignon and Merlot. Medium-full with excellent concentration, this offers aromas of black cherry, clove and myrtle and has a layered mid-palate and a finish with excellent persistence. There is good acidity along with balanced tannins and the wine finishes with pleasing notes of tart cherry; this is generally at is best from five to twelve or fifteen years, depending on the strength of the vintage. I love the balance and sub-dued style of these two wines, as they are not made to be the most powerful examples, but simply the most accomplished. **BRV** (both): 2007, 2006, 2005, 2004.

ALTURA "ROSSO SAVERIO"

Here is one of the most unique red wines in all of Italy; given the end-less diversity of the country's viticultural products, that is really saying something! This is a red wine from the island of Giglio, a small outpost not far from the town of Grosseto. Today everyone knows the island in an unfortunate way, as it was the scene of a terrible luxury cruise disaster in early 2012, but in reality, some pretty special wines have been produced here, primarily by cooperatives. Francesco Carfgana is one of the few individuals growing grapes and making wine on his own on the island; his vineyards on sandy soils lie close to the sea with roots reaching deep under rocks. He farms naturally, without the use of weed killers or chemical fertilizers and utilizes cover crops such as clover and wild flowers.

This is a blend of more than fifteen grapes, primarily red, such as Sangiovese, Ciliegiolo, Grenache, Aleatico and Trebbiano Nero along with some white, such as Malvasia, Grecanico and Procanico; all of these varieties have been grown on Giglio for many years. The first unique qualities of this wine are some intriguing aromas, which start out as though you were trying a white wine, as yellow peaches come to the forefront. Yet a few minutes later, strawberry, currant and milk chocolate notes emerge. Medium-full with a long, delicate finish, this is somewhat Burgundian in character, given its sensual texture and medium-weight tannins, yet it also has some Rhone-like qualities to it as well, especially with its earthy, slightly gravelly finish. I'd be hard pressed to choose just the right food match for this wine; instead, I'd prefer simply to drink this wine and be dazzled by everything about it. If greatness relies in part on originality, then this is an outstanding, singular wine! This is enjoyable upon release, but I can only imagine how special this wine must taste after seven to ten years of age. **BRV**: 2010, 2009, 2008, 2007, 2006.

SAN FELICE PUGNITELLO
Pugnitello is an ancient red Tuscan variety that San Felice rediscovered in the early 1990s; there are now three other estates in the region that have planted this grape. The name is translated as "little fist," a reference to the shape of the clusters. There are a few acres planted in four vineyards at the estate in Castelnuovo Beradenga; the vines are now twelve to fifteen years old. Aged in French barriques, the wine has

distinct brown spice and red cherry fruit with balanced acidity and moderate tannins. As there have only been a few releases, it's difficult to judge optimum drinking on this wine; five to seven years seems a safe bet, though that may increase as the vines mature. **BRV**: 2008, 2007, 2006.

CASTELVECCHIO "NUMERO 8"

At this estate in San Casciano Val di Pesa, just southeast of Florence, siblings Stefania and Filippo Rocchi specialize in producing lush bottlings of Chianti Colli Fiorentini, but they also introduce a few new wines from time to time. Numero 8 is Canaiolo Nero in *purezza*; the Rocchis have produced this since 2003. Named for the number of months the wine spends in used barriques, this is a charming, slightly spicy red with moderate tannins and aromas of cherry, strawberry and a hint of rosemary. It's meant to be consumed young – perhaps two to five years after the harvest – and this personable team has made this a wine of typicity and excellent varietal character. **BRV**: 2009, 2008, 2007.

SALUSTRI MONTECUCCO "GROTTE ROSSE"

The Montecucco wine zone is located in the province of Grosseto between Montalcino and Scansano; the principal red variety here, as with all local DOC reds, is Sangiovese. There are various styles of Montecucco, ranging from very soft and approachable to more deeply concentrated wines meant for a decade of aging. The Salustri family produces several versions, the most striking of which is the "Grotte Rosse," produced exclusively from Sangiovese from 70-year old vines; these are planted to a special Salustri clone of Sangiovese with very small berries that yields deeply flavorful wines. Morel cherries, strawberry preserves and red roses highlight the aromas; there is excellent persistence, very precise acidity and subtle wood notes, as this is aged for two years solely in large casks. This is a striking wine that should be better known; an excellent vintage such as 2008 will be at its best at 10-12 years of age. **BRV**: 2008, 2007, 2006, 2004.

FATTORIA MANTELLASI MORELLINO DI SCANSANO "MENTORE"

While Brunello di Montalcino and Chianti Classico are very famous, historical DOCG wine territories, Morellino di Scansano is a relative newcomer. This wine zone, situated in the province of Grosseto, is named for the town in the middle of the district; it was awarded DOC status in 1978 and then DOCG in 2007. Once home to the Etruscans, this area has been planted to vineyards for the past several hundred years. While there are some lowland plantings not far from the sea, most estates are on rolling hills with ideal exposure to the sun. Morellino di Scansano must contain a minimum of 85% Sangiovese, although numerous versions are made only with this variety. Some producers use traditional local varieties such as Colorino or Canaiolo in their blend, while others opt for international grapes, such as Cabernet Sauvignon, Merlot and Syrah.

Styles vary, as there are some wines meant for a decade of cellaring, but the classic Morellino di Scansano is a charming wine meant for early consumption; these wines, moderately priced, are among the most successful in wine stores throughout Italy. The "Mentore" offering from Fattoria Mantellasi offers fresh morel cherry with a light hint of tobacco, is medium-bodied and finishes with classic tart acidity and moderate tannins associated with Sangiovese. This version, although containing some Cabernet Sauvignon, is a wine meant for early drinking; given no wood aging, this is a simple pleasure made in a style that is too often forgotten in Tuscany these days. **BRV**: 2010, 2009, 2008, 2007.

PROVVEDITORE MORELLINO DI SCANSANO
MORELLINO DI SCANSANO RISERVA "PRIMO"

At his medium-size estate just south of Scansano, complete with fifteen cats and one very active dog, Alessando Bargagli has been producing lovely examples of Morellino di Scansano since the late 1970s. The regular bottling is simply one of the appellation's finest introductory efforts, a 100% Sangiovese (or Morellino, as the variety is known here), aged solely in stainless steel that offers ripe black plum, black cherry and violet perfumes, while finishing with modest tannins and typical tart acidity. It's a delicious wine meant for consumption within two to three years of age. For the Primo, this has small percentages of Alicante and Cabernet Sauvignon in the blend; deeper in color and slightly beefier, this is no less elegant or appealing, as there are some inviting licorice flavors to accompany the black cherry flavors. This has excellent structure with medium-weight tannins along with good freshness and roundness; it's meant for peak consumption at seven to ten years of age. The Morellino di Scansano zone has more famous estates, but few make wine as special as Provveditore. **BRV:** 2008, 2007, 2006.

PODERE 414 MORELLINO DI SCANSANO

This farm, established in 1998 by Simone Castelli, derives its name from the parcel number given it by the land authorities. Castelli farms organically and uses native yeasts; his wines have great purity and cleanliness. The regular Morellino, aged in both small and mid-size oak casks, offers attractive morel cherry and strawberry fruit with an intriguing touch of turmeric in the nose. The mid-palate is complete and round, while the wood notes are subdued, acidity is very good and the tannins are round and soft. This is a lovely Morellino made in a modern style, aimed at anyone who wants to understand what this wine zone represents; enjoy within three to five years of age. **BRV:** 2010, 2009, 2008, 2007.

LA MOZZA MORELLINO DI SCANSANO "I PERAZZI"

La Mozza was founded in 2000 by New York restaurateurs Joseph Bastianich and his mother Lidia along with chef Mario Batali. Their "I Perazzi" Morellino di Scansano – named for the pear-like fruit that grows on their property in Magliano in Toscana – is positioned between the simple versions of Morellino meant for short-term consumption and the *riservas*, structured for seven to ten years of cellaring. There are several things to like about this wine; its complexity (this is a blend of five varieties), its subtle use of oak (only 30% of the wine is aged in used French barriques for six months) and the overall balance. The tannins are medium-weight, there is good acidity and overall, this is a wine in which all the components meld together extremely well. While approachable two years after the harvest, this rounds out and offers greater complexities at five to seven years of age. **BRV**: 2010, 2009, 2008, 2007.

MORIS FARMS MORELLINO DI SCANSANO RISERVA

Established in 1971, Moris Farms has become one of the most recognized producers in Grosseto. While they produce a fine DOC Monteregio di Massa Marittima red, it is their Morellino di Scansano Riserva that is year in and year out, their most consistent wine. A blend of 90% Sangiovese with the rest a mix of Cabernet Sauvignon and Merlot, this has excellent ripeness with a distinct floral note; slightly forward, this has some touches of modern winemaking, as it spends one year in barrique, but the wood notes are slight. Nicely balanced with very good complexity, it is a nicely made middle ground for this wine type and is best consumed at five to seven years of age. **BRV**: 2009, 2008, 2007.

POGGIO BRIGANTE MORELLINO DI SCANSANO RISERVA "ARSURA"

The Rossi family has been operating this 50-acre estate in Magliano in Toscana since the early 1950s; today Franco and his son Leonardo manage the property; having produced their initial Morellino di Scansano in 2001. Their Arsura offering, a 100% Sangiovese aged in barriques, is a wonderful updating of Morellino, with ripe strawberry and cherry fruit, excellent persistence and impeccable balance. The oak notes are perfectly integrated and the wine is quite stylish. Medium-weight, this is at its best in the short term, some three to five years after release. **BRV**: 2009, 2008, 2007, 2006.

FATTORIA LE PUPILLE MORELLINO DI SCANSANO RISERVA "POGGIO VALENTE"

Fattoria Le Pupille – "the butterflies" – is a success story of a woman with a dream. Elisabetta Gepetti has been producing Morellino di Scansano at her lovely farmhouse (the cellars are situated in a former stable) since 1985 and has been refining her wines little by little each vintage. Critics have noticed and today, the winery is clearly one of the most famous in this zone. While the regular Morellino and the *riserva* are beautifully made offerings, it is Poggio Valente that has become a reference point for the area.

The wine is made from a small vineyard near Pereta in the middle of the zone that Gepetti purchased in 1996. She immediately replanted half the vineyard with four select clones of Sangiovese and left the remainder alone. More replanting was carried out a few years later and today, the wine is made entirely from these clones. This is ripe, assertive Morellino, aged in barriques, that is one of the more age-worthy wines from this DOC; while the oak can be a bit forceful upon release, older wines are evidence of the quality fruit and excellent winemaking with this offering. Blended with a small amount of Alicante for color, this demands a few years after release to settle down, but it is quite elegant a decade down the road. **BRV**: 2008, 2007, 2006, 2005, 2004.

POGGIO ARGENTIERA MORELLINO DI SCANSANO "CAPATOSTA"

Since 1997, Gianpaolo Paglia has made Poggio Argentiera one of the most recognized labels of Morellino di Scansano. Today, with quality as high as ever, Paglia is doing his best to lead his fellow producers to craft more representative offerings, as he decided a few years ago to elimitate the barriques and age his wines in large casks. "The Maremma is a place where you can make beautiful, true Mediterranean wines without having to show the muscle, without all this new oak, without all this body from concentration. Just let the wines be what they are without forcing them," Paglia told me during my most recent visit to his estate.

This philosophy of traditional aging is communicated beautifully in his Capatosta bottling of Morellino di Scansano. This is a blend of 85% Sangiovese, 10% Ciliegiolo and 5% Alicante; all of the fruit is from vineyards at least 20 years of age, while the Ciliegiolo vines are more than 50 years old. Aged in 10 and 20hl casks, this has a lovely pale garnet color – Paglia is adamant about the proper color of his wines – and attractive aromas of dried morel cherry, rhubarb, nutmeg, currant and tea leaf. Medium-full with excellent concentration and balance, this has a superb sense of place along with outstanding complexity and is a pleasure to drink. This wine simply oozes finesse! Morellino di Scansano has been a success in Italy and a few countries in Europe; yet these wines are not as well known in America. Examples such as this can only help this wine area's visibility in terms of standing alongside other quality Tuscan reds. This can be enjoyed upon release (usually at three years of age), although it is at its best from seven to ten years. **BRV**: 2009, 2008.

ANTONIO CAMILLO CILIEGIOLO "VALLERANA ALTA"

At Poggio Argentiera, proprietor Gianpaolo Paglia loves to work with numerous varieties in the Morellino di Scansano district. He is particularly fond of the Ciliegiolo variety, a local specialty, using it in his Morellino blends and also producing it as a stand-alone variety. He produces two offerings, named for Antonio Camillo, his winery manager and while both are beautifully crafted, it is this "Vallerana Alta" selection that is superb. Ciliegiolo means "cherry" or "cherry like" and it is this fruit that emerges with great identity of this wine; the fact that this particular vineyard is more than 50 years old ensures lovely varietal character. The aromas are particularly lovely with notes of Queen Anne cherry, strawberry preserves, carnation and red roses; medium-full, this has excellent depth of fruit, very good acidity, a generous mid-palate, silky tannins and excellent persistence. This is a classy wine, one that is easily the most impressive bottle of Ciliegiolo I've had the pleasure to enjoy! Displaying great complexity, this is at its best at seven to ten years of age. **BRV**: 2010.

Gianpaolo Paglia

STEFANIA MEZZETTI "PRINCIPE"

Stefania Mezzetti established this company in far southern Tuscany in the Cortona DOC; she owns 25 acres of vines along with a villa and guesthouses not far from Lake Maggiore. The "Principe" wine is 100% Syrah, a variety that has become synonymous with the Cortona zone. Medium-bodied, this has lovely varietally pure aromas of black and red plum, black mint and a note of menthol. Medium-bodied, this is aged in barriques, giving it a slightly modern feel, but unlike some examples of Syrah from this area, this is not overly ripe or showy. Instead, it is a pleasantly styled Syrah meant for consumption within its first four or five years. **BRV**: 2009, 2008, 2007.

MARCHESE PANCRAZI "SAN DONATO"

Imagine how surprised Marchese Vittorio Pancrazi was on the day in 1989 when he was informed that the Sangiovese vines at his estate east of Florence were actually Pinot Noir! For more than a dozen years, he had labeled the wine as Sangiovese, but from that time on, it would be bottled separately as Pinot Noir. Today, his most famous wine is the Villa di Bagnolo Pinot Noir, a medium-full, barrique-aged version of this variety. While I admire this wine, I prefer the "San Donato," a blend of 50% Pinot Noir and 50% Gamay; the latter undergoes carbonic maceration, which results in a more fruity, less tannic wine. There are appealing black plum, black raspberry and cherry aromas and flavors, moderate tannins, delicate red spice and very good acidity. It's a charming red, meant for white meats and lighter game birds (quail, duck); enjoy it from two to five years of age. **BRV**: 2011, 2010, 2009, 2008.

GUADO AL TASSO SCALABRONE

The *rosato* made at the Guado al Tasso estate in Bolgheri is one of my favorite in all of Italy. A blend of Cabernet Sauvignon, Merlot and Syrah, this has a pretty pink color with delicious strawberry and pear fruit along with very good acidity and impressive weight on the palate. It's nicely balanced, quite dry and simply delicious! What a fine partner for just about any meat or game dish when you don't want the tannins or weight of most red wines; enjoy within 12-18 months of the harvest. **BRV**: 2011, 2010.

BIBI GRAETZ CASAMATTA ROSE´

There have been a number of wineries in Italy that have jumped on the rosé bandwagon as of late. Perhaps it's the fact that they have too many red grapes left over or perhaps they need some cash flow, but too many of these examples are wines that are the result of a marketing decision. I believe if you are going to produce a rosé, make one that's got some character and richness, which is exactly why I enjoy the Bibi Graetz version. This is made from Sangiovese and Canaiolo grapes from Graetz' estate near Fiesole a bit north of Florence and it's got a deep cherry color with fresh morel cherry and currant fruit and a dry finish with very good acidity. It's nothing terribly complicated, but it is a well made rosé that's a pleasure to enjoy at one to two years of age. **BRV**: 2011, 2010

CASTELLO DI BROLIO VIN SANTO DEL CHIANTI CLASSICO

Vin Santo, "the wine of the saints", "the holy wine," is one of Tuscany's greatest vinuous pleasures. Produced in several wine zones in the region, it is most famous in Chianti Classico, although there are also some notable examples from other districts in Chianti as well as in Montepulciano. Castello di Brolio, now under the leadership of Francesco Ricasoli, has been crafting a marvelous version for decades. The wine is made from grapes – Malvasia (a white variety once used in the production of Chianti) along with a small percentage of Sangiovese – that have been naturally dried on mats for several months over the autumn and winter before being fermented. Aging – in small barrels known as *caratelli*, generally no bigger than 50 liters and sometimes as small as 20 liters – takes place for five years before bottling and then release, which is typically when the wine is six years old. Amber gold in color, this has sumptuous aromas of apricot, honey and almonds and is lightly sweet on the palate, thanks to cleansing acidity. I have tasted versions of this wine that are 12-15 years old and they are in amazing shape, still with a beautiful freshness; it is only after that that the wines start to resemble a dry sherry to a small degree. While some examples of Vin Santo are quite lush and almost butterscotchy in nature, the Brolio version is elegant and beautfully harmonious. **BRV**: 2005, 2004, 2003, 2001, 1999 (exceptional).

CASTELLO DI CACCHIANO VIN SANTO DEL CHIANTI CLASSICO

Located in Monti in the commune of Gaiole in Chianti not far from Castello di Brolio, Cacchiano is managed by Giovanni Ricasoli-Firidolfi, cousin of Francsco Ricasoli of Brolio. Produced from Malvasia and Canaiolo Nero, this is a slightly lusher and nuttier style of Vin Santo than that of Brolio, but it is equally delicious. Vintages in the late 1990s were quite intense with powerful butterscotch flavors, but over the past few years, the style here has lightened and the wine is much better balanced. Generally, this wine is at is best from 12-15 years after the harvest; medium-sweet, this has delicious caramel and apricot flavors along with notes of crème caramel with a rich mid-palate and a lengthy, satisfying finish. **BRV**: 2005, 2004, 2003, 2001 (exceptional), 1999, 1998.

ROCCA DI MONTEGROSSI VIN SANTO DEL CHIANTI CLASSICO

This is another outstanding Vin Santo from Gaiole in Chianti; coincidentally, the proprietor here is Marco Ricasoli-Firidolfi, brother of Giovanni at Castello di Cacchiano and cousin of Francesco Ricasoli at Brolio. Given this fact, one wonders what there is in the family DNA that allows for such lovely versions of this iconic dessert wine! The Montegrossi Vin Santo may be the finest of all three, if not the most accomplished in all of Chianti Classico. Produced from Malvasia and a small percentage of Canaiolo, the grapes here are not dried on mats, but rather placed on nets that are hung from poles in a special humidity-controlled room. Marco ages the wine in *caratelli* made of various woods, including oak, cherry and mulberry for a period between six and seven years, longer than the required minimum. The result is spectacular, with butterscotch and maple syrup flavors, and though this is quite lush, it is also elegant and graceful with a delicately sweet finish, thanks to lively acidity. Generally the wine drinks well upon release and all throughout its life, with 15-20 years being the absolute peak. **BRV**: 2005, 2004, 2001 (exceptional), 1999, 1998 (exceptional), 1997.

SELVAPIANA VIN SANTO DEL CHIANTI RUFINA

Selvapiana is famous for their Vin Santo for several reasons, the most important being that is a great example of how sublime this wine can be. A blend of Trebbiano, Malvasia and Sangiovese, this is appealing from first sight (brilliant burnt orange/amber) to initial smell (apricot, caramel, butterscotch) to its lengthy, flavorful finish. This is a lush, yet elegant Vin Santo that has extraordinary varietal purity as well as lovely finesse. There are many styles of Vin Santo; I love this as it is about as clean and elegant a version as I've ever tasted. Proprietor Francesco Giuntini Antinori is a stickler for quality and someone that pays attention to the smallest details, so if the final result is not up to his standards with this wine, he will not bottle it as Vin Santo, but declassify it. **BRV**: 2004 (exceptional), 1999, 1998.

AVIGNONESI VIN SANTO DI MONTEPULCIANO "OCCHIO DI PERNICE"

Avignonesi produces different versions of Vin Santo; this one is called Occhio di Pernice, meaning "eye of the partridge," a reference to the deep orange/reddish color of the wine. This hue is a by-product of the Sangiovese grape (known in Montepulciano as Prugnolo Gentile) which is the only variety in this wine; the other Vin Santo from Avignonesi is produced solely from white varieties. While this wine has outstanding depth of fruit and tremendous weight on the palate, it is a bit of an extreme style. It is undoubtedly a bit of a show-stopper, but it also has the consistency of motor oil in certain vintages, meaning one can only enjoy a small sip. While I do enjoy a more refined style of Vin Santo, this is undoubtedly a special wine, especially for its aging potential, as 15-20 years is not out of the question. **BRV**: 1998, 1997, 1995.

ROMEO VIN SANTO DI MONTEPULCIANO

Massimo Romeo is a vastly underrated producer of wines from the Montepulciano zone; his versions of Vino Nobile are always elegant with first-rate varietal character and balance. His Vin Santo rivals the best examples of the area; a blend of Malvasia, Pulcinculo (a synonym for Grechetto, a white variety) and Trebbiano. Romeo places the grapes on mats and dries them for a minimum of 120 days. He then places the must in small barrels (50 to 75 liters in size), where they ferment and age for five years. The resulting wine is marvelous, with honey and caramel flavors, a lengthy finish, excellent acidity and a light butterscotch note in the finish. This is a graceful example of Vin Santo; it's difficult to find outside of Montepulciano, but it's clearly worth the search! **BRV**: 1992, 1991.

BINDELLA VIN SANTO DI MONTEPULCIANO "DOLCE SINFONIA"

Swiss native Rudi Bindella, from a family that has imported Tuscan wines into his native country for years, purchased an estate a bit east of Montepulciano in 1984; he has acquired more land over the past twenty plus years and today has about 100 acres planted to vines. His Vin Santo "Dolce Sinfonia" – "sweet symphony" – is dedicated to Giuseppe Verdi and has a clever label featuring musical notation. A blend of 80% Trebbiano and 20% Malvasia, the grapes hang from the rafters of a drying room; maturation in small 50-liter barrels for three years is followed by one year of aging in the bottle prior to release. Medium-full with evocative aromas of apricot, mandarin orange and honey, this is a rich, yet very elegant *dolce* with a light hint of almond in the finish. This is nicely balanced and quite delicious! Savor this upon release or as long as ten to fifteen years after the harvest. **BRV**: 2006, 2004, 1999, 1998.

Pairing Local Wines and Foods – A Chef's Perspective

I sincerely believe that the combination of food and wine in Italy is a wonderful thing and at the same time extraordinarily natural and intimate. Our good fortune is to have a nation bathed in sunshine and history, which allows us to appreciate and cultivate products of superior quality that are born on earth, grow on plants and matured by the climate from the sun and light. This includes extra virgin olive oil that is the basis of the Mediterranean diet sanctioned by UNESCO.

The profession of cook pushes me to be curious and always looking and comparing with raw materials that my country offers every day when we are at the table. The simplicity of foods linked to pleasant sensations of smell is a great satisfaction that comes just from enjoying great food and a great wine.

I am also convinced that we have to dispel the notion of matching white wine with fish and red wine for meat. I know great Italian wines that allow you to enjoy a fish dish with a red wine, quite a wonder!

In my restaurant I give guests maximum flexibility in order to choose from the wine list even the major labels by the glass, as this is a useful way to understand the differences between the wines and the differences between the different years, because linking the wine and the food is a great pleasure for the palate and for arousing one's sense of smell.

Italy, my country, has many recipes that are suitable for pairing with wine; recipes with pigeon are wonderful, *Maremmani tortelli* with ricotta and spinach with white truffles seem born to be married to Sangiovese. These dishes were based on cooking *"fuoco al parole,"* when people would gather in homes and talk while the meat and soup slowly simmered. This helped create the recipes of our tradition, but nowadays one prefers shorter cooking.

In short, I believe that in recent years, we have the pleasure of staying at the table more so than in the past, not for sustenance but to enjoy the pleasures of nature and life - surely this allows us to make the best choices.

Roberto Rossi
Chef/ Proprietor
Restaurant Silene, Seggiano (Province of Grosseto)

Marche

Principal Varieties:

White:
Verdicchio, Pecorino, Passerina, Bianchello, Sauvignon Blanc

Red:
Montepulciano, Sangiovese, Lacrima, Ciliegiolo, Merlot, Syrah

———

GAROFOLI VERDICCHIO DEI CASTELLI DI JESI SUPERIORE "PODIUM"

The Verdicchio grape is most famously planted in the region of Marche and its best known appellation is Verdicchio dei Castelli di Jesi, named for the town of Jesi near the region's center. While most versions of this wine are steel-aged and seem like just another white to be consumed early rather than later, the truth is that wines made from Verdicchio are among the longest-aging whites in all of Italy. The Garofoli firm, which was established in 1901, making it the oldest wine company in Marche, has been one of the leading producers of Verdicchio from Jesi. Their *superiore* "Podium" offering has been among the top examples of this wine type for years; steel-aged, this displays inviting aromas of golden apples and flowers such as peony and acacia. Medium-full with tart acidity reminiscent of a freshly picked apple, this has a very dry finish with notable persistence, along with a touch of white spice. Enjoy this upon release and for five to seven years of age.

UMANI RONCHI VERDICCHIO DEI CASTELLI DI JESI SUPERIORE "CASAL DI SERRA VECCHIE VIGNE"

Umani-Ronchi, one of Marche's largest wineries, has been producing a Verdicchio from the Casal di Serra site since the 1983 vintage. Starting with the 2001 harvest, they have produced this special wine from the oldest parts of this vineyard (*vecchie vigne*), planted in 1973. The grapes are picked just as they become slightly overripe; a few of the bunches are often affected by botrytis. The wine does not go through malolactic fermentation and is matured on its own lees for several months in cement tanks. This is a wine of marvelous texture with a lengthy, beautifully structured finish with distinct minerality. The wine is released after two years and drinks well for five to ten years, depending on the vintage. **BRV**: 2009, 2008, 2007, 2006.

LA DISTESA VERDICCHIO DI CASTELLI DI JESI CLASSICO SUPERIORE "TERRE SILVATE"

Proprietor Corrado Dottori produces this marvelous wine from three vineyards at his estate in Cupramontana, a bit west of Jesi. This is a blend of 90% Verdicchio with the remainder Trebbiano and Malvasia - this mix is an ancient tradtion in this area - and the grapes are farmed organically. Aged on the lees for six months, this offers beautiful aromas of Anjou pear, fennel and chamomile and has a rich, lush mid-palate. There is lively acidity and excellent persistence with notes of white spice in the finish. This is an absolutely delicious Verdicchio, one with excellent complexity, striking varietal purity and a lovely delicacy on the palate. Drink this upon release or up to five years of age.

VILLA BUCCI VERDICCHIO DEI CASTELLI DI JESI RISERVA

Ampelio Bucci has been one of the standard bearers of Verdicchio dei Castelli di Jesi, crafting outstanding examples that show not only the complexities of this wine, but also their aging potential. The Riserva is sourced from 40-year old vineyards that severely limit yields, but offer excellent concentration. Aged for about one year in large casks, the wine displays beautiful aromas of dried pear, chamomile and hawthorn, there is ideal texture and persistence along with lively acidity and a very long finish. This has superb complexity and richness, all the while offering great finesse. Only produced from the finest vintages, this is generally at is best from seven to ten years, though a few great bottles drink well for a few years beyond that. **BRV**: 2008, 2007, 2006, 2004, 2001

SANTA BARBARA VERDICCHIO DEI CASTELLI DI JESI CLASSICO "LE VAGLIE"
"RISERVA"

Here are two examples of Verdicchio di Jesi from the same producer that typify this wine as well as any example. Founded by Stefano Antonucci in 1984, the winery derives its name from the town of Barbara where the cellars are located, in the Ancona province some 18 miles from the Adriatic sea. Antonucci produces several lines of wines in various price ranges; all of them display great typicity. I am most impressed with the purity and appealing nature of these two examples of Verdicchio dei Castelli di Jesi. The steel-aged "Le Vaglie" offers lovely Anjou pear, green apple and honey aromas; medium-bodied with very good acidity and a light touch of minerality, this is an alluring wine. The *riserva*, matured for about one year in barriques, takes things up a notch, yet never comes across as intense or heavy. The sensual perfumes of golden apple, Bosc pear, magnolia blossoms and a hint of cinnamon lead to a beautifully textured mid-palate with layers of flavor, while the finish is ultra long with very good acidity and a distinct note of minerality. I had to check the notes on this wine about the wood aging, as I can barely find any oak notes – the depth of fruit is that impressive. Exceptionally delicious, this is a great Verdicchio; enjoy from two to seven years of age (the 2010 *riserva* is outstanding). Bravo Stefano!

BISCI VERDICCHIO DI METALICA

Verdicchio di Metalica is the "other" Verdicchio of Marche; the DOC zone is south and further west of the Castelli di Jesi area. One of the best producers of Verdicchio di Metalica is the family estate of Bisci, situated in Fogliano. The regular offering (there are two *selezioni* as well as a *passito* also produced) is a delightful, steel-aged only wine with lovely perfumes of melon, Anjou pear, lemon oil and jasmine; one could get lost in these aromas! Medium-bodied with very good persistence and acidity, this is a delightful wine that is best enjoyed by its third birthday. This is a everyday wine that offers excellent complexity and is a sheer pleasure to drink; it should be much better known.

TENUTA COCCI GRIFONI PECORINO "PODERE COLLE VECCHIO"

Founded in 1970, Tenuta Cocci Grifoni has always been one of the most important producers of the Ascoli Piceno area in far southern Marche. Today Guido Cocci Grifoni and his two daughters Paola and Marilena manage wine and business affairs at their estate in Ripatransone, not far from the town of Offida. While they are well known for their Rosso Piceno reds, their white Pecorino – a variety named for the sheep (*pecora*) that once roamed these hills – is a consistent gem. A blend of several clones and sourced from vineyards comprised of sand and clay, this is aged solely in steel tanks and has inviting aromas of pear, golden apple and yellow flowers (nasturtium, golden poppy). Medium-full, this has an earthy finish with a hint of minerality, lively acidity and always very good persistence; this is best enjoyed from two to five years of age.

LE CANIETTE PASSERINA "LUCREZIA"

While this firm dates back to the late 1890s, it was reworked in the 1990s when Giovanni Vagnoni modernized the winery with state of the art equipment that was housed in a building of striking architecture. Located in Ripatransone in southern Marche, the winery is known for its Rosso Piceno reds as well as two whites made from local indigenous varieties: Pecorino and Passerina. The Passerina variety is of unknown origins, though it is believed to be a genetic relative of Trebbiano Toscano. Passerina from the Offida zone in Marche (DOCG) has much more to offer than a simple Trebbiano, especially when made as stylishly as with this version. The aromas are of dried pear, orange blossom and a touch of biscuit. This has a generous mid-palate with rich texture, excellent persistence, very good acidity and a note of honey in the finish. This is a unique, flavorful wine that offers a great amount of character and complexity for very little money; enjoy this from two to five years of age with lighter seafood.

CLAUDIO MORELLI BIANCHELLO DEL METAURO "LA VIGNA DELLE TERRAZZE"

At his winery near Fano not far from the Adriatic Sea in northeastern Marche, Claudio Morelli produces another regional white, Bianchello del Metauro, named for the grape and a local river. In fact, he produces three different versions of Bianchello (also known as Biancame) from his rolling estate vineyards of silt and clay; each offering is matured solely in steel tanks. The "La Vigna delle Terrazze" is from the lowest yields; the aromas are rather simple with delicate pear and yellow flower notes, while the mid-palate has good concentration. But the wine sells itself in the finish with impressive persistence along with bright acidity and a touch of minerality. Enjoy this over its first three to four years with rich seafood.

VELENOSI LACRIMA DI MORRO D'ALBA

Angela and Ercole Velenosi manage this very successful winery in far southern Marche, working with the renowned Attilio Pagli as consulting enologist. They produce several typical regional wines, such as Pecorino, Verdicchio and Rosso Piceno; my favorite is the delightful Lacrima di Morro d'Alba. Produced from the eponymous grape, grown a bit north of Jesi, this has a bright purple color, seductive myrtle, maraschino cherry and violet aromas and ripe, delicious fruit on the palate. The tannins are quite soft and the balancing acidity keeps this light and fresh. This is a distinct, lovely wine that is entirely drinkable upon release and should be enjoyed by its fourth or fifth birthday. **BRV**: 2010, 2009, 2008, 2007.

CLAUDIO MORELLI SANGIOVESE "LA VIGNA DELLA TERRAZZE"

This tank-aged Sangiovese (no wood) from the Claudio Morelli estate north of Ancona is a very different animal than a typical Sangiovese from Tuscany. Rather than simple cherry fruit and tart acidity, this is a meaty style of this variety with slightly wild, rustic aromas of grilled meat and dried cherry with notes of tar and cumin. Medium-bodied with moderate tannins and good acidity, this has strong notes of oregano and dried brown herbs in the finish. This is not meant for cellaring, but rather for pairing with lighter game or pastas with mushrooms from two to four years of age. **BRV**: 2010, 2009.

MORODER ROSSO CONERO "AION"

Rosso Conero is one of Marche's most beloved reds, a wine made primarily from Montepulciano with Sangiovese being allowed in lesser percentages. Named for Mount Conero near Ancona, the hillside vineyards have the benefit of being very close to the Adriatic Sea, which helps moderate temperatures and lengthen the growing season. One of this wine type's best producers is Alessandro Moroder, who established his firm in 1984; he produces easy-drinking versions as well as *riserva* offerings that age for more than a decade. I absolutely love his "Aion" bottling, a 100% Montepulciano aged only in steel tanks before being bottled. It's got a lovely garnet color, fresh Queen Anne cherry and red plum fruit and ends with a clean finish with modest tannins, good acidity and lovely varietal character. This is not a wine to think about – just drink it and enjoy this tasty red in its youth, generally by four or five years of age. **BRV**: 2009, 2008, 2007.

FAZI BATTAGLIA ROSSO CONERO RISERVA "PASSO DEL LUPO"

Established in 1949, this huge firm is most closely associated with Verdicchio dei Castelli di Jesi, helping spread the fame of this wine around the world. Lately the company has introduced several new wines including this Rosso Conero Riserva. Produced from 85% Montepulciano and 15% Sangiovese, this is a barrique-aged version that is sleek and ripe with appealing aromas of black cherry, tar, toffee and vanilla. While the oak is a bit evident, the depth of fruit and notable persistence in the finish balance things out. This is best enjoyed at seven to ten years of age when it displays greater complexities. The name means "wolf's passage," a reminder of the wolves that inhabit nearby protected lands. **BRV**: 2008, 2007, 2005, 2004.

UMANI RONCHI ROSSO CONERO RISERVA "CUMARO"

Since their founding in the mid-1950s, Umani Ronchi has been best known for its expertise with Verdicchio; today that proficiency has extended to some notable releases of Rosso Conero. Their Riserva "Cumaro" offering (Cumaro is derived from an ancient Greek word meaning Conero, referring to a local evergreen shrub). This is 100% Montepulciano from the San Lorenzo vineyard, originally planted in 1965. Produced only in the finest vintages, this is a ripe, modern red aged for approximately sixteen months in barriques. The aromas of black cherry, bramble, blackberry and mocha leap out of the glass, while there is excellent depth of fruit along with firm tannins and balanced acidity. This needs a few years after release to settle down; peak enjoyment is from five to ten years of age, depending on the strength of the vintage. **BRV**: 2008, 2007, 2006.

SALADINI PALASTRI ROSSO PICENO SUPERIORE "MONTETINELLO"

While Rosso Conero must have at least 85% Montepulciano in the blend, that percentage is lower for Rosso Piceno, which also has a higher percentage of Sangiovese. Saladini Palastri, established in the town of Spinetoli, not far from Asoli Piceno in far southern Marche, is a specialist with Rosso Piceno, producing as many as five versions per vintage. The "Montetinello" from thirty year-old vineyards situated very close to the Adriatic sea, is a blend of 70% Montepulciano and 30% Sangiovese; displaying a bright scarlet color and excellent ripeness, this has zesty fruit notes of black cherry and plum with a hint of licorice. Medium-full, this has subdued tannins and good acidity; enjoy this from three to seven years of age. **BRV**: 2008, 2007, 2006.

BUCCI ROSSO PICENO "PONGELLI"

At this estate, Verdicchio receives most of the headlines, but make sure to try this delightful red as well. The "Pongelli" Rosso Piceno is a 50/50 Montepulciano/Sangiovese blend that is a charming, delicately fashioned version with appealing strawberry jam and bing cherry aromas backed by good acidity, persistence and modest tannins. Aged for six months in large casks, the focus here is on the tasty fruit as well as its sleek entry on the palate and elegant finish. Enjoy this from three to five years of age. **BRV**: 2010, 2009, 2008, 2007.

BRUNORI ROSSO PICENO "TORQUÍS"

Here is another charming, very approachable version of Rosso Piceno from this family firm situated in San Paolo di Jesi. Matured in cement vats to preserve varietal freshness, this Montepulciano/Sangiovese blend offers toned down dried cherry fruit with light brown herb notes in the aromas and in the finish. The tannins are moderate, while there is balanced acidity and good persistence. Enjoy this with *salumi* or ligher red meats. **BRV**: 2011, 2010. Brunori also crafts several excellent versions of Verdicchio del Castelli di Jesi, especially the "San Nicoló" Riserva.

SANTA BARBARA ROSSO PICENO "IL MASCHIO DI MONTE"

From this renowned Verdicchio producer, here is a distinctive Rosso Piceno. 100% Montepulciano from vineyards in the village of Barbara some 750 feet above sea level, this is rich and beautifully balanced with an emphasis on ripe black fruit along with notes of tar and hints of tobacco. While it is matured for eighteen months in barriques, the wood notes are so beautifully meshed with the fruit that the oak here is barely noticeable. The tannins are round and supple and there is good, cleansing acidity. I hesitate to call this a "modern" wine, yet that is what it is; thankfully it is *not* an international wine that is overripe or manipulated for high ratings. The harmony and purity of this wine are its keys to success; this could spark a great deal of interest in Rosso Piceno. Just lovely, this can be enjoyed from two to ten years of age. **BRV**: 2009, 2008, 2007, 2006.

IL POLLENZA "PORPORA"

At his spectacular estate in Tolentino in central Marche, Aldo Brachetti Peretti produces a few flashy, powerful reds, but my favorite is this medium-bodied blend of Merlot and Montepulciano. Sourced from estate vineyards planted in 2001, this wine is aged partly in used barriques and partly in cement tanks, giving this a nice varietal focus without having dominant oak sensations. The tart acidity and round tannins make this wine approachable upon release; this is not a forceful wine, but one that charms you with its subtleties; this is best enjoyed when it is four to seven years old. **BRV**: 2009, 2008, 2007, 2006.

IL POLLENZA VINO PASSITO "PIUS IX MASTAI"

Any study of the world of Italian wines leads to some fascinating discoveries; here is one of my favorite. This is a glorious dessert wine, a blend of Traminer aromatico and Sauvignon Blanc made in a *passito* style where the grapes are naturally dried over the course of several months. Harvest takes place over the course of two weeks to insure the best berries; the wine is aged only in cement tanks for optimum varietal purity. The color is light amber gold and there are lovely aromas of candied apricot, honey and crème caramel. Medium-full with excellent concentration, this is quite elegant; it is never heavy or cloying. Medium-sweet, the wine actually finishes somewhat dry on the palate, thanks to ideal cleansing acidity. This is ultra clean and very delicious; you don't hear much about dessert wines from Marche, but this is among the best in all of Italy! Enjoy this from five to seven years of age. **BRV**: 2008, 2007.

Abruzzo / Molise
Principal Varieties

White:
Trebbiano, Pecorino, Cococciola, Passerina, Malvasia,
Moscato, Chardonnay, Sauvignon

Red:
Montepulciano, Cabernet Sauvignon, Sangiovese, Merlot,
Aglianico, Tintilia

———

LA VALENTINA TREBBIANO D'ABRUZZO "SPELT"
Trebbiano, in its various forms and guises, is the most widely planted white variety throughout Italy. A few strains, such as Trebbiano di Soave, have a great deal of character, yet the truth remains that most clones of Trebbiano have little to offer besides acidity. Thankfully a few producers take enough care in Abruzzo to craft a very nice wine from Trebbiano; the "Spelt" offering from La Valentina is among the most enjoyable I've tasted. Medium-bodied, the wine has the typical pear and melon aromas along with subtle herbal notes, such as rosemary and thyme, along with a slight nuttiness. This also has nice richness on the palate, thanks to low yields. It's nothing terribly complicated, but it is a well made example of Trebbiano that is consistent from year to year; drink within one to two years of the harvest.

MARRAMIERO TREBBIANO D'ABRUZZO "ANIMA"
The Marramiero family has been growing grapes in Abruzzo since the 1960s, but it was only in the 1990s that Dante Marramiero estab-

lished the cantina. The "Anima" Trebbiano is a selection of the finest Trebbiano grapes from their estate vineyards at Rosciano in the province of Pescara. Aged only in steel tanks, this has stylish perfumes of lemon oil and hyacinth and a lovely texture; the finish has impressive persistence and there is excellent complexity and freshness. This is a much more complex and interesting version of Trebbiano d'Abruzzo that most examples; enjoy upon release and up to four years of age.

MASCIARELLI TREBBIANO D'ABRUZZO MARINA CVETIC
Gianni Masciarelli was one of the true dreamers of Abruzzo, who in a short time realized the true potential of his region's wines. He established his state-of-the-art winery in the hills of San Martino sulla Marrucina in 1981 and immediately won raves for his intensely flavored reds and whites. Sadly he passed away in 2008; today, his wife Marina Cvetic and daughter Miriam, along with enologist Romeo Taraborrelli manage the winery. One of their most striking products is this Trebbiano; a wine far removed from the everyday examples of this local product. Produced from a pergola vineyard some 50 years old, the wine is fermented in wood and matured entirely in new barriques for 22 months. This style is clearly a bit extreme and will not please everyone, but I believe this to be a beautifully balanced wine. Full-bodied, with aromas of Bosc pear, vanilla and honey, this is multi-layered with a long finish that offers a trace of smokiness. Enjoy this at three to five years of age.

ILLUMINATI PECORINO
While Trebbiano d'Abruzzo is the region's most famous white wine, there is a district called Controguerra in the far northern reaches of Abruzzo where several vintners produce excellent examples of other whites, such as Pecorino and Passerina. The Dino Illuminati Pecorino is a stellar one, sourced from hillside vineyards at an elevation of 800 feet. The wine is predominantly fermented and aged in steel tanks, with 10% of the must fermented in barriques; in this fashion, a bit of texture emerges without losing the delightful aro-

matic profile. Those perfumes are quite captivating, as there are notes of guava, pineapple, lemon oil and a hint of almond on the nose; medium-full, this has a rich mid-palate, excellent ripeness, very good acidity and excellent length and balance. This is a distinctive wine with beautiful focus, complexity and clarity; enjoy at three to five years of age.

CONTESA DI ROCCO PASETTI PECORINO
The Contesa Pecorino from Rocco Pasetti is among the best examples of this variety in Abruzzo. Fermented partly in oak and partly in steel, there are expressive aromas of lemon, vanilla and peaches and cream. This has excellent concentration, a rich mid-palate and a long, flavorful finish with very good acidity. Offering great focus, this has some of the characteristics of Condrieu, a white wine from France's Rhone Valley made from Viognier. Drink in its youth, from two to three years of age.

VALLE MARTELLO COCOCCIOLA "PRIMA TERRA"
Situated in Villamagna, southeast of Chieti in central Abruzzo, Valle Martello is a specialist in the rare white variety Cocacciola, producing a steel-aged and a barrel-aged version. The "Prima Terra" is the latter; offering aromas of lemon, pear and a hint of saffron, this has subtle spice, a hint of jasmine in the finish and is beautifully structured. The wood notes are delicate and the varietal character is nicely captured; enjoy this from three to five years of age.

CONTESA DI ROCCO PASETTI MONTEPULCIANO D'ABRUZZO CERASUOLO "VIGNA CORVINO"
One of Italy's most famous versions of rosé is Cerasuolo of Montepulciano d'Abruzzo; the name comes from the word *ceresa*, meaning "cherry red." Most producers of Montepulciano d'Abruzzo produce at least one bottling, ranging from quite dry to lightly sweet. One of the most flavorful and beautifully balanced of these is the "Vigna Corvino" from the Contesa winery of Rocco Pasetti; the grapes are from the Collecorvino estate, a bit west of Pescara, not far from the sea. The red Montepulci-

ano grapes are macerated on the skins for twenty-four hours, resulting in a deep pink color. Medium-bodied, with lovely aromas of fresh cherries and resin, this has very good acidity and persistence; it's dry and delicious- enjoy this from one to two years of age.

LA VALENTINA MONTEPULCIANO D'ABRUZZO CERASUOLO

There's no real secret to the reason why I've included this particular Cerasuolo; I love this wine! It's got a light copper/strawberry color with intriguing aromas of dried cherry, tar and clove. Medium-bodied, this has delicious fruit, impressive texture and a rich finish. It's so well balanced and it's also ultra clean and sleek. Enjoy this from one to two years of age.

CATALDI MADONNA MONTEPULCIANO D'ABRUZZO CERASUOLO

I absolutely love this Cerasuolo after it's been in the market for a year's time, as the ripe cherry flavors become a bit more developed and subtle, while the wine still maintains its freshness. This has a light strawberry color and plenty of flavor with a dry, elegant finish. While it's certainly lovely upon release, this really does improve with a bit of time in the bottle. This producer is as consistent with this wine as any firm.

SAN LORENZO MONTEPULCIANO D'ABRUZZO "ANTARES"

The Montepulciano variety dominates the Abruzzese wine scene, as it is far and away the dominant red grape planted throughout the region. Naturally Montepulciano d'Abruzzo is the signature wine of the region; offerings vary from the mass-produced versions bottled for airlines to beautifully structured wines that can improve for more than a decade. One of the most delightful everyday versions I've tasted is the Antares from San Lorenzo, a solid producer that makes a full line of fresh, flavorful whites, reds and rosés from the region. Deep ruby red with a light purple tint, this ripe blackberry, black plum and black raspberry aromas with pleasant black spice notes. Medium-bodied, this is straightforward with moderate tannins and balanced acidity. It's value priced and a fine introduction to this wine type; consume over its first two to three years for maximum pleasure.

MASTRANGELO MONTEPULCIANO D'ABRUZZO "RISERVA DEL VICARIO"

Filiberto Mastrangelo is one of the new generation of producers in Abruzzo and like most of his generation, he combines youthful passion as well as great respect for the tradition of his land. He established his small estate in 2000 and today produces about 35,000 bottles from nine acres of estate vines. The Riserva del Vicario bottling, made from ancient clones of Montepulciano, is a well-made wine that straddles the line between traditional and modern styles of this wine. It is aged in barriques for as long as fifteen months, but this is a more-toned down version, definitely not as ripe as some examples from nearby producers; the medium-weight tannins are refined and the acidity is very good. Mastrangelo has made a wine for food here, not for glowing reviews; we should be thankful for that and hope that more of the area's producers would do the same. Enjoy this from four to seven years of age.

MASCIARELLI MONTEPULCIANO D'ABRUZZO "VILLA GEMMA"

The Villa Gemma Montepulciano is the showcase red at Masciarelli; a powerful wine with explosive fruit. Produced from a high-density vineyard planted twenty years ago, the wine is fermented in various sizes of *botti* and then matured entirely in new French barriques, the aromas are the classic *frutti di bosco* such as blackberry and raspberry along with notes of vanilla, red roses and bitter chocolate. There is excellent richness on the palate and impressive persistence with seductive tannins. This clearly needs time to settle down; ten to twelve years of age is when this is at its best. **BRV**: 2007, 2006, 2005, 2004.

VALLE REALE MONTEPULCIANO D'ABRUZZO "SAN CALISTO"

For some producers of Montepulciano d'Abruzzo, there has been a shift in their thinking over the past fifteen years, moving from everyday, value-priced wine to products of greater complexity and character. For Valle Reale, founded in 1999, that has not been the case, as the Pizzolo family has sought to be among the area's finest producers since day one. Their "San Calisto" bottling, made from grapes sourced from a vineyard located in a national park amidst the Gran Sasso mountain range, has been a signature wine for the firm ever since its initial release from the 2000 vintage. Matured for one year in *tonneaux*, this is a forward, very appealing effort with flavors of black raspberry, black cherry and mocha; the finish is quite long, the tannins are polished and there is good balancing acidity. This is a sleek, modern, delicious wine that is structured for peak enjoyment from five to seven years of age. **BRV**: 2008, 2007, 2006, 2005, 2004.

BARBA MONTEPULCIANO D'ABRUZZO "I VASARI"

The Barba brothers – Vincenzo, Giovanni and Domenico – manage this estate situated in Scerne di Pineto between Teramo and Pescara in northern Abruzzo. Several businesses, including a dairy farm are part of the estate, which has 165 acres of vineyards. The signature wine is the "I Vasari" old vine Montepulciano d'Abruzzo, offering a deep purple color, powerful aromas of black raspberry, mytle and anise supported by excellent depth of fruit. Though aged for sixteen months in barriques, the wood only emerges a bit in the aromas, as the varietal purity shines through in the lengthy finish; structured for time in the cellar, this peaks around ten years of age. **BRV**: 2008, 2007, 2006.

ZACCAGNINI MONTEPULCIANO D'ABRUZZO "SAN CLEMENTE"

Marcello Zaccagnini operates this ultra modern estate in Bolognano, a little ways south of Pescara. His premium Montepulciano is the "San Clemente" bottling, a modern, ripe, somewhat showy wine, but one that is true to its type. Sourced from low yielding vinyards of clay and limestone soils, this is fermented in wood and then matured for eighteen months in barriques. Aromas of black cherry, violets, roses and vanilla lead to a rich mid-palate and a powerful, yet elegant finish, as the tannins are beautifully polished. While this impresses with its forward nature when released, this really needs several years in the bottle to display its complexities and grace; enjoy this up to ten to twelve years of age. **BRV**: 2008, 2007, 2006, 2004.

ILLUMINATI MONTEPULCIANO D'ABRUZZO RISERVA "PIELUNI"

As more producers of Montepulciano d'Abruzzo are crafting limited release wines that are more "serious" than the honest, everyday wines of the past, they are turning out deeply colored, highly extracted, "modern" wines in certain instances. That may or may not be a good thing, depending on your point of view – as well as your palate. This *riserva* from Dino Illuminati (from the DOCG Colline Teramane zone) is a robust wine with aromas of licorice, black plum, black raspberry and cocoa powder backed up by ample oak (the wine was matured in barriques for two years). There is notable persistence and balancing acidity with medium-weight tannins, but this is a wine that needs to settle down for a few years after release, as there is often some bitterness from the oak treatment. This wine is definitely a modern, international style that has little to do with tradition, but if you love this approach, you will find lots to admire in this wine, especially when consumed some seven to ten years after the vintage date, when it has had time to round out and display greater complexities. **BRV:** 2007.

FARNESE "CINQUE AUCTOCONI"

Founded in 1994, Farnese is a large firm, producing more than ten million bottles per year. While Montepulciano d'Abruzzo and Pecorino are their most famous wines, they are also known for this marvelous blend. A mix of five indigenous varieties: Montepulciano, Primitivo, Sangiovese, Negroamaro and Malvasia Nera, the grapes are primarily from Abruzzo, but some are sourced from Puglia. Barrique-aged in French and American barrels for approximately one year, this is bright purple with aromas of black raspberry, licorice and myrtle; the layered mid-palate features flavors of loganberry and damson plum. There is impressive persistence, good acidity, nicely integrated oak and round, sleek tannins; notes of tobacco and tree bark highlight the finish. All told, this is a fruit forward, harmonious red aimed at giving the wine drinker a stylish interpretation of today's southern Italian red scene. This is at is best from five to seven years after the vintage, sometimes a year or two more if from a top growing season. **BRV:** 2007, 2006.

VALENTINI MONTEPULCIANO D'ABRUZZO
CERASUOLO D'ABRUZZO
TREBBIANO D'ABRUZZO

Edoardo Valentini was one of Italy's legendary winemakers; his reputation earned with stunning examples of the three most famous wine types of Abruzzo. Sadly he passed away in 2006 at the age of 72; fortunately he trained his son Francesco well, as he admirably continues the work of his father at this tiny estate in Loreto Aprutino in the province of Pescara.

There is not much I can add to his story, as anyone who has tasted his wines knows the amazing complexity of these wines as well as the remarkable varietal purity. This is minimalist winemaking with long aging in large casks that results in wines of splendid suppleness and finesse. I did meet Edoardo Valentini at his estate a few months before his death; I asked him about how he made his wines. He looked directly at me and in a booming voice that could be heard some 30 or 40 feet away – I was only five feet from him at the time – he replied "I don't make the wines, the earth makes the wines." That simple emphatic statement summed up his philosophy; his work in his pergola vineyards was – and remains – impeccable. The results are striking as even his Trebbiano drinks well at ten to twelve years of age, while the Cerasuolo, very dry and powerful, is often in top shape at five to seven years, while for the Montepulciano, 15-20 years is when these wines truly shine! Production is extremely limited, but you must try at least one of these wines if you are to be thought of as a true Italian wine lover!

DI MAJO NORANTE "DON LUIGI" RISERVA
Founded in 1968, Di Majo Norante is the most famous wine producer of Molise; for some time, it was the only one! Named for the patriarch of this firm, the Don Luigi Riserva is a blend of 90% Montepulciano

and 10% Aglianico that is an intriguing mix of modernity and tradition. Matured in barriques for eighteen months, this is a big, spicy wine with strong notes of tar, clove and tobacco in the finish; there is impressive persistence as well as nicely tuned acidity and balanced tannins. The black plum and myrtle aromas carry through nicely on the palate and there is a bit of a rustic note in the finish. The Don Luigi does not fit neatly into one winemaking philosophy; like it or not, it is unique! This is structured for several years of enjoyment; drink from five to ten years of age. **BRV**: 2009, 2008, 2006, 2005.

DI MAJO NORANTE MOSCATO REALE "APINAE"

It's difficult not to be won over by the mesmerizing aromatics of a well made Moscato; I'd say it would be also impossible not to be seduced by this dazzling example! Produced from Moscato Reale grapes (a strain of Moscato found in Molise and Puglia), this has heavenly aromas of mandarin orange, orange zest and crème caramel; medium-full and quite lush on the palate, this has a long finish with excellent concentration. This is lightly sweet and thanks to the cleansing acidity, perfectly balanced; there is a subtle pleasant bitterness in the finish, as the wine finishes dry. Offering outstanding complexity, this has gorgeous varietal character and is an inspired choice with simple *biscotti*, blue cheeses or even on its own after a meal. Given the depth of fruit and the excellent natural acidity, this will age well; peak enjoyment should be from seven to ten years of age. **BRV**: 2009, 2008.

Lazio
Principal Varieties

White:
Grechetto, Malvasia, Bombino Bianco, Trebbiano

Red:
Cesanese, Sangiovese, Merlot, Cabernet Sauvignon

———

SERGIO MOTTURA GRECHETTO "POGGIO DELLA COSTA"

There are several whites and reds produced at this leading estate in Lazio; these include the traditional Orvieto – dry and slightly sweet – as well as a charming 100% Pinot Nero and an elegant Merlot/Montepulciano blend. But year in and year out, the two wines that best typify Mottura are the *selezioni*, made entirely from Grechetto. This variety, grown throughout Lazio and Umbria, is a local mutation of Greco from Campania and delivers beautiful aromatics. Mottura produces two versions from vineyards in Civitella d'Agliano, located about 45 miles northwest of Rome, on the border with Umbria. The "Latour a Civitella" offering is aged in oak, while the "Poggio della Costa" is aged solely in steel tanks; while both wines are excellent, I prefer the latter for its remarkable varietal purity and vibrancy. Offering luxurious aromas of quince, Anjou pear and honeysuckle, this is a wine of richness on the palate and beautiful texture, thanks in part to the six months of lees aging. There are so many outstanding whites from Italy that are famous – especially from Friuli and Alto Adige – but here is a relatively undiscovered white that can stand in comparison to those more celebrated examples. Peak consumption is between five and seven years, although the finest versions can be enjoyed up to a decade or slightly longer.

FALESCO FERENTANO

Riccardo Cotarella is one of the most renowned enologists working in Italy; currently he consults for approximately 75 wineries, not only in Italy, but also in France and the United States. Yet of all the companies for which he labors, his pride and joy is his own estate Falesco, on the border between Lazio and Umbria; his brother Renzo is co-owner. This wine is made entirely from the Roscetto grape, a rare indigenous variety of the Greco (Grechetto) cultivar that Cotarella has single-handedly saved from extinction. From a vineyard planted in 1987 in the Montefiascone zone of far northern Lazio, this wine was first produced in 1998. Cotarella ferments in steel and barriques and then matures the wine for four months in barriques. There are distinct aromas of banana, pear and vanilla and the wine is quite creamy and lush on the palate; the finish is rich with excellent persistence. Cotarella is very familiar with many Italian white varieties that deliver wines for the short term; with this wine, he wanted to produce an Italian white capable of more than immediate drinking. Given that this wine is at its best at five to seven years of age, I would say that he has succeeded. **BRV**: 2008, 2007, 2006.

FONTANA CANDIDA FRASCATI SUPERIORE "LUNA MATER"

Founded in 1958 and currently owned by Gruppo Italiano Vini, the firm that owns more than a dozen wineries throughout Italy, Fontana Candida is arguably the best-known producer of Frascati, Lazio's most quaffable and recognized white wine. Like most producers, Fontana Candida makes a simple, drink-me-now style of Frascati; production of this most basic wine is in the millions of bottles. However they also produce three other versions that display more weight on the palate as well as complexity; the "Terre dei Grifi" and "Vigneto Santa Teresa" are quite elegant and refreshing. Their most singular Frascati is the "Luna Mater", a blend of Malvasia di Candia, Malvasia Puttinata, Bombino Bianco, Greco and Trebbiano that is produced in very limited quanties of approximately 1400 cases per year. The grapes used are from the best vineyards and are late harvested in two stages; that combined with fermentation on the skins gives this wine a very different sensation than the typical Frascati. The aromas are of banana, spiced pear, applesauce and cinnamon and the mid-palate is quite expressive; there is good acidity and excellent persistence with almond notes in the finish. A lovely wine that will surprise anyone who is used to a routine Frascati; this is best between three to five years after the harvest. **BRV**: 2010, 2009, 2008 (exceptional), 2007.

CORTE DEI PAPI CESANESE DEL PIGLIO "SAN MAGNO"

Cesanese is Lazio's most famous red indigenous variety; there are at least two separate cuttings, namely Cesanese Afflile (named for the place where it was first planted) and Cesanese Comune. There are three DOC zones for the variety, all situated close together near the town of Frosinone in south central Lazio; the Cesanese del Piglio is the most highly regarded. The "San Magno" version from Corte dei Papi is a typical version with strawberry and cherry aromas backed by notes of small oak. Medium-full with notable tannins, this has balanced acidity and good persistence, while the finish has a note of roasted meat. Time will help soften the tannins; enjoy this from seven to ten years of age. **BRV**: 2009, 2007.

DAMIANO CIOLLI CESANESE "SILENE" / "CIRSIUM"

Here are two very different versions of Cesanese from Damiano Ciolli, a winery south and slighly east of Rome that started production in 2001; the family has been growing grapes for more than fifty years. The "Silene" is a charming wine, aged in used barrels, that has a pale garnet color and inviting aromas of fresh raspberry, currant and carnation. Medium-bodied with delicate tannins and good acidity, this is meant for consumption over its first three to five years. The "Cirsium" from vineyards planted in 1955, is a richer, oakier style with bigger tannins; the aromas veer toward black fruits with some herbal notes (oregano, coriander). Matured in barriques, this is a more forward wine with riper fruit; each is well made, but styled for different foods. **BRV** (both): 2009, 2008, 2007.

SOLONIO "FONTANAPIANA"

This winery, owned by the Le Tenute di Genagricola group, produces a variety of wines from indigenous and international varieties from their vineyards in the Colli Lanuvini area just south of Rome. Their red Fontanapiana, is Montepulciano *in purezza* that is a graceful, elegantly styled red with very good acidity, round tannins and a nicely balanced, lengthy finish with impressive persistence. There is excellent varietal character – the aromas feature notes of dried cherry, thyme and tobacco – and overall, this is a lovely food wine; enjoy this from three to five years of age.

FALESCO "MONTIANO"

Winemaker Riccardo Cotarella has often been referred to as "Mr. Merlot," given his proclivity for incorporating that variety into many of his blended reds that he crafts at the dozens of wineries at which he consults. Perhaps his finest version of Merlot is the "Montiano" bottling he produces at his own estate, Falesco. Sourced from a single vineyard with volcanic soils, this has all the prototypical characteristics Cotarella is looking for with this variety: sweet red fruit, an elegant mid-palate and polished tannins. From the inviting aromas of black cherry, menthol, marmalade and tar to the lengthy, supple finish with excellent persistence, this is an irresistible Merlot! Approachable upon release, this will drink well anywhere from five to ten years and longer in the very best vintages. A special "30 Anni" offering from the 2009 vintage (this in honor of 30 years of Falesco), made from the vines that were 45-50 years of age, is simply stunning. **BRV**: 2009, 2008, 2007, 2006, 2004.

Umbria

Principal Varieties

White:
Grechetto, Trebbiano, Procanico, Verdello, Viognier, Vermentino, Chardonnay, Sauvignon, Riesling, Moscato

Red:
Sagrantino, Sangiovese, Gamay, Cabernet Sauvignon, Merlot, Canaiolo, Syrah, Cabernet Franc

———

PALAZZONE ORVIETO CLASSICO SUPERIORE "TERRE VINEATE"
ORVIETO CLASSICO SUPERIORE "CAMPO GUARDIANO"
While Orvieto is undoubtedly Umbria's most recognized white wine, too many producers do little to enhance its image, preferring to make the most basic wine they can to please the tourists who want to sip a glass at an outdoor trattoria near Orvieto's grand cathedral.

Enter Palazzone, a winery that actually takes great care with this wine. There are two special bottings, each made with a blend of the five varieties allowed in this wine, with Grechetto and Procanico representing the majority of the cuvée.

The "Terre Vineate" has seductive aromas of Bosc pear, magnolia and mango and offers a beautifully textured mid-palate and a harmonious finish. The "Campo Guardiano" takes things up a notch, both in weight as well as aromatic profile. The main difference here is that this wine is aged in bottle for twenty-four months in an underground cave of tufo rock; this is much like the Etruscans would have made this wine. The aromas are quite distinctive, offering notes of turmeric, golden apple and saffron; medium-full, this is quite rich and offers a well-structured finish of excellent length. Both wines show what can be done when an ordinary wine is treated in an extraordinary way. The "Terre Vineate" is meant for consumption within two to three years after the vintage, while that increases to three to five years for the "Campo Guardiano." **BRV**: Terre Vineate: 2011, 2010, 2009. Campo Guardino: 2010, 2009, 2008.

DI FILIPPO GRECHETTO "SASSI ARENARIA"
Back in 1971, Italo and Giuseppina Di Filippo left the city for the country and established their wine estate in Cannara on the road between Torgiano and Montefalco. Today Roberto and Emma Di Filippo manage this property with 75 acres of vines, producing Montefalco reds as well as some notable whites; the vineyards were certified organic in 1994. The "Sassi d'Arenaria" is their special *selezione* of estate Grechetto; aged on its lees for a six months and matured in older *botti*, this combines enticing aromatics (mango, Anjou pear and geranium) with a lovely textured mouthfeel. There is very good acidity, excellent persistence and beautiful complexity and balance. Grechetto in Umbria is too often little more than a pleasant wine, but Roberto di Filippo has made a first-rate version! Enjoy this from three to five years of age.

CASTELLO DELLA SALA "CERVARO DELLA SALA"
This celebrated white is from the Antinori estate Castello della Sala in Umbria; Renzo Cotarella, brother of famed consulting enologist Riccardo, is the head winemaker. This is a blend of 85% Chardonnay and 15% Grechetto that is fermented and aged in French barriques; there is marvelous texture and richness in the mid-palate with appealing pear, fig and mango flavors with beautifully integrated wood notes and subtle spice in the finish. Appealing upon release, this tends to improve over the course of five to seven years, while a few older bottles from great vintages (2001, 1999) are still in fine shape. How nice to taste a wine structured for the long term, while

still offering great pleasure upon release! **BRV**: 2009, 2008, 2006, 2004, 2001, 1999.

VITALONGA ROSE´

The Vitalonga ("long life") estate is located in Ficulle, in the Oriveto hillsides in western Umbria, not far from the borders of Tuscany and Lazio. Brothers Gian Luigi and Pier Francesco Maravalle produce several reds from indigenous and international varieties, as well as this impressive Rosé, a blend of Merlot and Cabernet. Crafted from early ripening grapes, this is quite flavorful with fresh black cherry flavors and has very good acidity and a very dry finish. While this needs to be consumed within one or two years of release, this is a bit more serious than many other similar examples.

LUNGAROTTI RUBESCO TORGIANO RISERVA "VIGNA MONTICCHIO"

Any history of Umbrian red wine must tell the story of Lungarotti and Torgiano wine. Founded in the early 1960s by Giorgio Lungarotti, this is the winery that gave birth to Torgiano, a red wine from hillside vineyards just south of Perugia. Today Chiara Lungarotti and her sister Teresa Severini manage the estate and continue this company's great work with Torgiano. A blend of 70% Sangiovese and 30% Canaiolo (these are the only two varieties allowed in a Torgiano *rosso*) aged for one year in barriques, this is a rich, ripe, vibrant red with black cherry, currant and tar aromas, impressive concentration and persistence, very good acidity and round tannins. The wood notes stay in the background and there is very good freshness; the 2005 bottling, tasted in mid-2012 seemed like a much younger wine. Impeccably balanced, this is a lovely wine of great complexity; enjoy this from five to twelve years of age, depending on the strength of the vintage. **BRV**: 2006, 2005, 2004.

COLLEALDOLE MONTEFALCO SAGRANTINO

The most distinctive red indigenous variety of Umbria is Sagrantino, a grape planted in the commune of Montefalco, not far from the towns of Spoleto and Assisi. This is a variety that is among the most tannic in the world, making this wine a challenge for producers that want to offer a product that does not need years after release to be appreciated. Collealdole, managed by Francesco and Frabrizio Antano, is one of the producers that opts to mature Sagrantino in large casks, so as to help soften the wine. The grape itself offers a beautiful array of aromas, which the Antanos capture; notes of red cherry, currant, tobacco, sage and myrtle are evident. Medium-full, this is a wine that coats every part of your palate and finishes with distinct herbal notes. The tannins are quite evident and while the wine is at its best after a decade, it can be enjoyed upon release, usually three to four years after the harvest. **BRV**: 2009, 2008, 2007, 2006.

ANTONELLI SAGRANTINO DI MONTEFALCO "CHIUSA DI PANNONE"

Filippo Antonelli is a gentleman and a wonderful businessman who has slowly seen the growth of his winery take shape over the past twenty years. He has always been a producer that wants his wines to express varietal purity as well as a sense of place, thus producing wines in a traditional style and resisting the urge to adopt a flashier, more international approach. His regular Sagrantino, aged for one year in 25 hl casks, is a model of balance and restraint. The Chiusa di Pannone offering maintains those characteristics in a wine of greater weight and complexity. First produced from the 2003 vintage, the grapes are sourced from a vineyard at an elevation of 1300 feet above sea level comprised of limestone, clay and gravel; the plants are a massal selection and yields are very low, some 30 hl per hectare or one kilo per plant. This wine takes Sagrantino di Montefalco to new heights with a more beautifully defined mid-palate with layers of fruit and a finish of great length with silky tannins, very good acidity and subtle wood notes. Although this has only been produced for a few years, the track record of what Antonelli has done with this variety gives one confidence that this may one day be recognized as one of Italy's very finest reds. **BRV:** 2006, 2005, 2004 (exceptional), 2003.

COLPETRONE SAGRANTINO DI MONTEFALCO "GOLD"

Colpetrone is the Umbrian property of the giant Saiagricola firm, which also owns wineries in Montepulciano and Montalcino in Tuscany. The Gold bottling of Montefalco Sagrantino is a special selection of what winemaker Riccardo Cotarella (he took over in 2010 after a long, successful run from Lorenzo Landi) considers the finest lots of wine. Deeply colored, this is very rich and a bit tightly wound upon release, yet has a round, elegant finish with supple tannins. This has rich flavors of black plum, marmalade, licorice and black cherry backed by a generous mid-palate. Aged for one year in barriques, there is ample fruit to counteract the wood notes, with the result being a ripe, gutsy Sagrantino built for the long haul; this wine is at peak at ten to twelve years of age. **BRV**: 2007, 2006, 2005, 2004.

ARNALDO-CAPRAI SAGRANTINO DI MONTEFALCO "COLLEPIANO"

Marco Caprai, son of Arnaldo, who founded this estate in 1971, has done a great deal for Montefalco di Sagrantino. Through his efforts, he has received a great deal of media attention and critical acclaim, prompting one local producer to name him, "our Angelo Gaja." At his state-of-the-art winery, Caprai produces very modern wines, aging his Sagrantino in French barriques, as opposed to many local producers who opt for the traditional *botti*. While his "25 Anni" offering has received numerous high marks, I find the wine to be terribly overoaked with sharp, extremely bitter tannins. Much better is his Sagrantino di Montefalco "Collepiano," in which the wood notes are much better intertwined with the fruit. Offering considerable amounts of fruit on the palate and in the finish, this is an excellent example of the richness and spice of this type of wine, as there are notes of tobacco, balsamic and sage in the finish. The wine starts to reveal much of its complexity at age seven or eight and is usually at peak some 10-12 years after the vintage. **BRV**: 2008, 2007, 2006, 2005, 2004, 2001.

TIBURZI MONTEFALCO SAGRANTINO "TACCALITE"

It's an adventure tasting the wines of Tiburzi with winemaker Tiziano Vistalli at this small estate located in a business zone in Montefalco, as meat refrigerators are right next door to the tasting area. Perhaps it's the power of suggestion, pairing beef with these wines, but it works! The style of the "Taccalite" bottling is unmistakably modern, given its deep ruby red color and bright aromas of ripe black cherry fruit along with notes of marmalade, tar and melted chocolate. Matured for 18-24 months in new barriques, this is a somewhat flashy wine, but a well-balanced effort with good acidity and silky tannins. It's best to give this wine a bit of time after release; enjoy from seven to ten years of age. **BRV:** 2007, 2006.

TABARRINI MONTEFALCO SAGRANTINO
"CAMPO ALLA CERQUA / "COLLE ALLE MACCHIE"

At his estate in Montefalco established in 2001, Giampaolo Tabarrini produces three separate versions of Montefalco Sagrantino, each with their own unique personality, based on different cellar approaches. I am focusing on two of these wines: the "Campo alla Cerqua," which is aged solely in large casks and released after four years, while the "Colle alla Macchie" is aged in barriques and then an additional two years in the bottle before release; thus in 2012, the "Cerqua" was the 2008 vintage, while the current vintage of the "Macchie" was the 2006.

The "Cerqua" is a brilliant styling of Sagrantino, offering expressive aromas of menthol, myrtle, black raspberry and tar. Medium-full with a layered mid-palate, this has outstanding persistence, very good acidity, rich, youthful tannins and beautiful varietal purity and structure. Supremely made, this is meant for peak enjoyment from seven to ten years of age. The "Macchie" has black plum, bitter chocolate and purple iris perfumes, excellent concentration, perfect ripeness and balanced acidity. Best of all, this expresses a sense of place – this is a first-rate version of Montefalco Sagrantino. This is structured for peak enjoyment from seven to twelve years of age. **BRV:** Cerqua- 2008 (outstanding), 2007, 2006. Macchie - 2006 (outstanding), 2005, 2004.

PAOLO BEA MONTEFALCO ROSSO RISERVA

There are modern producers in Montefalco (Caprai, Colpretone) and there are traditional producers (Antonelli, Collealdole) and then there is Giampiero Bea. Son of Paolo, he has a philosophy of treating the earth with great respect, adopting organic as well as biodynamic practices with the result being wines of great breeding, finesse and perhaps above all, restraint. It is difficult to select only one wine from Bea, as all of his wines are outstanding, be they white, red or sweet. I have opted for the Montefalco Rosso Riserva, a blend of primarily Sangiovese with the remainder a mix of Montepulciano and Sagrantino. Aged for two years in *botti*, this is a gorgeous red with a light garnet color, fresh cherry and currant fruit, subtle red spice, delicate tannins and very good acidity. This has a lovely mid-palate and an exceedingly long finish with excellent persistence. This wine along with all the other reds from this great producer are all about delicacy instead of power; this drinks well for seven to ten years and often longer in great vintages, proving that a wine that is not powerful on the palate can age successfully. **BRV**: 2006, 2005, 2004.

CASTELLO DELLE REGINE MERLOT

Milan attorney Paolo Nodari purchased a sprawling estate about 40 miles north of Rome in the late 1990s and began producing wine from the 2000 vintage. Nodari wisely hired famed enologist Franco Benabei as his winemaker and decided to focus on varietal wines. To date, his most successful have been the Sangiovese "Selezione del Fondatore" along with his Merlot. Sourced from grapes grown in clay soils that are ideal for the variety, this is an instantly appealing wine with deep color and ripe red cherry aromas that are joined by notes of menthol and herbal tea. This is ripe and forward, made in a modern style, as it ages for one year in barriques, yet the wood notes perfectly complement the fruit, while there is good balancing acidity and round, elegant tannins. This is at its best anywhere from five to ten years of age. **BRV**: 2007, 2005, 2004, 2003, 2001.

LUNGAROTTI "SAN GIORGIO"

Here is one of Umbria's most renowned reds, a blend of Sangiovese and Canaiolo along with a prevalance of Cabernet Sauvignon. Medium-full with aromas of dried black currant, thyme and black plum, the wine is aged for one year in barriques and then at least three years in the bottle before being released. The mid-palate is nicely developed, while the tannins are polished and there is excellent persistence and very good acidity. A wine of breeding and class, this is meant for anywhere from a dozen to twenty years of enjoyment; the 2004 tasted at eight years of age has at least another ten years of life ahead of it. **BRV**: 2005, 2004, 2001.

CASTELLO DI CORBARA "CASTELLO DI CORBARA"

Castello di Corbara produces an array of white and reds from the Lago di Corbara zone, just north of Lago Corbara and east of Orvieto. My favorite red from them is their signature red named for the estate, a blend of Sangiovese, Merlot and Cabernet Sauvignon (and sometimes with a small percentage of Montepulciano). Matured both in barriques and *botti*, this offers ripe fruit aromas of black cherry along with notes of menthol, black olive and violets. While this is in the modern vein, as with numerous reds from Umbria and Toscana, this is more toned-down in its fruit presentation and is elegantly styled to accompany food, as it has good balancing acidity. This is best consumed from five to ten years of age. **BRV**: 2008, 2007, 2006, 2004.

VITALONGA "PHI"

"Phi" is the expression of the finest wine that can be produced at Vitalonga. It is an unabashedly modern red with small oak aging and very ripe grapes, but it is quite well done in that style. Primarily Cabernet Franc, this is aged in barriques (a portion of them new) for fifteen months and offers excellent concentration and persistence with balanced acidity and youthful, rounded tannins. The mid-palate is nicely developed and there is the structure to age for seven to ten years. It may have little to do with tradition, but it is a notable wine. **BRV**: 2010, 2009.

PERTICAIA SAGRANTINO MONTEFALCO PASSITO

Perticaia, named for a word that means "plow," is a visually stunning estate in the heart of the Sagrantino Montefalco territory. Owner Guido Guardigli produces the typical wines of the area; most impresssive is his *passito*. Just as in Valpolicella, it is the sweet wine that is the most historically significant, as this was the original Sagrantino; today of course, it is the dry version that is more famous. This *passito*, made from Sagrantino grapes that have been naturally dried for 40 days and then fermented and aged in French oak, offers lush blackberry, black cherry and black plum fruit with a lightly sweet finish and moderate tannins. It's not as spicy as some versions, but it is a highly appealing wine for enjoyment after dinner or with chocolate; it's usually at its best at five to seven years of age. **BRV**: 2008, 2007, 2006, 2004.

SCACCIADIAVOLI MONTEFALCO SAGRANTINO PASSITO

You've got to love the name of this winery, which means "devil hunters." Members of the Pambuffetti family own this marvelous winery, which dates back to 1884, though some of the structures here are centuries older. The wines here are made by Stefano Chioccioli, who does a marvelous job capuring the red fruits of the Sagrantino grape while rounding out the harsh tannins of the variety. The *passito* is a lovely wine, medium-sweet with appealing red plum and dark chocolate flavors and precise acidity to keep everything in balance. This is best at seven to ten years of age. **BRV**: 2008, 2007, 2006, 2004, 2001.

Campania

Principal Varieties

White:
Greco, Fiano, Falanghina, Aspirinio, Fenile, Ginestra, Biancolella

Red:
Aglianico, Piedirosso, Tintore, Merlot

———

GROTTA DEL SOLE LACRYMA CHRISTI DEL VESUVIO BIANCO

Lacryma Christi means "the tears of Christ"; the story of how this wine received its name is directly tied in with the area. The legend has it that when Lucifer the devil was kicked out of eternal paradise and banished to hell, he grabbed a piece of heaven as he was evicted. God saw this and cried; his tears landed in the Gulf of Napoli. There are actually three different types of Lacryma Christi produced: bianco, rosso and rosato; it is the white that is the most popular, especially at lunchtime in *trattorie* near the sea in Napoli. The grape here is Coda di Volpe which means "tail of the fox," referring to the shape of the grape's clusters (note: this variety is also known as Caprettone). Grotta del Sole, a producer located in the Campi Flegrei area just north and west of Napoli, makes a typically delightful version of Lacryma Christi white, with fresh lemon and melon fruit, medium-body and a clean finish with moderate acidity. Enjoy this wine within one to two years of the harvest.

DE FALCO LACRYMA CHRISTI DEL VESUVIO BIANCO

Established in 1990 within the National Park of Vesuvius – the estate vineyards are rich in lava deposits – the De Falco winery is a medium-sized firm that offers a wide array of well made Campanian wines that are crafted by Mario Ercolino, one of the region's most renowned enologists. This is a blend of 90% Coda di Volpe and 10% Falanghina; featuring bright lemon and pear aromas, there is beautiful complexity with a light touch of minerality in the finish. Medium-bodied with very good acidity, enjoy this within a year or two of the vintage.

VADIAPERTI CODA DI VOLPE

While Coda di Volpe is the principal variety in Lacryma Christi del Vesuvio, you don't find too many producers that bottle it as a stand alone variety; perhaps it doesn't have a lot of allure on its own. Thankfully a few vintners such as Raffaelle Trosi at Vadiaperti think enough of the variety to fashion an excellent version. "It has its own identity," Troisi told me about the wine. Displaying aromas of stone fruit, lemon and a hint of almond, this is medium-full with a lengthy finish with a trace of minerality. This offers much more complexity than the typical Coda di Volpe and should be enjoyed with *vongole* and lighter shellfish over its first two to three years.

CANTINA DEL TABURNO FALANGHINA DEL SANNIO

Falanghina is an indigenous Campanian variety first thought to have been planted by Greek colonists more than 2000 years ago. One of the best areas for this variety is the inland area of Sannio in the province of Benevento in northern Campania. Cantina del Taburno, which first bottled its own wines in 1972, is one of the finest cooperative producers in all of Italy; Falanghina is of one of their specialties. Featuring exotic jasmine and honey aromas, this has impressive depth of fruit and a lengthy finish with lively acidity, which is characteristic of this variety. The balance is impeccable as is the varietal purity; enjoy this delightful wine within two to three years of the harvest.

VILLA MATILDE FALERNO DAL MASSICO BIANCO

At Villa Matilde, located in Cellole in the province of Caserta, Salvatore Avallone has continued the work of his father who was an instrumental figure in keeping the vines of this small appellation flourishing. The principal white grape here is Falanghina; the name is derived from the word *falerna*, meaning "pole" or "stick," a reference to the first vines that were supported by such a measure. Avallone produces different versions of his Falerno dal Massico Bianco (there is also a Rosso); for those who want to experience this wine given barrique aging, there is the Caracci offering. I prefer the steel-aged version, one that is well-textured with a rich, persistent finish and complex aromas ranging from pear and melon to acacia flowers and almond. This drinks well for anywhere from three to seven years after the vintage date.

MUSTILLI FALANGHINA SAN'T AGATA DEI GOTI "VIGNA SEGRETA"
This traditional producer, located in the ancient town of Sant'Agata dei Goti in northern Campania, is headed by Leonardo Mustilli and his daughter Chiara. During the winery's first few years in the 1970s, Leonardo planted the local hills with traditional grapes such as Greco, Fiano, Aglianico, Piedirosso and Falanghina; this last variety is a local specialty. Sourced from a single vineyard and aged solely in steel tanks, this has lovely aromas of pear, melon, lemon and hawthorn and is quite rich on the palate with a long, persistent finish and vibrant acidity. How nice that we can enjoy this wine and recall the dedication of signore Mustilli some 40 years ago! Enjoy from three to seven years of age.

SAN PAOLO FALANGHINA SELEZIONE "ARIA" / "ACQUA" / "TERRA" / "FUOCO"
San Paolo, located in Torrioni near Tufo, is a member winery of the Magistravini group, headed by Claudio Quarta. A relatively new project here concerns various offerings of Falanghina produced by this estate. In fact there are four separate selections, all from different sites in Benevento, designed to display how the variety performs in various microclimates. The wines, made by Vincenzo Mercurio, one of Campania's most gifted enologists, do show varying styles with the Aria (air) and Acqua (water) bottlings being a bit lighter on the palate than the Terra (earth) and Fuoco (fire). The Aria, from rocky clay and calcaire soils is medium-bodied with banana and peach aromas and is best consumed within a year or so, while the Acqua from sandy soils offers

a bit more lush fruit and greater mineral finish while the Fuoco, originating from sandy soils with volcanic influence, is a more intense wine with kiwi aromas and distinct minerality; this will peak in five years. All in all, this is a fascinating study into the bloodlines of Falanghina.

I CACCIAGALLI FALANGHINA "AIORIVOLA"
Diana Iannaconne and Mario Basco are the caretakers of this small property near Roccamonfina, an extinct volcano near Campania's northern border with Lazio. The approach here is biodynamic or what the couple like to refer to as "non invasive" methods of farming. The Falanghina, named for the small zone some 900 feet above sea level where the vines are planted, is fermented and aged in oak barrels; the red apple and honey aromas are backed by excellent depth of fruit and a rich finish. Acidity is very good, though not as high as a typical example of this variety. One gets the feeling from tasting this wine that while quite special now, future vintages of this wine will become much more distinctive. Enjoy from two to five years of age.

LA SIBILLA FALANGHINA "CRUNA DEL LAGO"
As more producers throughout Campania work with Falanghina, we are starting to see some pretty special bottlings. One of the best is the "Cruna del Lago" offering from La Sibilla, a small estate in the Campi Flegrei zone just north of Napoli. Luigi di Meo is the visionary here; he also produces a regular Falanghina and an enticing Piedirosso. This wine is a *selezione* of the finest bunches; the soils here, situated so close to Mount Vesuvius are volcanic, giving this Falanghina a distinct minerality and vibrancy. Matured in steel tanks on its lees for nine months, this has exotic aromas of kiwi, mango and stone fruit; the mid-palate is quite rich and there is lively acidity and outstanding complexity. This is one of the most expressive and invigorating examples of Falanghina I've ever tasted. Depending on the vintage, the wine can be enjoyed from five to ten years of age.

TENUTA CAVALIER PEPE GRECO DI TUFO "NESTOR"
Greco di Tufo is one of Campania's signature whites, produced from the Greco grape – literally "Greek" for the colonists who planted it

several millenia ago – from a small area in the province of Avellino, also known by its ancient name of Irpinia. There is a town called Tufo, which is one of seven where this DOCG wine is produced; tufo is also the name of the soil – clay that can be easily broken up – that is prevalent in the vineyards. There are dozens of excellent examples, most of them fermented and aged in stainless steel. At Tenuta Cavalier Pepe near Luogosano in eastern Irpinia, Milena Pepe crafts an excellent representation of this wine with her "Nestor" Greco di Tufo. Offering aromas of lemon zest, acacia and a hint of kiwi, this is medium-full with excellent concentration, good acidity and hints of white spice in the finish. The varietal focus is exemplary; enjoy this wine from two to five years after the vintage, depending on that year's qualities.

TERREDORA GRECO DI TUFO "LOGGIA DELLA SERRA"

Walter and Lucio Mastroberardino left their famous family estate in 1978 to establish Terredora; Lucio passed away in January 2013. There are excellent Irpinian whites and reds; most notable are the Fiano di Avellino "Campo Re" and this selection of the best Greco grapes from the firm's vineyards in Montefusco. Aged on its lees in stainless steel, this is a textbook Greco di Tufo with marvelous aromas of quince, lemon peel, golden apples and that quintessential touch of almond that is a hallmark of this variety. This is a wine of freshness and vibrancy, one of outstanding varietal purity and complexity; it generally drinks well up to five to seven years after the harvest.

FEUDI DI SAN GREGORIO GRECO DI TUFO "CUTIZZI"

Feudi di San Gregorio is a winery that revolutionized the Campanian wine industry. Before the Capaldo and Ercolino families founded this company near the town of Sorbo Serpico in 1986, Irpinian white wines as a whole were pleasant and nicely balanced, yet rather straightforward and undemanding in nature. The owners pitted themselves against the local wine establishment, opting for riper, more expressive wines made from grapes that would be harvested seven to ten days later than normal. The results for both their whites and reds were immediately praised by wine critics in Italy and around the world; success in the marketplace soon followed.

Today, Antonio Capaldo, son of the original owners, manages this estate and has made it a reference point for Campania; indeed it is one one Italy's most renowned. One of their top wines is the Greco di Tufo "Cutizzi" from a single vineyard in the town of Santa Paolina. The wine offers lovely aromas of honeydew melon, spearmint and Bosc pear and has marvelous texture and richness on the palate that continues all the way through the lengthy finish. The acidity is excellent and it is important to note that this wine never sees any oak; the weight on the palate being a combination of excellent concentration from small yields as well as several months of lees aging. The result is a splendid white wine, quite enjoyable on its own, thanks to its impeccable balance, but also a perfect partner for a number of dishes, from shellfish to pasta with fresh ricotta and *bufala mozzarella* cheeses (a dish you might enjoy at the winery's Michelin-starred restaurant, Marennà). Enjoyable upon release, the wine displays exotic dried fruit qualities after two or three years in the bottle. The finest examples drink well for as long as a decade.

Cutizzi Vineyard, Santa Paolina, Greco di Tufo zone

VADIAPERTI GRECO DI TUFO "TORNANTE"

Antonio Troisi and his son Raffaele manage this excellent company that excels with both Greco di Tufo and Fiano di Avellino. Antonio, an ardent supporter of all things Campanian, took over the estate from his mother in the 1980s and produced his first bottle of Fiano di Avellino in 1984. The finest wine here on a regular basis is the Tornante bottling of Greco di Tufo, a wine that offers captivating aromas of lemon oil, peony and ginger. Medium-full, this is quite generous on the palate and is one of the more complex and varietally pure versions of Greco di Tufo I have tasted. This opens up two or three years after release and is generally at peak from seven to ten years of age, thanks to its overall balance and excellent structure.

VILLA RAIANO GRECO DI TUFO "CONTRADA MAROTTA"

Recently, this consistent Irpinian producer has decided to produce a few special versions of local whites, *selezioni* offerings of Greco di Tufo and Fiano di Avellino. Each of these wines is quite impressive and have won instant acclaim in Italian media circles. I have selected the "Contrada Marotta" Greco di Tufo, sourced from the eponymous site in Montefusco in the heart of this DOCG zone; the vines sit slightly more than 2000 feet above sea level and the soils are classic tufaceous chalk. Matured on its lees in steel tanks in order to heighten the varietal perfumes of lemon zest, melon and hibiscus, this is medium-full with outstanding persistence, lively acidity, distinct minerality and even a subtle note of saltiness in the finish. Quite elegant, this is a wine of class, breeding and beautiful complexity. This is quite good upon release, but it is much better with time in the bottle; peak enjoyment should be seven to ten years after the vintage.

PIETRACUPA GRECO DI TUFO

It's been quite a pleasure seeing the development of Irpinian whites such as Greco di Tufo and Fiano di Avellino emerge from their status as pleasant dry whites to their current notoriety as truly unique offerings with great personality and character. One of the individuals that has been at the center of this renaissance has been Peppino Loffredo,

who began producing his Pietracupa wines at his cellar in Montefredane in 1989. Today with his son Sabino, his wines have become
reference points in the area. Their Greco di Tufo is steel aged with several months of lees contact, yielding a wine with lovely texture. There
is great depth of fruit along with outstanding persistence and distinct minerality. This is a white wine of amazing complexity, one with
a soul and character all its own. It is ideal at five to seven years of age;
though the finest vintages drink well some ten years after release.

VILLA DIAMANTE FIANO DI AVELLINO "VIGNA DELLA CONGREGAZIONE"

Antoine Gaita, a native of Belgium, is the owner/winemaker at this
tiny estate in Montefredane, known best for this single vineyard Fiano
d'Avellino, named for his wife Diamante. The vineyard, which was
originally owned by the church, is situated some 1200 feet above sea
level and is certified organic and farmed to very small yields. Gaita
does not filter the wine and ages it solely in stainless steel. This is a
powerful, lush Fiano with aromas of stone fruit, mandarin orange and
grapefruit that literally fill the room. There is excellent acidity and the
finish seems to go on forever. This is one of Italy's finest white wines!
Best consumed within five to seven years of the harvest.

MASTROBERARDINO FIANO DI AVELLINO "RADICI"
FIANO DI AVELLINO "MORE MAIORUM"

When writing the history of Campanian wine, you have to start with
Mastroberardino, a family firm that produced its first wines in 1878.
For much of the 20th century until the late 1980s and early 1990s, the
only examples of Irpinian wines you could find outside the area were
from this winery; indeed most of today's producers owe a great deal
of thanks to this family as Antonio Mastroberardino and his father
did a great deal of work rescuing the ancient indigenous varieties
that were threatened with extinction after the Second World War.

Today, Antonio's son Piero manages the winery with one eye on tradition and the other on his firm's role as a leader in today's local wine

scene. These two versions of Fiano di Avellino are prime evidence of what Mastroberardino represents, as they are vastly different models of what can be done in the cellar with this variety. The Radici bottling – *radici* meaning "roots" – is a first-rate example of a modern style of Fiano di Avellino; sourced from a prime vineyard in Santo Stefano del Sole, the wine is steel aged and has lemon, pear and yellow tea aromas, lively acidity and impressive persistence. The More Maiorum – loosely translated as "the ways of the past" or "as the ancients did" – is made in a manner replicating Fiano of years ago. This wine, from a single vineyard, is fermented in both steel tanks as well as barriques, which yields complex aromas of fennel, anise seed and lemon peel; there is marvelous texture and richness on the mid-palate as well as a note of honey in the finish. Both examples age quite well; I have tasted 10-12 year old versions of the Radici Fiano that were in excellent shape.

Fiano Vineyard of Mastroberardino, Santo Stefano

DONNACHIARA FIANO DI AVELLINO

The Donnachiara winery and estate vineyards are stuated below the town of Montefalcione, one of the finest sites for Fiano di Avellino. Proprietor Ilaria Petito captures the tropical fruits (mango, kiwi) of this variety in the aromas along with notes of lemon and ripe apples. Medium-full with impressive weight on the palate, this is an exquisite wine that offers instant pleasures, but improves dramatically with one to five years in the bottle. The 2010 tasted in late 2012 displayed more depth of fruit in the finish along with greater complexities than upon its release, while the 2007, sampled at the same time, is really quite a stunner, showing how well this wine ages. Given that 2005 was the first year of production at Donnachiara, the progress in quality has been rapid and very impressive. Brava Ilaria!

PIETRACUPA FIANO DI AVELLINO "CUPO"

Cupo is from a single vineyard in Montefredane, in the heart of the Fiano di Avellino zone. This is a wine of intense perfumes of citrus fruit, honey and notes of yellow flowers and mint; the aromas evolve over several minutes in the glass. There is deep concentration and a rich mid-palate, offering layers of flavor that coat the mouth. The finish is quite long with outstanding persistence, vibrant acidity and a strong note of minerality. This is a great Fiano, one with superb varietal character and wonderful texture as well as a strong sense of place. Enjoy within five to seven years of the vintage, though some bottlings will drink well for a decade.

CIRO PICARIELLO FIANO DI AVELLINO

Ciro Picariello is a winemaker in love with Fiano. He produces both a DOC Irpinia Fiano as well as a DOCG Fiano di Avellino. This latter wine has received tremendous critical approval from local writers; more international acclaim would certainly come his way if there were more bottles available, as there are only 2000 cases of this wine (about half his total production) made each vintage. This is a blend of two low-yielding vineyards in Summonte and Montefredane; the grapes are harvested about two weeks later than is typical in this area. Picariello is a minimalist winemaker, adding only small amounts of sulfites and aging only in steel tanks; he does not filter or fine the wines. There are the typical aromas of ripe lemons, but also notes of mint, rosemary and even almond and hazelnut. Medium-full, this has a strong mineral note in the finish. Picariello's Fiano di Avellino ages extremely well, as 12 and 15-year old versions are in fine shape.

LUIGI MAFFINI FIANO "KRATOS" / "PIETRAINCATENATA"

While the examples of Fiano from Avellino are the most famous, there are also excellent offerings from other zones in Campania. Two of the finest examples are made by Luigi Maffini at his estate in Cenito in the province of Salerno south of Napoli. The two wines are complete opposites as the Kratos is aged in stainless steel, while the Pietraincatenata matures in barriques. The Kratos offers perfumes of kiwi and melon and has excellent varietal purity and a clean finish with excellent acidity, while the Pietraincatenata has aromas of honey and beeswax backed by a generous mid-palate and a bright finish with impressive persistence. While I generally prefer the Kratos for its straight ahead flavors, I am also won over by the richness and texture of the Pietraincatenata. Both wines age well, with the latter typically improving for 5-7 years.

DECONCILIIS FIANO "DONNALUNA"

Bruno de Conciliis is a man that loves life; always smiling, he salutes his origins by producing wines of great focus and elegance from vineyards in Cilento in the province of Salerno. The "Donnaluna" offering is 100% Fiano from vineyards ranging from eight to thirty years of age. Fermented and aged only in steel, the intense aromas of pear, acacia flowers and almond are dazzling, leading to a beautifully structured finish with very good acidity and length along with hints of white spice. Delicious upon release, this drinks well for three to five years after the vintage.

FEUDI DI SAN GREGORIO "CAMPANARO"

This is one of Feudi's groundbreaking wines, a Fiano/Greco blend from vineyards within Irpinia. Fermented and aged in stainless steel and matured for five months on its own lees, this offers the richness of Fiano with the minerality of Greco; the kiwi, green apple and chamomile aromas are very seductive. There is impressive persistence, very good acidity and a long, textured finish. This wine is released one year after the standard winery bottlings of Greco di Tufo and Fiano di Avellino and is at its best within five years of the harvest. This is a white wine that can be paired with a wide variety of dishes including poached scallops, sea bass, risotto with vegetables or roast chicken or veal.

VINOSIA "DOCEASSAJE"

Brothers Mario and Luciano Ercolino were part of the original team and owners at Feudi di San Gregorio back in the 1980s and '90s. They left to open their own winery in 2002, locating in San Potito Ultra in the Taurasi zone. While their reds have been the story, another noteworthy release has been this white blend of Greco and Fiano, similar to the Campanaro made by Mario Ercolino during his time at Feudi. The Greco is sourced from rock-strewn vineyards with clay and calcium deposits, while the Fiano is from local plantings in San Potito with volcanic soils. The grapes are harvested in late October, giving the wine exotic aromas of passion fruit and pineapple. The wine is round and soft with good, but not exceeedingly high acidity and is fairly restrained, despite it being made from late harvest grapes. This is delicious upon release and drinks well for an additional three to five years.

JOAQUIN "JQN 23"

At Joaquin, proprietor Raffaelle Pagano does things *his* way. His wines reflect his personality, which is to say they're not shy. This doesn't mean they are fruit bombs or they are out of balance; on the contrary, these are very harmonious wines. It's just that these are wines that grab you and show you the potential of the Campanian varieties. The JQN 23 is a 100% Fiano with grapes sourced from a number of vineyards, most of them between ten and twelve years old. The grapes are harvested during the second and third weeks of October with a portion of them cryo-macerated to deliver more intenste perfumes in the wine. Aged in barrique, this is a powerful, spicy version of Fiano with a rich, persistent finish. This is a wine that makes you sit up and notice. While enjoyable upon release, this improves greatly after three to five years.

TERRE DELLE PRINCIPE PALAGRELLO BIANCO "FONTANAVIGNA"

Terre delle Principe specializes in the indigenous varieties of the Caserta province where they are located; these cultivars include Casavecchia as well as Palagrello Rosso and Bianco. Mistakenly iden-titified for some time as Coda di Volpe, Palagrello Bianco was planted by the Greeks thousands of years ago and delivers a wine with lively acidity and marvelous aromatics, with perfumes of lemon zest, grapefruit and yellow flowers. The Fontanavigna version is steel-aged only and offers lovely texture and precise acidity. It's a delicious aromatic white meant for consumption within two to three years, though a few examples age for as long as five years. Enjoy this on its own or with lighter shellfish.

GIUSEPPE APICELLA TRAMONTI BIANCO "COLLE SANTA MARINA"

Giuseppe Apicella produces small lots of remarkably flavored white, red and rosé wines from his vineyards in the town of Tramonti in the Costa d'Amalfi DOC, located just a few hundred meters from the sea. Here varieties such as Biancolella, Ginestra and Pipella are the most common white varieties, while grapes from Irpinia, such as Greco and Fiano are not planted. When I asked Apicella why local farmers used these varieties, he said that these are the ones that worked best in this area; the high winds from the sea dictating hearty vines. This particular blend, made with Falanghina (known locally as Bianca Zita) and the three local varieties mentioned above, has vibrant acidity, a distinct minerality and a delicate saltiness. The aromas offer pineapple and grapefruit flavors along with a note of white pepper. Enjoy this up to three years of age with shellfish.

MARISA CUOMO COSTA D'AMALFI FURORE BIANCO "FIORDUVA"

Marisa Cuomo and her winemaker/husband Andrea Ferraioli, produce a number of vibrant offerings at their estate in Furore, one of the most spectacular towns in all of Italy. Situated on the Amalfi Coast between Amalfi and Positano, this is for all intents and purposes a vertical town, as the main road winds back and forth among vines from sea level to almost 2000 feet in elevation. (A point of trivia; the 1948 film *Amore*, directed by Roberto Rossellini and starring Anna Magnani was filmed in Furore.) The vines here are terraced and cling to the sides of hills, making them exposed to the stiff breezes coming off the sea, making the pergola system – overhead canopy – necessary to protect the bunches.

The estate white known as Fiorduva, named for the local fiord in this town, is a mesmerizing white wine that is among Italy's most renowned. A blend of local varieties Fenile, Ginestra and Ripoli, the wine is fermented and aged in small oak; the aromas of lemon, banana, acacia, figs and chamomile leap from the glass, while the rich mid-palate, outstanding persistence, vibrant acidity and powerful minerality combine to create a highly individualistic white that is unforgettable! While many Amalfi Coast whites are delicately styled and are ideal with shellfish, the power of this wine is best suited to lobster, sea bass or even certain veal preparations. This ages well, as long as seven to ten years from the best vintages. I have tasted this wine on several occasions, always with Andrea; the smile on his face tells you all you need to know about the pride he feels about battling the local elements to realize such a special offering such as this. **BRV**: 2010, 2009, 2008, 2006, 2005.

Pergola Vines at Marisa Cuomo estate, Furore, Costa d'Amalfi

I BORBONI ASPIRINIO DI AVERSA "VITE MARITATA"

The Aspirinio grape is an indigenous white variety found primarily in the northern Campanian province of Caserta (there are also some plantings in the province of Napoli). Grown for centuries in this area, the vines are planted on poplars that reach as high as 15 meters (50 feet) above ground! As you might imagine, pickers have to climb up ladders to harvest most of the bunches; in a region where heritage and tradition are so important, here is one of the most amazing sights!

Aspirinio has very high acidity,which makes it ideal for production as a sparkling wine as well as a dessert wine (*passito)*; it is also produced as a dry white. I Borboni produces all three wine types; I have selected this offering, a dry white. The grapes are harvested at the end of September or as late as the first few days of October and then fermented and aged in steel for six months before bottling. Offering aromas of fresh lemon and apple with notes of thyme and rosemary, the wine is medium-bodied with a lightly herbal finish and vibrant acidity. Enjoy this within two to three years of the harvest.

GIUSEPPE APICELLA TRAMONTI ROSATO

While I've tasted some nice versions of rosé from all over Italy, it's generally the ones from the south that interest me the most. Pugila is famous for rosé made from Negroamaro and I've also had some beautiful versions produced from the Aglianico variety in Campania. But this version from Giuseppe Apicella from the Amalfi Coast is one of the few I've ever given a 5-star (outstanding) rating to - it's been my favorite from Italy for several years. This is a blend of Sciascinoso and Piedirosso made to excite your senses with its deep strawberry/copper color and strawberry and maple aromas. Medium-full, this has outstanding richness on the palate, it's very dry and has excellent acidity with a lightly earthy finish. I tried this once with Giuseppe for lunch at his estate; it was paired with fresh local beans and it was an amazing experience! There's no need to wait on this wine- enjoy it right upon release and within the first one to two years after the harvest.

MONTE DE GRAZIA ROSATO

Monte de Grazia is a lovely estate in the hills of Tramonti, high above the Amalfi Coast. Owner Alfonso Arpino, a doctor, was passionate enough about producing limited offerings of local wine, that he purchased two old vine plantings in Tramonti in the 1990s. *Nce stanno vigne ca teneno cchiú 'e 100 anne e 'e vite veneno riprodotte pe propaggene* – (Nnapulitano, i.e., Neapolitan dialect meaning "some of the vines are over 100 years old and cared for in an ancient way.")

The vines are farmed organically with very low yields; these are impeccably made products with superb varietal character. His *rosato* is made entirely from the local Tintore grape (the grape probably got its name from the "tint" or dark color it owns); because of strange DOC laws, this must be labeled as an IGT Campania wine. This has a lovely deep cherry/light strawberry appearance with aromas of tart cherry, strawberry and herbal tea. Medium-full, this has notable depth of fruit, excellent persistence, very good acidity and even a touch of minerality in the finish. The 2010 tasted in mid-2012 was excellent, displaying very good freshness, so this is a *rosato* that can drink well for two to three years.

VILLA DORA LACRYMA CHRISTI DEL VESUVIO ROSSO "GELSONERO"

Lacryma Christi Rosso is made primarily from a local variety named Piedirosso, which literally means "red feet," a reference to the feet of the birds that tend to feed on these grapes. The grape yields wines that are medium-bodied with juicy black cranberry and raspberry fruit and very tart acidity with very light tannins. It can be blended in Taurasi in Irpinia (no more than 15% of that blend), but as many producers of that wine now go exclusively with Aglianico, your best chance of tasting a wine with Piedirosso is this charming red wine from vineyards not far from Vesuvius.

Villa Dora, located just east of Vesuvius, produces two excellent versions of Lacryma Rosso, this wine and a more full-throttle version called "Forgiato." I have selected this wine, as it is the more typical example of this wine type. A blend of 80% Piedirosso and 20% Aglianico, this is medium-bodied with minimal wood, fresh cherry-berry fruit and expressive acidity with a light herbal finish. This is best consumed over the first two to three years of its existence, although the wines from the best years surprise and drink well on their fifth or sixth birthday.

GROTTA DEL SOLE PIEDIROSSO RISERVA "MONTEGUARO"

Piedirosso is a Campanian variety that offers fresh berry fruit, tart acidity and moderate tannins. It is sometimes used in small percentages in

Taurasi to soften the impact of the Aglianico grape; it is also famously used in Lacryma Christi del Vesuvio Rosso as a lighter red to accompany simple foods.

The Martusciello family at Grotta del Sole produce this version of Piedirosso that shows the true potential of this variety. The grapes are grown on vineyards along the shores of Lake Averno in the Campi Flegrei zone just north of Napoli; the vines are ungrafted (planted on their own roots) and the soils are volcanic with traces of pomace. The zesty aromas are textbook Piedirosso, with notes of black raspberry, bitter chocolate and myrtle; matured for one year in French barriques, this is medium-full with very good acidity, slight wood notes and lively fruit flavors on the palate. This is a sensual, delicious, beautifully structured red that displays admirable harmony and is a pleasure to drink; enjoy this from five to ten years of age.

I CACCIAGALLI PIEDIROSSO "BASCO"
This Piedirosso from the province of Caserta near the border with Lazio, is from vineyards situated at 650 foot elevation that are farmed to organic and biodynamic methods. There are textbook red cherry, plum and thyme aromas; the volcanic soils of this area imbue the wine with a slight rugged quality, though the tannins are quite reserved. Offering notable complexity and balance, this is a well made, charming wine with good acidity and freshness. Enjoy this from three to five years of age.

MASTROBERARDINO TAURASI "RADICI"
Taurasi is Campania's most renowned red wine, one that can age for decades. Produced in a small zone in Irpinia including the town that gives the wine its name, Taurasi must be made from a mimimum of 85% of the Aglianico variety, while up to 15% can be Piedirosso. While some producers do use both varieties, it it quite common today at most estates to make a Taurasi exclusively from Aglianico. The variety has appealing dark cherry and bitter chocolate flavors, healthy acid-

ity and firm tannins; the wines from the most concentrated years can routinely be cellared for 25 years or even longer.

Once again, the firm of Mastroberardino is the beginning chapter of the story of Taurasi. This family firm was the one that put this wine on the map, especially with some of the great offerings from the 1940s and '50s; their 1968 bottling is considered a legendary wine. I tasted this wine in 2006 at VinItaly and noted that it probably had another 10-12 years of life ahead of it; not bad for a 38 year-old wine at the time! Back then, aging was solely in *grandi botti*, so the wines had the potential to drink for 40-50 or more years. Today, the wines are just as rich as ever, but now the maturation process includes both small and large oak, adding a touch of modernity to the wine. Aside from this difference, the current versions of Mastroberardino Taurasi are still first-class wines, offering excellent weight on the palate along with firm tannins and impressive persistence. In certain years, you can find a note of black pepper to go along with the chocolate/cherry flavors; this wine starts to show its complexities five to seven years after the harvest and peaks in 15-25 years. **BRV**: 2008, 2007, 2006, 2004, 2001, 1999 (outstanding).

VILLA RAIANO TAURASI

Villa Raiano has always been an Irpinian winery on the cusp of greatness; certainly their recent work with single vineyard Greco di Tufo and Fiano di Avellino has brought them added attention among local media. But their Taurasi is the wine that garners great international acclaim, as this is a striking, classically-styled offering. 100% Aglianico aged in large French oak casks, the grapes are from Venticano in the heart of the DOC zone. Offering sumptuous aromas of black cherry, strawberry, sweet tobacco and a hint of licorice, this is instantly recognizable as not only Aglianico, but also as a Taurasi. Medium-full with perfect ripeness, a generous mid-palate and a lengthy finish with impressive persistence, this has very good acidity and youthful, well balanced tannins. The harmony of all the components is impeccable as is the sense of local terroir. This is a beautifully realized wine upon release (four years after the vintage), but it is clearly meant for consumption at 12-15 years of age. **BRV**: 2008 (outstanding), 2007, 2006, 2005, 2003, 2001.

CANTINE LONARDO - CONTRADE DE TAURASI TAURASI

Sandro Lonardo is dedicated to producing a traditional Taurasi at his small estate in the heart of the DOCG zone. He has a mixture of older vines in the pergola system along with the more modern Guyot training system. Sadly, he was forced to rip out some of the older plantings because of a decree; thankfully, that decree was later rescinded, though it came too late to save some of his vines. Lonardo firmly believes these 60 and 70 year-old vines add great character to his Taurasi. He only takes his best lots of Aglianico grapes for his Taurasi, opting to use the remainder in a declassified wine he labels as Aglianico IGT (he also produces a small amount of Riserva Taurasi from the finest vintages). Aged for 18-24 months in large casks, this is an elegantly styled wine with ripe cherry and plum fruit and finely tuned acidity, which helps preserve freshness. Displaying a fine sense of terroir, this wine is at its best some seven to twelve years after the harvest. **BRV**: 2008, 2007, 2006, 2005, 2004 (outstanding).

ANTONIO CAGGIANO TAURASI " MACCHIA DEI GOTI"

Antonio "Nino" Caggiano is a delightful individual, a former fashion photographer who turned to wine in 1990 with the founding of his quaint cellar in the heart of the town of Taurasi. His finest wine is this offering from his estate vineyard, only a hundred or so meters from his winery. Caggiano has become a serious student of the Taurasi area and understands that the various sub-zones yield very different wines; for him, the Taurasi commune delivers the most typical versions of this wine. Beautifully balanced, the wine offers complex aromas of black cherry, red plum, myrtle, mint and vanilla. Medium-full, the wine has a long finish with delicate spice and refined tannins. The wine peaks at 12-15 years after the harvest and can sometimes be enoyed on its 20th birthday. **BRV**: 2008, 2007, 2006, 2005, 2004 (outstanding), 2001.

Antonio Caggiano

IL CANCELLIERE TAURASI "NERO NE'"

Romano Soccorso, his wife and his son Enrico produce a few thousand bottles of Taurasi from their meticulously farmed vineyard in Montemarano, in the far southern reaches of the DOCG zone. First produced from the 2005 vintage, this is 100% Aglianico, aged for two years in large oak casks and then one in barriques; there is a regular version as well as a *riserva*. These are powerful, deeply concentrated wines that are dominated by ripe fruit – black cherry, black raspberry and bramble – as well as notes of anise and thyme along with strong bitter chocolate notes in the finish. The regular Taurasi should be consumed by its 10th or 12th birthday, while the *riserva* should peak another three to five years after that. **BRV:** 2008, 2007, 2006, 2005.

FEUDI DI SAN GREGORIO TAURASI RISERVA
"PIANO DI MONTEVERGINE"
"SERPICO"

Producers in Avellino craft all sorts of wines from the Aglianico grape. While Taurasi is the most famous, there are other versions that are aged for a shorter period of time (three years of aging in the cellar is the minimum requirement for Taurasi). Here are two excellent 100% Aglianico wines from this famous Irpinian producer. The Taurasi is from a single vineyard in the commune of Taurasi with vines averaging 15-20 years of age. Aged for three plus years in French barriques, this is a rich, forward wine with bitter black cherry, plum and raspberry aromas and a rich mid-palate. The Serpico is aged for only two plus years before release, and while not as intense as the Taurasi, it is just as ripe and with less oak, the fruit is more forward upon release. Both wines, however have the structure and backbone for several years of aging. As the Piano di Montevergine has been refined longer at the cellar, the tannins are silkier and more refined, while the Serpico upon release is slightly more bitter. Both wines are at their best from 12-20 years of age. **BRV**: Piano di Montevergine – 2007, 2004, 2002 (one of the most successful of the vintage), 2001, 2000. Serpico – 2008, 2007, 2006, 2004, 2001, 1999 (exceptional).

While these wines have been aged in barriques, proprietor Antonio Capaldo recently told me that he believes Aglianico is better suited to large oak casks, so the aging regimen will change and so undoubtedly will the style of the wines, back to a more traditional approach. Given the success of these two wines at Feudi, this may be somewhat of a risky move, but it is one that Capaldo thinks is correct and I applaud him for this philosophy.

TERREDORA TAURASI "FATICA CONTADINA"

Terredora produces three separate versions of Taurasi; my favorite being the "Fatica Contadina," from the company's own vineyards in Lapio and Montemiletto. Matured first in barriques and then in large casks, this is a less powerful, more restrained style of Taurasi as compared to the producer's other bottlings. Medium-full with classic black cherry, tar, black chocolate and cedar aromas, this has a rich mid-palate and very good acidity with round tannins and impressive length in the finish. This is not a showy wine, but rather a well made Taurasi of very good typicity; it's best qualities are its balance and drinkability. As with the best examples of this famous Campanian red, the wine is better with time; enjoy this from seven to twelve years of age. **BRV**: 2006, 2005, 2004.

VINOSIA "MARZIACANALE"

Mario Ercolino loves Aglianico and produces at least three different versions per year at Vinosia in Luogosano, only a few miles from the town of Taurasi. The "Marziacanale" is 100% Aglianico of deep color and extract, rich tannins and powerful persistence; new oak is present, but it is nicely integrated. The bitter chocolate and cherry aromas of the Aglianico grape are brought to the front here; this may remind you of the best chocolate cake you ever tasted in your youth! As forward and ripe as this wine is, this is not meant for immediate pleasure; rather this is best enjoyed from seven to ten years of age. **BRV**: 2007, 2006, 2005, 2004.

DONNACHIARA AGLIANICO IRPINIA

Many producers of Taurasi also make a bottling of Aglianico that is aged for a shorter period of time; this wine is meant for drinking early on, while one lays the Taurasi away for a few years down the road. I love the purity of the Aglianico produced by Donnachiara; there is a Campania version (IGT) as well as an Aglianico Irpinia (DOC). It is this latter that I opt for, as it is richer and more complex than the former. Offering typical black cherry and dark chocolate aromas, this is medium-bodied with a touch of oak (four to six months of maturation in barriques), good acidity and a lightly bitter finish. This is all about crafting an Aglianico with ideal varietal character, yet still making it approachable upon release. Enjoy this from two to seven years of age.

FONTANAVECCHIA AGLIANICO DEL TABURNO RISERVA "VIGNA CATARATTE"

The other great Aglianico-based wine in Campania is Aglianico del Taburno from the northern inland province of Benevento. Fontanavecchia, located near the town of Torrecuso, is one of the essential wineries of this area, operated by Libero Rillo and his father Orazio. Among their products are Falanghina, an excellent *rosato* made from Aglianico and several splendid reds, also from this variety. My favorite is the *riserva* offering Vigna Cataratte, a 100% Aglianico. This has textbook Aglianico aromas and flavors - black cherry and chocolate along with notes of menthol and tar. Medium-full, this is beautifully balanced with young, firm tannins and nicely integrated oak. Libero Rillo told me that the examples of Aglianico from Taburno – because of a specific clone that is used here – tend to have deeper color, higher alcohol and lower acidity than the wines from Taurasi; thus Aglianico dal Taburno is generally more approachable upon release, although they do not tend to age quite as long as examples of Taurasi. The Vigna Cataratte is at its best seven to ten years after the vintage. Fontanavecchia also produces two more explosive reds; Grave Mora, which is a selction of the best estate Aglianico and Orazio, a 60/40 blend of Aglianico and Cabernet Sauvignon. These wines are more powerful and are also highly recommended. **BRV** (Vigna Cataratte): 2008, 2007, 2006, 2004, 2001.

CASEBIANCHE "CUPERSITO"

Casebianche is the vision of husband and wife Pasquale Mitrano and Elisabetta Iuorio, who experimented with several wines at their estate in Torchiara not far from the sea in the Cilento zone of the Salerno province south of Napoli. Their first wines, made by enologist Fortunato Sebastiano were from the 2006 vintage. Pasquale and Elisabetta farm organically with minimal intervention; this natural approach is evident in their 100% Aglianico called "Cupersito," sourced from vineyards planted in 1999 and 2006 (note: the 2008 vintage was the first 100% Aglianico - previous offerings were a blend of Aglianico, Piedirosso and Primitivo). Aged in a combination of new and used *tonneaux*, this is a supple, refined style of Aglianico, much less powerful than Taurasi or as forceful as Aglianico del Taburno. Medium-bodied, with aromas of morel cherry, bitter chocolate and mulberry, this is about complexity, harmony and varietal purity; this is a very distinctive Aglianico! Congratulations to the team at Casebianche for their purist approach that results in such a lovely wine. This is best consumed from five to seven years of age.

MONTE DI GRAZIA COSTA D'AMALFI ROSSO

Alfonso Arpino, a physician in the small town of Tramonti in the Amalfi Coast wine zone, began work in the vineyards during the 1990s. His production remains small, so he can focus on handcrafting elegant wines with impressive nervous acidity that typifies the wines of this area. He produces a white and a rosato, but his most complex is this red, a blend of indigenous varieties Tintore along with Piedirosso, known locally as Per' e Palumno. The vineyards he works with have a few vines that are over a century old; these huge trunks rise only a few feet above the ground in some cases with shoots spreading in several different directions. The red is medium-bodied and has an aroma that makes you believe you have just stepped into a forest with notes of bramble, myrtle and clove with a hint of bitter chocolate. The acidity is high and the tannins are moderate, resulting in a rustic red that is best consumed three to five years after the harvest. This is not a powerful wine, but a charming, surprisingly complex wine that is totally distinct.

GIUSEPPE APICELLA COSTA D'AMALFI RISERVA "A' SCIPATTA"

One of the delights of tasting the wines from the Amalfi Coast is discovering the largely unknown gems made from indigenous varieties. At his estate in Tramonti, Giuseppe Apiecella produces a unique red known as A' Scipatta; in local dialect this means "stolen," which refers to this particular vineyard from which the grapes are sourced. This is a steep hillside that had to be uprooted for planting of vines; thus the soils were stolen, so to speak, for viticulture, when it was planted in 1933. The wine is a blend of Tintore and Piedirosso; this has a bright purple color with aromas of ripe black fruit – raspberry, plum and cherry – with notes of pepper and chocolate. Medium full, there is a beautifully structured mid-palate and a lengthy finish with excellent persistence. This is quite stylish and displays outstanding harmony of all components; the tannins are particularly silky and smooth. This generally is at its best some 10-12 years after the harvest; for my money, this is one of the most underrated red wines of Campania. **BRV**: 2007, 2006, 2004, 2001, 1999, 1995 (exceptional).

GROTTA DEL SOLE GRAGNANO

Here is one of the most charming examples of Campanian wine. Gragnano is a slightly sparkling (*frizzante*) red wine; named for the town of Gragnano in the Sorrento Peninsula south of Napoli, this is made with local red varieties. The Grotta del Sole version is produced from Piedirosso, Aglianico and Sciascinoso and has a deep purple color with a light mousse and only a small amount of bubbles. The bright aromas are of black raspberry, cranberry and myrtle, which leads to a dry finish with a hint of bitterness and notes of cacao and black mint. While this could be paired with *salumi* and lighter pastas with tomato sauces, the overwhelming pairing in Sorrento, Napoli and all along this seaside area is with the classic Neapolitan pizza; you'll find Gragnano served at virtually every pizzeria in the area. This is, above all, a fun wine that calls to mind the simple pleasures of Napoli and the surrounding seaside.

CANTINE FEDERICIANE LETTERE

Lettere is something of a companion wine to Gragnano, a red frizzante wine also from the Sorrento Peninsula; the wine is named for the eponymous town located a bit east of the seaside town of Castellammare di Stabia. Cantina Federiciane produces both a Gragnano and a Lettere and while the wines have obvious similarities – they are made from the same varieties - the Lettere is a touch drier in the finish with a bit more depth of fruit. As with Gragnano, enjoy the wine in its youth and pair it with Neapolitan pizza; you'll feel just like one of the natives!

Pairing Campanian Wines and Food –
A Chef's Perspective

My land: land of farmers, land of aromas, a land of wines. I, a cook of memories; memories of my grandmother's kitchen made of flavors and odors, made especially for lunches and dinners that woud always accompany our wines of Irpinia.

Today if I think of a Falanghina, what comes immediately to mind is a tart of turnips and potatoes with smoked sausage. For a Fiano di Avellino, onion soup with *caciocchiato* (a local cheese from cow's milk), crusty bread and a *pecorino bagnolese*.

For Greco di Tufo, cream of chestnuts with *tabacchini* beans and toast with lard. Or perhaps *fusilli Avellinesi "Allardiati"* with San Marzano tomatoes, basil and salted ricotta. To accompany a Taurasi, a filet of *ferrochina* with red Hawaiian salt and red beets.

A good dinner cannot finish without a *dolce*, so with a Fiano *passito*, a delicious pie made from *annurche* apples with Neapolitan pastry cream.

My territory – in order to say you know it, you have to discover it through drinking and eating its products.

Antonella Iandolo
Chef, Avellino

Puglia
Principal Varieties

White:
Fiano Minutolo, Bombino Bianco, Greco, Chardonnay,
Verdeca, Falanghina, Malvasia, Sauvignon

Red:
Negroamaro, Primitivo, Nero di Troia (Uva di Troia),
Susumaniello, Aglianico, Montepulciano, Syrah,
Cabernet Sauvignon, Cabernet Franc, Merlot

———

ALBERTO LONGO "LE FOSSETTE"

Puglia is not known for white wines, so thank goodness there are a few individuals who take white varieties seriously in this region. Alberto Longo produces a lovely version of steel-aged Falanghina that is truly a product imbued with his passion. The wine certainly retains the lively acidity this variety is known for, yet it does not taste like the examples from Campania, the variety's most famous home. The Longo wine has exotic aromas of guava, mandarin orange and lime – the perfumes alone of this wine makes it special – while there is impressive concentration and a round, lightly spicy finish. Enjoy this in its youth- over its first two to three years. Longo also recently started producing a classical method sparkling Falanghina; this wine is also called Le Fossette.

Alberto Longo

MASSERIA LI VELI VERDECA

Here is a wonderful story about one family's love for rare, indige-nous varieties. The Falvo family, at the time in 1999 the owners of the Avignonesi estate in Montepulciano in Tuscany, purchased a 128-acre propery in southern Puglia on the Salento peninsula. They concentrated on the typical wines of the area, including Salice Sal-entino and various offerings made from Negroamaro and Primitivo; all the wines to date have been very appealing, ripe offerings that have been fairly priced. About a decade into their work, the family decided to craft limited amounts of wine from ancient varieties of the area that have been largely forgotten. They called their project Askos, which is the name of a wine jar used by the Greeks in their production some two millenia ago. For a white variety, they selected Verdeca, from local vineyards planted in the late 1970s (there is also

10% Fiano Minutolo in the blend). There is no oak aging and everything possible is undertaken in the cellar to preserve the variety's aromatics. They have done a dazzling job, as the wine features perfumes of tangerine, Bosc pear and yellow flowers. This has a lovely texture, great richness and lively acidity; it is unique and quite well balanced and and excellent example of this uncommon variety; it is capable of five years of aging.

RIVERA BOMBINO BIANCO "MARESE"

While other Italian regions have dozens of wineries that have wide-ranging appeal in the marketplace, the same is not true for Puglia. Rivera is one of the few, best known for its stylish Castel del Monte reds; this indigenous white is not something most people know about, but it's equally good. It's very light in appearance with pleasant, straightforward melon and pear aromas, but there is impressive concentration with lovely texture, lively acidity and notable persistence. Enjoy this in its youth - within its first two years.

FARNESE GRECO "BIANCO SPINOMARINO"

This tanatalizing white is from a producer famous for their marvelous versions of Primitivo. This Greco is sourced from 20 year-old vines some 1100 feet above sea level. The aromas are just lovely with notes of lemon merinque, spearmint and magnolia blossoms - this is aged solely in steel tanks to preserve the perfumes. Medium-full, this has good acidity and balance as well as notable varietal purity. It's just a pleasure to enjoy up to three or four years of age, though it's quite delicious upon release.

POLVANERA FIANO MINUTOLO

There is a lot of mystery about the origins of Fiano Minutolo, a rare white variety of Puglia. Some say it was brought into the region from Campania, others not. There is talk of changing the name to simply Minutolo, but one of the best producers of this wine, Filippo Cassano at Polvanera in the Gioia del Colle area, still labels the wine as Fiano Minutolo. This has lovely aromatics of chamomile, pineapple and mandarin orange, good concentration, lively acidity and excellent persistence in the finish. This is such an appealing wine to be enjoyed in its youthful freshness, from one to three years of age.

LEONE DE CASTRIS "FIVE ROSES"

While *rosato* is not an important part of most wine Italian wine regions, the Pugliese take them a bit more seriously. In particular, rosés produced from the Negroamaro grape are quite famous in this region. The Five Roses bottling – made from 90% Negroamaro and 10% Malvasia Nera – was the first rosé made and bottled in Italy, way back in 1943 (the name of the wine refers to the five children several generations of the DeCastris family had over the course of many years). In 1993, on the 50th anniversary of the inaugural release of this wine, the winery created a special Five Roses Anniversario bottling, one with a slightly different blend of 80% Negroamaro and 20% Malvasia Nera; this wine been produced every year since. Both wines are excellent, with fragrant cherry and geranium aromas and a flavorful, dry finish with very good acidity. The Anniversario version, is a bit fuller on the palate, as you would imagine, but both are quite delicious and are meant for consumption within two years.

SCHOLA SARMENTI ROSATO "MASSEREI"

At this estate in the Nardò, in far southwestern Puglia only a few miles from the Ionian sea, owner Lorenzo Marra looks to the past for inspiration for his wines. He produces a range of wines from local varieties, most of them from *albarello* ("little tree") vines, with some of them as much as 80 years old. This *rosato* is 100% Negroamaro; the aromas are lovely, encompassing notes of maraschino cherry and pear. Offering good concentration and a dry, clean finish, this is a well-made *rosato* that drinks well for two years after the vintage. This is straightforward, nicely balanced and very refreshing.

CEFALICCHIO ROSATO

One of Puglia's greatest wine farms is Cefalicchio, located in Canosa di Puglia, about midway between the towns of Bari and Foggia in the southern province of Barletta-Andrea-Trani. Proprietor Fabrizio Rossi employs biodynamic agriculture and is the only winery in Puglia to be Demeter certified. Their *rosato* is in the great tradition of Apulian rosés; produced entirely from Montepulciano (also known locally as Morellone) planted in limestone/clay soils at elevations ranging from 800 to 1000 feet. Displaying a bright cherry/strawberry color and aromas of maraschino cherry, currant and white flowers, this is medium-full with beautiful ripeness, excellent persistence, lively acidity and a big, gutsy, flavorful finish with plenty of character. The 2010 tasted in mid-2012 was very fresh and quite delicious; this is an outstanding rosé that can age for up to three years, perhaps even a bit longer. One other note on this wine: there are no added sulfites. **BRV**: 2010, 2009.

FATALONE PRIMITIVO "TERES" (ROSATO)
At Fatalone, proprietor Pasquale Petrera calls this his "light" Primitivo. Perhaps he doesn't care for the term *rosato*, but that's what it is; it just happens to be one of the most distinctive examples of this wine in all of Puglia. Displaying a deep garnet/bing cherry color with aromas of red plum, cherry and nutmeg, this has an appealing ripeness along with impressive persistence. His current release in 2012 was the 2009 (yes, the 2009!) and it shows remarkable freshness and character; this will drink well for another year or two. This is a lovely wine - bravo, Pasquale! **BRV**: 2009.

ALBERTO LONGO CACC'E MMITTE DI LUCERA
Alberto Longo is one of only three producers to make a red wine called Cacc'e Mmitte di Lucera, a DOC that represents among the smallest production totals in all of Italy. This wine is made from grapes in the Lucera area in northern Puglia, not far from the famous Castel del Monte. Longo's work with this wine probably helped save this DOC from extinction and while still a tiny appellation, it is at least alive. His version is a blend of the local Nero d'Troia (a mainstay of Castel del Monte reds), Montepulciano d'Abruzzo and the white variety, Bombino Bianco. Vinified in steel tanks, the aging takes place in cement vats for 6-8 months; as these are inert

containers, they preserve the aromatics and varietal character of the wine. This is a medium-bodied red with inviting aromas of black raspberry, red plum and marmalade; offering moderate tannins and very good acidity with distinct red spice in the finish, this is a wine that combines the tangy, ripe fruit of a Dolcetto with the spice and earthiness of a French Cotes-du-Rhone. Enjoy this in its youth – generally within three to five years of the harvest. **BRV:** 2010, 2009, 2008, 2007.

RIVERA CASTEL DEL MONTE "PUER APULIAE"

At Rivera, Carlo di Corato produces several reds from the Castel del Monte zone; this DOC is named for the famous 13th century octagonal-shaped structure atop a hill in northern Puglia. While his most famous wine is the "Il Falcone" bottling, a blend of Nero di Troia and Montepulciano, my favorite is the "Puer Apuliae" ("son of Apulia"), a 100% Nero di Troia from an old clone that produces small berries. Matured in new French barriques for fourteen months, there are black plum, blackberry, vanilla and a hint of dark chocolate in the aromas; medium-full with notable persistence, the acidity is quite good while the youthful tannins are nicely balanced. Give this time to shed some bite; it is generally at its best from seven to ten years of age. **BRV:** 2007, 2006, 2004.

TORRE VENTO CASTEL DEL MONTE RISERVA "VIGNA PEDALE"

Torre Vento – "the tower of the wind" – was established in 1948 when brothers Francesco and Domenico Liantonio purchased this property in the Murgia sub-zone north of Bari. Their Castel del Monte Riserva "Vigna Pedale" is a 100% Nero di Troia that gets your attention right away with its seductive aromas of black raspberry, crème di cassis, black plum and violets; medium-full, with lively acidity, nicely integrated oak and notes of tar and black spice in the finish, this is a delicious red with great appeal upon release, although its offers greater complexity five to seven years down the road. **BRV:** 2009, 2008, 2007, 2006, 2005.

CEFALICCHIO NERO DI TROIA "ROMANICO"

The biodynamic viticulture employed by Fabrizio Rossi at Cefalicchio results in some lovely, refined reds, especially the wines made from the Nero di Troia variety. The "Romanico" bottling is a DOC Rosso Canosa Riserva, matured in *grandi botti*; offering aromas of dried cherry, red plum, cedar and just a hint of tar, this is a low-key, traditional red with middle weight tannins and a distinct herbal edge in the finish. It's nice to see this style still being made in Puglia, a region that is too often turning away from its wine traditions. Enjoy from five to ten years of age. **BRV**: 2007, 2006.

ALBEA NERO DI TROIA "LUI"

Nero di Troia – sometimes known as Uva di Troia - is found primarily in northern Puglia, as it is the principal variety of Castel del Monte DOC reds. The Albea winery, named for the town of Alborello in the province of Bari where it is located, produces this ripe, lush, modern style of Nero di Troia that features a bright purple color with aromas of black plum, anise and vanilla. Medium-full with excellent depth of fruit and persistence, this is a muscular, barrique-aged wine that is a bit showy, but one that is nicely balanced and has five to ten years of staying power. **BRV**: 2009, 2008, 2007, 2006.

LI VELI SUSUMANIELLO

Along with their white Verdeca, Li Veli also produces a Susumaniello as part of their Askos project, aimed at a renaissance of largely unknown indigenous Puglian varieties. Sourced from a vineyard in the province of Brindisi planted in the *albarello* system just over a decade ago, this barrique-aged wine has a strong note of bacon in the aromas along with black cherry, cumin and oh, did I mention bacon? To that degree, the bacon notes may make you think of Pinot Noir and you're actually not far off, given the delicate tannins, although the acidity here is not as high as with Pinot Noir. Medium-bodied, this has a nice burst of fruit on the palate and in the finish and it's a stylish wine that benefits from being open for a good thirty minutes to allow a bit more complexity to emerge. Enjoy this from three to seven years, depending on the strength of the vintage. **BRV**: 2010, 2009.

TORMARESCA "BOCCA DI LUPO"
Established in 1998, Tormaresca is the Apulian estate of Piero Antinori of Tuscany. What I like about this company is their wide range of products in various price ranges and the attention that goes into each wine. For example, there is a basic red called Neprica, named for the initials of the three varieties that comprise the blend: Negroamaro, Primitivo and Cabernet Sauvignon. This is an instantly appealing wine, especially at around $12 a bottle. Then there is the Torcicoda – "tail twister" – a 100% Primitivo that's ripe, round and gutsy. But to date, the finest red wine produced at Tormaresca is the Bocca di Lupo, a wine made exclusively from Aglianico, from the company's estate in the Castel del Monte DOC zone, very near the border with Basilicata. Medium-full with excellent depth of fruit, this has great varietal purity with its black cherry and bitter chocolate notes. Aged for fifteen months in a combination of French and Hungarian oak, this is a ripe, sleek, robust style of Aglianico that can drink well for 12-15 years. This has become one of Puglia's most prominent reds. **BRV**: 2008, 2007, 2006, 2004.

CANTELE SALICE SALENTINO RISERVA
Salice Salentino, named for the town situated a bit west of Lecce in far southern Puglia, is one of the region's most famous red wines (there are also white and *rosato* versions). Produced from a minimum of 85% Negroamaro, most examples are medium-weight wines that drink well over the course of five to seven years, a bit longer for a *riserva* bottling. The 100% Negroamaro *riserva* from Cantele, one of the area's most consistent producers, is a typical example with black cherry, tar and clove aromas nicely integrated oak and a moderately tannic finish with good acidity and impressive persistence. Ripe and a bit forward, but with good backbone for aging, this is not flashy or massively concentrated, simply a wine of very good typicity. **BRV**: 2009, 2008, 2007, 2006.

LEONE DI CASTRIS SALICE SALENTINO RISERVA "DONNA LISA"

The charms of Salice Salentino, with its ripe black fruits and velvety tannins, have not escaped the senses of consumers throughout Italy and many countries. The Donna Lisa Riserva has become something of a classic version of this wine; medium-full with ample fruit aromas and flavors along with subtle hints of brown spice (nutmeg, cinnamon), this is a supple, beautifully balanced wine with big persistence and polished tannins; barrique aging adds some toasty notes, but they are subdued. This renowned producer has been as consistent with this wine as any of its fellow producers. Despite its early appeal, this is generally at its best from five to twelve or even fifteen years of age. **BRV**: 2007, 2006, 2005, 2001, 1999.

CASTELLO MONACI "ARTAS"

Castello Monaci is a large company that focuses on the varieties of Salento in southern Puglia; the wines combine excellent varietal focus with admirable pricing. The "Artas" bottling, a 100% Primitivo, is a fine example of what this producer aims for; displaying plum and black cherry aromas with very good concentration and nicely balanced acidity and tannins with subtle black spice notes, this is appealing upon release, yet has the structure to improve for three to five years. Aged in small barrels, this is forward with good ripeness, yet power and intensity are not the main features here - those are impressive varietal character and balance. **BRV**: 2009, 2008.

FATALONE PRIMITIVO

The first Fatalone wines were from the 1987 vintage; today, this winery has made a name for itself for its authoritative versions of Primitivo from the Gioia del Colle district. This wine zone in central Puglia, about 25 miles from the sea, is comprised of soils that contain marine fossils that clearly add a minerality to the red wines; farming at the Fatalone plantings is organic. While the *riserva* bottling is quite good, I am opting for the elegance and purity of the regular Primitivo. Deep ruby red with aromas of black cherry, black plum and tobacco leaf, this is medium-bodied with beautiful ripeness and varietal character.

There are young, nicely balanced tannins and an expressive finish with good grip and acidity. What I like most about this is the precise varietal character and sense of place displayed in this wine. Enjoy from five to seven years of age. **BRV**: 2008, 2007, 2006, 2005.

FEUDI DI SAN MARZANO PRIMITIVO DI MANDURIA "SESSANTANNI"

The Primitivo di Manduria DOC zone is in far southern Puglia, situated between the towns of Taranto on the west and Brindisi on the east; the zone is named for the town of Manduria in the center of this area. Feudi di San Marzano, established in 2003, is one of the best known producers of this wine; the "Sessantanni" has become their signature wine. Sourced from *albarello* vines averaging sixty years of age (*sessantanni* is "sixty years" in Italian), this is a ripe, deeply colored, robust red, aged in barriques for six months; black fruit flavors and tobacco notes dominate, while the oak in nicely integrated. It's definitely a modern red with polished tannins and not exceedingly high acidity and it delivers a lot of chocolate, coffee and black spice notes. This is generally at is best from five to ten years of age. **BRV**: 2009, 2008, 2007, 2006.

RACEMI PRIMITIVO DI MANDURIA "FELLINE"

The Racemi project, headed by Gregory Perrucci, is based on the preservation and research of traditional Puglian varieties and wines. This Primitivo di Manduria is excellent evidence of this work, sourced from 40-50 year-old *albarello* vines. An elegantly styled example of this wine with aromas of black cherry, sweet red plum and licorice, this features polished tannins and admirable balance and ripeness. There is some spiciness here, but not too much as the focus is on the appealing flavors of the Primitivo grape. Enjoy this from three to seven years of age. **BRV**: 2010, 2009.

CASTEL DI SALVE "PRIANTE"

Castel di Salve is a very modern winery in an ancient land, situated in the small town of Depressa, south of Lecce, almost at the most southern point of Italy's heel in Puglia. Their Priante – emblazoned with a bright copper red "P" – is a 50/50 blend of Negroamaro and Montepulciano. This is, without doubt, a modern Apulian red with black plum and cherry fruit, rich, round tannins and balanced acidity. Though aged in a combination of French and American barriques, the casks are all second and third year, so the wood notes do not overwhelm the fruit. There are plenty of brown spice and tobacco notes in the finish – this is a big, gutsy red. This is at its best five to seven years after the harvest. **BRV**: 2009, 2008, 2007, 2006.

CANDIDO "DUCA D'ARAGONA"
Candido is a medium-sized producer located in the southern province of Bari that makes several tiers of wines; their best bottles rank among the most special of Puglia. This blend of 80% Negroamaro and 20% Montepulciano is reminiscent of rustic Puglian wines that were commonplace twenty or so years ago; this despite being aged in barriques for one year. The aromas are quite complex, combining notes of dried brown herbs, dried cherry, thyme and a hint of cigar. This has a nicely defined mid-palate, subtle wood notes and distinct earthiness with rich, but elegant tannins. This is quite subtle in its approach and is at its best some five to seven years after the harvest. **BRV**: 2004, 2003, 2001, 1999.

TORRE VENTO MOSCATO DI TRANI "DULCIS IN FUNDO"
This sweet white from northern Puglia is made entirely from the Moscato reale di Trani strain; unlike some versions of Moscato from the south, this is not a *passito* wine. Light yellow with exotic aromas of pineapple, musk oil and guava, this is medium-bodied with moderate sweetness and a light bitterness in the finish. This is an amiable, low-key dessert wine to be enjoyed from two to five years of age. **BRV**: 2009, 2008, 2007.

CANDIDO ALEATICO
There are a few producers left in Puglia that still make a sumptuous dessert wine from the Aleatico grape; my favorite is the offering from Candido. Made from naturally ripe grapes, this has intriguing aromas

of currant, almond, caramel and orange peel. Medium-full with very good to excellent concentration, this is a very sexy wine! There is very good acidity, moderate sweetness and a lovely note of toffee in the finish. Unlike some versions of Aleatico in Puglia, this is not syrupy or over the top; rather this offers an elegant entry on the palate and a delicate, harmonious finish. Enjoy this from three to seven years of age.

Basilicata

Principal Varieties

White:
Fiano, Malvasia, Moscato,
Chardonnay, Sauvignon

Red:
Aglianico

———

CANTINE DEL NOTAIO ROSE´ BRUT "LA STIPULA"

Aglianico is overwhelmingly the leading red variety of Basilicata, employed most famously in the region's most renowned wine, Aglianico del Vulture. The variety also works beautifully when produced as a rosé; here is a distinguished example of Aglianico rosé as a sparkling wine. Aged on its own yeasts for eighteen months, this has beautiful complexity and richness on the palate. The aromas are intense, offering notes of cherry, strawberry, orange zest and a hint of almond and there is a persistent stream of bubbles. There is impressive varietal character and notable persistence; enjoy this remarkable sparkler upon release and over the following two to three years. Bravo to proprietor Gerardo Giuratrabocchetti and his consulting enologist Luigi Moio for crafting such a special wine! **BRV**: 2009, 2008.

GRIFALCO AGLIANICO DEL VULTURE "DAMASCHITO"

Aglianico del Vulture (*voohl* - tur- ay) is by far the most famous wine of Basilicata; produced entirely from Aglianico from vineyards north of

Mount Vulture. Owners Fabrizio Piccin and his wife Cecilia sold their estate in Montepulciano in Toscana to focus on this wine and the results have been quite special. There are three different versions of Aglianico del Vulture produced, the "Damaschito" is the most accomplished, sourced from 40 year-old vines. Matured in large Slavonian oak casks, which yields very supple tannins, this has inviting aromas of Queen Anne cherry and mocha with a hint of tar. There is admirable ripeness and beautiful harmony, as the acidity leaves a clean finish. Medium-full, this is a beautifully made example of this wine that oozes finesse, especially after a few years in the bottle. Depending on the strength of the vintage, this can drink well from seven to fifteen years of age. **BRV**: 2007, 2006, 2005.

DONATO D'ANGELO AGLIANICO DEL VULTURE

Donato d'Angelo is the agronomist and winemaker at this small estate owned by Filomena Ruppi. They have been producing Aglianico del Vulture since 2001; this is the richer version, noted by a purple label. Sourced from 50 year-old vines in Rionero, this is matured for eighteen months in 50 HL *botti*. Medium-full, with aromas of dried cherry, sage and tobacco, this is a beautifully balanced wine with graceful tannins and distinct notes of black pepper in the finish. Depending on the strength of the vintage, this is at its best from four to eight years of age. **BRV**: 2008, 2007, 2006.

MACARICO AGLIANICO DEL VULTURE "MACARICO"

This tiny estate in Barile crafts several versions of Aglianico del Vulture; established in 2001, the quality was high from the start and has only improved. The Macarico bottling is my favorite of their wines, sourced from high density vineyards 1600 feet above sea level, it is matured in barriques for eighteen months. Deep ruby red/light purple, this has big black raspberry, black cherry and tar aromas, good acidity (typical for this zone) and young, firm tannins. This is clearly a modern wine, rich and gutsy with excellent varietal character. This is a touch bitter upon release, so give this a few years to settle down;

peak drinking is at five to ten years of age. **BRV**: 2008, 2007, 2006, 2005, 2004.

TERRE DEGLI SVEVI AGLIANICO DEL VULTURE "RE MANFREDI"

Established in 1998, Terre degli Svevi is owned by the large Italian firm Gruppo Italiano Vini, who has wineries in several regions of the country. The "Re Manfredi" Aglianico del Vulture has been a model of consistency here, a textbook version with a light touch of modernity (one year maturation in barriques) as well as ideal varietal focus. Medium-full, this has black cherry, menthol and tar aromas, firm, but nicely balanced tannins and good acidity with light black spice notes. This is not as intense as some examples of this wine type, but it will offer greater complexity at age four or five and can drink well at ten to twelve years. **BRV**: 2008, 2007, 2006.

PATERNOSTER AGLIANICO DEL VULTURE "DON ANSELMO"

Ever since 1925, when Anselmo Paternoster decided to sell Aglianico bottled separately, this has been arguably the signature estate of Aglianico del Vulture. Today, his grandchildren uphold his belief in the excellent of this variety and wine type; this latest generation honors him with their "Don Anselmo" offering. Ripe and powerful with lovely aromas of baked cherries, red plum, carnation and red roses, this has excellent persistence, good acidity and firm, youthful tannins. Matured 50/50 in large Slavonian casks and barriques, the wood notes can at times be a touch strong, but there is impressive depth of fruit at the wine's center that keeps this attractive. This needs a bit of time to shed its youthful bitterness; enjoy from five to twelve years, longer in a deeply concentrated vintage such as 2007. **BRV**: 2007, 2006, 2005, 2004.

CANTINE DEL NOTAIO AGLIANICO DEL VULTURE "LA FIRMA"

La firma in Italian means "signature," which should tell you a lot about how Gerardo Giuratrabocchetti, the proprietor of Cantine del Notaio, feels about this wine. Matured primarily in one year-old barriques in the volcanic undergound cellars, this is a robust Aglianico with blackberry, clove, tar and vanilla aromas. The acidity is generally quite good (especially so in the 2008) resulting in a powerful, but well balanced wine with typical notes of bitter chocolate in the finish. It can be a bit sharp upon release – this more so from the most powerful vintages – but it's never too tannic or oaky and there is marvelous complexity, grip and typicity. Depending on the vintage, enjoy this from seven to fifteen years of age. **BRV**: 2008, 2007, 2006, 2004, 2001.

Calabria

Principal Varieties

White:
Greco, Mantonico, Malvasia,
Chardonnay, Sauvignon

Red:
Gaglioppo, Magliocco, Greco Nero,
Nerello Mascalese, Nerello Cappuccio

———

STATTI MANTONICO

There just isn't much white wine produced in Calabria (about 10% of the total output) and much of that is made from the Greco variety, while a few producers work with Chardonnay and/or Sauvignon. However there are a few vintners that grow Mantonico, an ancient variety, thought to have been planted by the Greeks millenia ago. At Statti, brothers Alberto and Antonio produce an excellent example; fermented in large casks of acacia, the wine is then matured for four months, also in acacia barrels. Medium-full with distinctive aromas of fig, dried pears and green tea, this has good acidity and persistence along with a dry, earthy finish; there is impressive complexity and the wood notes come out more on the nose than on the palate. A wine of good freshness (the 2009 was in lovely condition in mid-2012), this is at its best at three to five years of age.

LIBRANDI EFESO

Another noteworthy example of a 100% Matonico from Calabria is the "Efeso" bottling from Librandi; the name Efeso comes from

Ephesus, a colony in Turkey where some believe this variety originated. Aged in new and one-year old French barriques, this sports aromas of baked apple, vanilla and pear; the persistence is admirable and the acidity is balanced. This is a very different style of Matonico than the Statti, given the oak treatment, so this is a wine that clearly needs rich seafood with cream sauces as its best showcase; enjoy from three to five years of age.

IPPOLITO 1845 CIRÒ ROSSO SUPERIORE "LIBER PATER"

Ippolito 1845, named for the year it was founded, is one of the leading producers of Cirò Rosso, easily the most famous wine of Calabria. The winery is still owned by the Ippolito family; Gianluca is the current proprietor and has the famed enologist Franco Bernabei in his employ. Produced entirely from the Gaglioppo variety and aged for six months in barriques, the wine has aromas that combine dried cherry fruit with notes of oregano and dried brown herbs. Medium-full, this is a slightly rustic style of Cirò Rosso with pleasing notes of porcini mushrooms and tobacco in the finish. There is good acidity, the wood notes are moderate and the tannins are medium-weight; this is an excellent representation of this wine. Enjoy this from three to five years of age, perhaps a year or two longer. **BRV**: 2009, 2008, 2007.

LIBRANDI CIRÒ ROSSO SUPERIORE "DUCA SAN FELICE"

Aguably the most famous wine producer in Calabria, Librandi is a family estate that has been bottling wines under its own label since 1950. Situated in Cirò Marina, in central eastern Calabria, only a few miles from the sea, the winery is best known for its Cirò Rosso made from the Gaglioppo variety. Their Duca San Felice version, named for the oldest vineyard planted by the family, is a delightful steel tank-aged wine with red cherry, cumin, currant and tobacco notes. Medium-full, this has excellent persistence, refined tannins, balanced acidity and distinct tobacco notes in the lengthy finish. Enjoy this from five to eight years of age from most vintages. **BRV**: 2009, 2008, 2007.

STATTI "ARVINO"
Here is a 100% Gaglioppo that is a real charmer. Aged only in steel tanks, this offers delightful aromas of tart cherries and carnations; medium-bodied, this has very soft tannins, good acidity and very good varietal character. It's not a wine to be laid away, but rather, to be consumed in its first two to three years with lighter pastas, pork and veal dishes.

LIBRANDI "MAGNO MEGONIO"
The Librandi "Magno Megonio," named for a Roman centurion who understood the potential for viticulture in the area, is produced solely from the Magliocco grape; the vines were planted in 1975. Matured for sixteen months in new and one year-old barriques, this has deep ruby red color with purple tints and intense aromas of black cherry, myrtle and hints of soy sauce. Medium-full, this does have ample oak as well as balanced acidity and medium-weight tannins. The finish offers a mix of red fruit, dark chocolate and pepper notes along with impressive persistence. This is a ripe, modern Calabrian red best enjoyed from five to seven years of age. **BRV:** 2009, 2008, 2007, 2006.

TRAMONTANA "PELLARO"
This family-owned winery in Gallico, just north of Reggio Calabria, was updated by Vincenzo Tramontana in the mid-1980s; their array of wines goes from value whites and reds to more limited *selezioni*. I'm a fan of their red "Pellaro," a blend of Nerello, Castiglione (the Calabrian name for Nero d'Avola) and Alicante. It's deeply colored with big aromas of tar, bramble and black plum. Aged only in steel tanks, it is fruit-forward with a pleasing rustic edge; this is a bit of a tribute to the old-fashioned Calabrian reds, but made in a more modern style. Enjoy this from three to seven years of age. **BRV:** 2009, 2008, 2007, 2006.

LIBRANDI GRAVELLO
Here is Librandi's "Super-Calabrian" red, a blend of Gaglioppo and Cabernet Sauvignon. Aged for one year in new and used barriques,

this has abundant black fruit (cherries, currants, plums) in the aromas along with notes of pepper and thyme. Medium-full with excellent persistence, this has very good acidity and round tannins, which makes this wine quite approachable upon release, although it is generally at its best from five to ten years of age. **BRV**: 2009, 2008, 2007, 2006.

Sicily
Principal Varieties

White:
Grillo, Carricante, Insolia, Cataratto, Moscato, Grecanico,
Viognier, Zibibbo, Malvasia, Chardonnay

Red:
Nero d'Avola, Nerello Mascalese, Nerello Cappuccio, Frappato,
Syrah, Merlot, Cabernet Sauvignon

———

PLANETA COMETA

Since 1995, Alessio, Francesca and Santi Planeta have realized a dream of making their family winery one of Sicily's most widely recognized. Along the way, they have gone from one estate to six and have produced first-rate wines – both white and red – from indigenous as well as international varieties. Cometa, made entirely from Fiano is prime evidence of the brilliant work this family has accomplished. Though not widely planted in Sicily, Alessio Planeta believed that this variety would work well in the clay and limestone soils at their home estate near Menfi; the limestone especially would be beneficial for the variety's aromatics. Initial vintages (the first was from 2000) were aged in oak, but the past few releases now mature only in steel tanks; the wine is much brighter, displaying gorgeous aromas of mango, yellow peach and geranium. This has wonderful texture and impressive depth of fruit as well as excellent balance. This is attractive upon release, but irresistible three to five years after the harvest. **BRV**: 2010, 2009 (exceptional), 2008, 2007.

BAGLIO DI PIANETTO "GINOLFO"

Established in 1997, Baglio di Pianetto is the Sicilian wine estate of Count Paolo Marzotto, former general manager of Santa Margherita in Alto Adige. Marzotto, one of the most charming, truly funny people I have ever met, decided on Sicily for his wine venture after leaving northern Italy, because as he told me, "everything grows in Sicily." He works with both indigenous and international varieties, which are planted at the winery estate near Palermo, as well as an estate near Noto in southeastern Sicily. The Ginolfo is a 100% Viognier, a rarity for the island; the wine receives three months of aging in barriques. The aromas are textbook with notes of honeysuckle, Bosc pear and pineapple and there is impressive richness on the palate, notable persistence and very good acidity. While there is not a long history with this wine, this is a Viognier that ages well; the 2004 tasted in 2011 offered good freshness. Immediately appealing upon release, this is at its best five to seven years of age. **BRV:** 2010, 2009, 2008, 2007, 2004.

TERRELÍADE GRILLO "TIMPA GIADDA"

For decades, Grillo was the overwhelming white variety planted in Sicilia, thanks to its use in the production of Marsala. While Grillo is still a major white variety on the island, the total acreage has decreased, in part due to less focus on Marsala as well as the plantings of other white varieties, especially Chardonnay. Many stand-alone bottlings of Grillo are quite simple, so it is especially nice to try this version from Terrelíade, located in Sambuca di Sicilia in southwestern Sicilia. Steel-aged, the winery labels this wine as "Timpa Giadda," referring to a local stone of that name that has a brilliant yellow color. This Grillo has such lovely perfumes of honeydew melon, spiced pear and hibiscus - these perfumes are so striking that it's a bit difficult to move ahead and actually taste the wine! Medium-bodied, this is ultra clean with balanced acidity and lovely freshness; this is a lovely dry white to be enjoyed right away, from one to two years of age. How nice that Terrelíade takes the trouble to make such a first-rate version of this variety!

BENANTI ETNA BIANCO "PIETRAMARINA"

While the Etna DOC wine zone is more famous for its red wines, there are a few notable whites made here, such as this highly praised offering from Benanti. Pietramarina is 100% Carricante, the district's most widely planted white – the name of the grape means "consistent" – and one that combines aromatics, richness on the palate and distinct minerality. The grapes are sourced from vineyards on the eastern side of Mount Etna; comprised of sandy soils, these are situated more than 3000 feet above sea level! The vines are albarello – basically, little trees that stand no more than a few feet above the ground and have an average age of 80 years; many of these are on their own original roots. This is a sumptuous, beautifully structured and textured white with perfumes of dried apricot and apple backed by impressive persistence and very good acidity. This wine has a marvelous track record and ages for more than a decade. The wine tends to open up some four to five years after the harvest and often peaks after 12-15 years. **BRV**: 2008, 2007, 2006, 2005, 2004.

TENUTA DI FESSINA ETNA BIANCO "A' PUDDARA"

Another impressive Etna Bianco made entirely from Carricante is the "A' Puddara" bottling from Tenuta di Fessina. Winemaker Federico Curtaz sources the fruit from a 45-year old vineyard on the southern slopes of Mount Etna, at an elevation of 3000 feet. Aged for a short time in very large oak casks, this is a juicy style of Carricante with expressive aromas of lemon custard, pear and a slight flintiness; there is good acidity and a finish with notes of fresh citrus fruit. Only a few vintages have been produced to date, but this is a winner! This is typically at its best at three to five years of age, though the best bottles may hold for another year or two. The name of the wine refers to the Pleiades constellation, which appears in the sky directly above the winery. **BRV**: 2010, 2009.

CORNELISSEN MUNJEBEL BIANCO

You only need to be with Frank Cornelissen for fifteen or twenty minutes to start to understand what drives this man. A former mountain climber from Belgium, Cornelissen brings the same determination he used to conquer the peaks of the Alps to his natural winemaking. Everything about what he does at his vineyards and winery in the Etna district is with the highest degree of purity; he does not add sulfites to any of his wines and he uses no oak barrels or stainless steel tanks in his cellar. Thus he needs to bring in the cleanest, purest grapes he can to produce his distinctly individual wines. The Munjebel Bianco – Munjebel is an old name for Mount Etna – is a blend of Grecanico Dorato, Coda di Volpe and Carricante from lava-strewn vineyards situated between 2000 and 3200 feet above sea level on the north side of Mount Etna. Cornelissen keeps the juice in contact with the skins – "everybody known the skins contain all the flavor," he told me – for anywhere from four to ten weeks on the skins. Combine that with the aging in terra cotta pots – *amphorae* – and the resulting appearance is a bright amber gold/orange color with a slight cloudiness, as the wine is not filtered.

The various bottlings of Munjebel Bianco are labeled with a number – 7 is made from grapes from the 2010 harvest – as none of Cornelissen's wines are vintage dated. The aromas fill the room with their perfumes of golden raisin, orange zest, apricot and heather along with a light smokiness. This is a white wine based on texture as it coats and caresses your palate and has a long sensual finish. Optimum drinking depends on individual tastes, as this is akin to tasting a traditional white wine from Georgia; some will prefer the newest release, while others can savor this wine some seven to ten years after the vintage. Whatever your preference, this has excellent freshness, no matter how many years it has been in the bottle. This is a great expression of a terroir told from the viewpoint of one man. **BRV:** Munjebel Bianco 7 (2010), Munjebel Bianco 6 (2009).

TENUTA DI TERRE NERE ETNA BIANCO
American-born Italian wine importer Marco de Grazia established this estate on the north slopes of Mount Etna in 2002. While his various versions of Etna Rosso have been the most celebrated of his

releases, his Etna Bianco has also been something quite special. The blend is 50% Carricante, 25% Cataratto, 15% Grecanico and 10% Inzolia, all from vineyards planted in 1947. Steel-aged only, this has delicate aromas of lemon, orange blossom and pear and is one of the most floral of all whites from Etna. Medium-bodied, there is wonderful freshness and a light touch of minerality, a by-product of the volcanic soils. This is best enjoyed within two to five years of the harvest.

PLANETA CHARDONNAY

Of all the first-rate wines crafted by this great producer, this is the one that put them on the map. This should not be a surprise given how few producers anywhere in Italy were producing a premium Chardonnay when this wine was first released from the 1994 vintage. Here was a wine that was rich and powerful with strong oak and spicy notes, displaying baked apple and toasted almond flavors, as in the style of modern Chardonnays from California and France. Today the wine is just as rich and stylish, but the oak influence has been lessened – fermentation and maturation takes place in 50% new and 50% used French barriques – making for a better balanced wine with more freshness. Approachable upon release, the wine is at its best three to five years after the harvest, though some bottles age up to a decade. **BRV**: 2010, 2009, 2008, 2007.

TASCA D'ALMERITA CHARDONNAY

The Tasca d'Almerita family winery is one of Sicily's most historic. Once known as Regaleali, this company now is represented by estates throughout the island, from Mozia near Marsala on the west to Mount Etna on the east. The Regaleali estate in northern central Sicily is the source for several of the company's best wines, including this barrel-fermented and aged Chardonnay. Offering aromas of banana, lime and vanilla, this has excellent richness on the palate, all the while displaying lovely subtleties. This has very good acidity and though the oak is noticeable, it is nicely integrated; the finish is quite full with delicate spice. This is at its best from three to five years of age.

TENUTA DI CASTELLARO "POMICE"

This small winery is located on the island of Lipari, just north of Sicily. While the most famous wine from this area is a sweet wine made from Malvasia, this dry white, a blend of Malvasia, Carricante and other selected local varieties, is also quite distinctive. Sourced from soils that are mix of sand as well as volcanic (the wine is named for the pomice stones that are plentiful in this area), this is medium-bodied with beautiful acidity, offering intense aromas of honeydew melon, pear and white flowers. Fermented in steel tanks and in oak, this has marvelous complexity and is quite unique; this is best enjoyed at three to five years of age. **BRV**: 2010, 2009, 2008.

DUCA DI SALAPARUTA "DUCA ENRICO"

Nero d'Avola has become the most highly regarded red variety in Sicily, but it wasn't until 1984 when it was first bottled as a stand-alone variety as a premium wine. That honor went to Duca di Salaparuta, who until then was best known for their everyday value offerings of Corvo red and white. This producer was among the first to recognize that if they wanted to produce a Nero d'Avola of deep color and ideal structure, they would have to plant the variety not near Marsala on the island's west coast, but much further east; they settled on an estate near the southeastern town of Gela. The wine has textbook aromas of maraschino cherry as well as notes of fig, sandalwood and even a hint of prosciutto. Medium-full, this has beautiful depth of fruit and ripnesss with the typical round, elegant tannins of Nero d'Avola along with good acidity and nicely integrated oak. Perhaps the nicest quality of this wine is the overall complexity, as Nero d'Avola had been thought of historically as a variety that was as its best blended with one or two other varieties, such as Merlot or Cabernet Sauvignon. The other great virtue of this wine is its aging potential, as the wine really starts to develop some seven to ten years after the harvest and reaches optimum drinking at 12-15 years of age. **BRV**: 2007, 2006, 2004, 2003, 2001, 1999, 1997.

PLANETA "SANTA CECILIA"

Santa Cecilia is Planeta's top example of Nero d'Avola; it is a wine that has undergone several changes since the first release from the 1997 vintage. The family early on decided to produce a premium version of this variety and planted vines at their Sambuca estate near Menfi in western Sicily; while the first bottling did include 15% Syrah, the wine would be Nero d'Avola *in purezza* for every future release. Wine-maker Alessio Planeta soon decided that Nero d'Avola would per-form better planted in southeastern Sicily and settled upon a small area near Noto for the new estate plantings of this variety. Beginning with 2003, every release of Santa Cecilia has been from this site; the wines now have brighter fruit and are fresher, a far cry from the more rustic early releases. Medium-full with nicely integrated oak, tanta-lizing black fruit, beautifully balanced tannins and very good acidity, Santa Cecilia has a graceful entry on the palate and a well structured finish. Optimum drinking time depends on the vintage; while the 2005 is a touch lighter and will be at peak in another five years, the more deeply concentrated 2006 will drink well for another decade. **BRV**: 2008, 2007, 2006 (exceptional), 2005, 2004.

MORGANTE "DON ANTONIO"

Established in 1998 in the province of Agrigento in south central Sicily, Morgante is a family owned winery specializing in Nero d'Avola. Three versions are produced; the Don Antonio, made by famed enologist Riccardo Cotarella, is the showcase wine. Produced from vineyards planted in 1970 and 1975, situated some 1700 to 1850 feet above sea level, the wine is aged in French barriques for one year. This is always quite rich with good ripeness; alcohol is usually around 14.5%, though in very warm vintages that can creep up to 15%. This is a Nero d'Avola that expresses the spicy side of the variety, with dominant notes of black pepper, menthol and leather along with a distinctive touch of cocoa. While often forward and approachable in its youth, it tends to harmonize some five to seven years after the harvest. **BRV**: 2009, 2008, 2007, 2006, 2005, 2004.

TENUTA RAPITALÀ NERO D'AVOLA "ALTO"

This is the newest wine from this winery that was established in 1968 after an earthquake destroyed the original property. Tenuta Rapitalà, situated in northwest Sicily near Camporeale has a nice mix of value and premium wines, made from a combination of indigenous and international varieties. This 100% Nero d'Avola is sourced from vineyards at an elevation between 1300 and 1700 feet; the vines are approximately ten years old. Medium-full with a firm backbone, this emphasizes the tobacco notes of this variety along with currant and dried cherry fruit. Matured in both small and large barrels, this has subtle spice, balanced acidity and impressive persistence. It's a wine that needs some time to settle down; the 2007 should be at peak around 2017 or so. **BRV**: 2007.

ARIANNA OCCHIPINTI NERO D'AVOLA "SICCOGNO"

Arianna Occhipinti is the niece of COS co-founder Giusto Occhipinti; both have wine estates are near Vittoria. Arianna produces an excellent Cerasuolo di Vittoria, but my favorite wine of hers is the Nero d'Avola "Siccogno." Produced from organically grown grapes, the vineyards are of clay and limestone soils, averaging 35 years of age. Pale garnet with inviting aromas of red currant, strawberry and mulberry, the wine is as generous as Arianna herself. Deeply concentrated with beautiful varietal purity, this has moderate tannins, subtle wood notes (the wine is aged in large Slavonian oak) and very good acidity and offers lovely complexity. This is not one of the most famous examples of Nero d'Avola from Sicily, but perhaps after a few more years, it will be! Best consumed within seven to ten years after the harvest. **BRV**: 2008, 2007, 2006.

GULFI NERO D'AVOLA "NEROBUFALEFFJ"

Established in 1996, the Gulfi winery is a producer of several typical reds from southeastern Sicily, including a lovely Cerasuolo di Vittoria. But it is with Nero d'Avola from vineyards near Noto, that this firm has made its name. There are several versions; I have singled out the "Nerobefaleffj" as it best represents the house style. The vineyards used for this wine are planted in the classic *albarello* style and average 35 years of age; yields are extremely low. Matured for eighteen months in *tonneaux*, this features aromas of red plum, bing cherry and a hint of tobacco. Medium-full with excellent persistence, this is a beautifuly balanced wine with excellent complexity and a lovely varietal focus. This is best enjoyed from five to seven years of age. **BRV**: 2007, 2006, 2005, 2004.

DONNAFUGATA "MILLE E UNA NOTTE"

The Rallo family, once solely producers of Marsala, has been expanding their portfolio of Sicilian wines over the past twenty years. Easily their finest red wine is this engaging red with a name that translates as "a thousand and one nights." This is primarily Nero d'Avola with a small percentage of local red varieties from the company's estate in the Contessa Entellina zone in Western Sicily. This is a big, bold, ripe, modern style of Nero d'Avola with aromas of damson plum, marmalade and licorice. While the wine is aged primarily in new French barriques, the wood notes are well integrated and there is quite a powerful punch of ripe varietal fruit in the nose and on the palate. The tannins are polished and sleek and the overall sensation is one of seduction. I've served this wine at classes and seminars and it's a real crowd pleaser. While it's appealing upon release, this tends to need a few years in the bottle to soften, so the best time to drink this is from five to seven years of age, though it has no problem staying the course for ten to twelve years in most instances. **BRV**: 2006, 2005, 2004, 2001 (exceptional), 2000, 1999.

CUSUMANO "NOA"

Established in 2000 by the Cambria family, Cusumano is a little giant of Sicilian viticulture, producing more than two million bottles per year from almost 1000 acres of vineyards at four sites across the island. Noa is one of their modern specialties, a blend of Nero d'Avola, Merlot and Cabernet Sauvignon from their Presti e Pregni estate in the western province of Trapani. Aged for barriques for 12 months, this is a ripe, gutsy red with black raspberry, black plum, licorice and tar aromas, impressive depth of fruit along with very good acidity. To me, this is a wine of much greater complexity than their 100% Nero d'Avola called "Sagana." This is generally best consumed at seven to ten years of age. **BRV**: 2007, 2006, 2005, 2004, 2001, 2000, 1999.

BAGLIO DI PIANETTO "RAIMONE"

Here is a red wine that is a great example of this underrated company's philosophy of matching the proper variety to the right growing area. This is a blend of 50% Nero d'Avola from their vineyards near Noto in southeastern Sicily with 50% Merlot from vineyards at the winery estate in Santa Cristina Gela at the northwestern reaches of the island. Notes of tar, black cherry and white pepper highlight the aromas of this medium-full wine with moderate tannins and very good acidity. This is aged for one year in barriques, but the depth of fruit takes precedent over the wood notes. This is a beautifully made, elegant blend that is one of this winery's most successful products. Drink at five to seven years of age. **BRV**: 2007, 2006, 2005, 2004, 2001.

TAMBURELLO PERRICONE "PIETRAGAVINA"

While Nero d'Avola is the premier red indigenous variety of Sicily, Perricone is a lesser-known, but very fine cultivar. This wine from Tamburello, an estate in the Monreale DOC, just east of Palermo, is sourced from twenty year-old vines situated 650 feet above sea level. Medium-bodied with a slight earthy, rustic character; this is not as forward or plummy as with a typical Nero d'Avola, rather it is more subdued with aromas of cedar, dried cherry and brown herbs. The wood notes are gentle, acidity is balanced and there are middle weight tannins. Braised rabbit or game will bring out the best in this wine. Enjoy this from five to ten years, depending on the strength of the vintage.

COS CERASUOLO DI VITTORIA "PITHOS"

Cerasuolo di Vittoria – "cherry of Vittoria" – is currently the only DOCG red wine of Sicily. A blend of Nero d'Avola and Frappato, the wine is produced in a zone in southeastern Sicily, not far from the town of Ragusa. Combining the richness of Nero d'Avola with the charm (light tannins) of Frappato, this is a wine that drinks well upon release, but can age. While most versions are meant to be consumed within three to five years, some of the best are extremely ageworthy. The Pithos bottling from COS is a great example of this. COS is named for the first initial of the last three names of the founders: Giambattista Cilia, Giusto Occhipinti and Pinuccia Strano; today the first two are the proprietors as Strano is no longer part of the company. Occhipinti and Cilia produce their wines according to very distinct methods; farming is biodynamic and the wines are aged in terra cotta pots called *amphaorae*, buried in the ground, much like the winemaking process of centuries past. What this leads to is a consistent elegance as well as remarkable varietal purity in the all the COS wines. The Pithos bottling, made from vines that are more than twenty years old, has strawberry and red cherry flavors with a nice mix of brown spice notes, moderate tannins and a long, sumptuous finish with outstanding persistence. I have tasted older versions – some 20 years of age – that are still in fine shape, as these wines tend to focus more on balsamic and coffee notes. **BRV:** 2009, 2008, 2007, 2006, 2005.

PLANETA CERASUOLO DI VITTORIA "DORILLI"

Planeta has been offering a lovely version of Cerasuolo di Vittoria since 2001; this special selection named for a river near the vineyards was first made from the 2009 vintage. Produced from a slightly different blend than the regular Cerasuolo – this has 70% Nero d'Avola and 30% Frappato as compared to the usual 60/40 blend in the regular bottlng – this has a deep garnet color with gorgeous aromas of maraschino cherry, black plum and lavender. Medium-full, this is a beautifully textured wine with moderate tannins, very good acidity and notes of red spice in the finish. This is a skillfully made example of Cerasuolo, displaying the potential of this wine, as it combines richness and complexity with elegance and finesse. The wine is approachable upon release and should drink well for three to five years. **BRV:** 2010, 2009.

VALLE DELL'ACATE FRAPPATO

Frappato, one of two varieties that make up the blend for Cerasuolo di Vittoria, is made as a stand-alone variety by a few producers in the Vittoria area. My favorite is that of Valle delle Acate, a first-rate estate a bit north of Vittoria. What makes this estate's Frapppato so special are the aromas, which offer not only lovely maraschino cherry and cranberry perfumes, but also a savory, slightly meaty edge to them. Medium-bodied and aged only in steel tanks, this has beautiful complexity, balance and varietal purity and is a delight! This is best enjoyed from two to five years of age. **BRV**: 2011, 2010, 2009.

TENUTA DELLE TERRE NERE ETNA ROSSO "SANTO SPIRITO"

One of the most exciting developments in Sicilian viticulture has been the renaissance of red wines from Etna. Importer Marco de Grazia is at the forefront of this movement with his Terre Nere reds, which range from a charming entry-level offering meant for early consumption to one remarkable release from a pre-phylloxera vineyard planted in 1870.

Another of his Etna reds that I love is the "Santo Spirito," from a vine-yard planted in 1950 and 1960 to Nerello Mascalese and a small percentage of Nerello Cappuccio, the two varieties of this DOC. Medium-full with an attractive garnet color, this offers lovely aromas of strawberry and red currant fruit along with hints of red pepper and anise. Offering wonderful harmony, this has polished tannins, very good acidity and a finish with excellent persistence that has a great deal of finesse. Burgundian in nature like the finest examples of Etna Rosso, this is a wine of great breeding! Optimum drinking is between seven to ten years of age. **BRV:** 2010, 2009, 2008 (outstanding), 2007.

TENUTA DI FESSINA ETNA ROSSO "MUSMECI"

Silvia Maestrelli, owner of Villa Petriolo in Tuscany, along with Federico Curtaz, an agronomist who once worked for Angelo Gaja in Piemonte, purchased a 15-acre vineyard in Rovitello in the Etna district in 2007. The vineyard is planted primarily to Nerello Mascalese, with gnarly vines ranging from 70 to 80 years of age; these are *albarello* plants that do not reach far above ground. The top red here is "Musmeci," named for the farmer who tended this site for many years. This is a typical Nerello blend that has a lovely garnet color, excellent concentration – a result of the limited yields of the old vines – beautifully integrated oak, very good acidity, round tannins and a lengthy finish. This has been made for only a few years, but the 2008 is outstanding and will clearly drink well for another seven to ten years. This is a stylish wine that I predict will become one of Etna's most famous in the not-too-distant future. **BRV**: 2009, 2008 (outstanding).

Nerello Mascalese vine from the early 1900s at
Tenuta di Fessina estate

COTTANERA ETNA ROSSO

While the Cottanera winery is in the heart of the Etna district, it took the Cambria family several years to produce an Etna Rosso. They have blended the two red grapes – Nerello Cappuccio and Nerello Mascalese – in a moderately priced wine known as Barbazalle *rosso* for some time, but it was only starting with the 2005 vintage that they released an Etna Rosso DOC. Medium-full with beautifully ripe red cherry fruit along with lovely red rose aromas; this has elegant tannins, very good acidity and impressive grip in the finish. You get the sense that as good as this wine is now, vine age and experience will combine to take this wine to another level in a few years. Approachable upon release, this tends to peak from seven to ten years of age. **BRV**: 2008, 2007, 2006, 2005.

GRACI ETNA ROSSO "QUOTA 600"

There are two versions of Etna Rosso produced at this small estate; this is the superior bottling, sourced from fruit some 2000 feet above sea level on the northeastern slopes of Mount Etna. Fermented and matured in large conical oak vats known as *tini*, this is a sensual red, Burgundian in style with enticing aromas of wild strawberry, lavender and cedar. The medium-weight tannins are quite silky and there is very good natural acidity, while the elegant lengthy finish has excellent grip. This is very seductive upon release and drinks well for five to seven additional years. **BRV**: 2009, 2008, 2007.

CORNELISSEN "MAGMA"

Every wine that Frank Cornelissen handcrafts is a unique product; Magma is his most remarkable wine, his *opus magnum*. The source of any great wine is the vineyard and for this wine, Cornelissen works with a 100 plus year-old site called Barbaecchi in the Etna district. Comprised of pure lava rock, this ungrafted vineyard delivers tiny yields (less than a pound of fruit per vine) of Nerello Mascalese, thanks to vine age as well as vigorous pruning by Cornellissen. His cellar technique does not involve steel tanks or oak barrels, rather he ferments in polyethylene tanks and matures the wine in *amphorae*; sulfites are never added.

This is a red wine of spectacular complexity, one that needs to be decanted, as the perfumes change rapidly over the course of just 15-20 minutes after it is opened, shifting from notes of bing cherry, marmalade and fig to Asian spice, clove and tar. Medium-full with excellent depth of fruit, this is a sensual red, quite Burgundian in style with medium-weight tannins that glide across your palate; needless to say, the acidity is vibrant and precise. Cornelissen only produces this wine from the finest vintages; the 2009 is labeled as Magma 8VA- this is the eighth release of this wine and the VA stands for *vigne alte* ("high vineyards"). This should be enjoyed from 15-20 years of age, though that is a bit of an educated guess, given the distinctiveness of this wine; it may drink well for several additional years. This particular product is more than a great red wine, it is a true reflection of the passion and rhythms of its architect Frank Cornelissen; indeed it may represent its originator as well as any wine in this book!

DONNAFUGATA "BEN RYE"

One of the most unique dessert wines produced anywhere in the world is Passito di Pantelleria, made from decades-old vineyards on the island of Pantelleria, south of Sicily. To say it is hot here during much of the year is an understatement, as northern Africa is only 70 miles away. To combat the heat, the vineyards here are in the *albarello* system, as the bunches reach only a few feet off the ground, so as to offer protection from the ever-present winds and often oppressive sun. For this wine, the Zibibbo grapes, a local strain of Moscato, are harvested in mid-August and then naturally dried on mats by the wind and sun. The resulting wine is stunning; quite lush, with intense aromas of candied apricot, orange zest, golden raisins and banana peel. This has outstanding depth of fruit and is medium-sweet with good acidity to balance things out and maintain freshness. This wine, first made from the 1989 vintage, has shown remarkable aging ability; 15-20 years is not out of the question. While this is a wine that is best on its own (alcohol is around 14.5%), this can be enjoyed with aged blue cheeses or some cakes and pastries that feature almond, hazelnut or honey. **BRV**: 2009, 2008, 2007, 2006, 2005, 2004, 2001.

The name incidentally is Arabic for "son of the wind," a reference to the constant winds that swirl around the plants.

ABRAXAS PASSITO DI PANTELLERIA

Abraxas is a small producer located on the island of Pantelleria that produces not only the famous *passito* from Moscato grapes here, but also a few special reds. This includes Kuddia di Zè, a spicy, tangy red that is a blend of Syrah and Grenache and Kuddia di Nero, produced from Nero d'Avola. But their preeminent release is their Passito di Pantelleria, made from *albarello* vines and harvested in the middle of August. This is not as forward or as ripe as the more famous Ben Ryé offering from Donnafugata, but the quality and distinctivness of this bottle is just as special. Displaying aromas of crème caramel, dried apricot and hazelnut, this is quite lush and sensual. There is excellent persistence and moderate sweetness, which is held in check by the cleansing acidity. There is also a nice touch of nuttiness in the finish that adds to the charm of this wine. While this marries well with pound cakes or apricot tartes, for me, this is best appreciated on its own, whether at four, five or ten years of age, as this is a wine that reveals more of its charms little by little as it ages. **BRV**: 2009, 2008, 2007, 2004.

FLORIO MARSALA SUPERIORE "DONNAFRANCA"

Any study of Sicilian wine must include Marsala, the famous dessert wine from the far western reaches of the island in the province of Trapani. But while Marsala was clearly the most famous wine of Sicily throughout the 19th and the first half of the 20th century, today it is more of a historical footnote, as the island's production has shifted to a predominance of table whites and reds from indigenous and international varieties. This is truly a shame as there are several outstanding versions of Marsala that compare favorably with other great Italian dessert specialties, especially Vin Santo from Tuscany. The historic Florio firm, established in 1833, crafts various offerings that have been aged for more than five years in oak. Their finest example is Donnafranca, a Marsala Superiore that has been aged for more than 15 years in small barrels. Produced entirely from Grillo, the finest local variety for Marsala (it with-stands the heat extremely well), this has a deep amber color with intoxicating aromas of caramel, hazelnut, orange peel, marzipan and even a hint of chocolate. This wine simply glides across the palate and ends in a long, long finish with moderate sweetness. This has outstanding complexity and richness, yet you are taken in not only by its sumptuous flavors, but also its finesse. Again, this is another great Italian dessert wine that is at its best alone; enjoy this over the course of ten to twelve years after you purchase a bottle (this is a non-vintage selection).

FLORIO MALVASIA DELLE LIPARI

Malvasia delle Lipari is an historic dessert wine produced from vine-yards planted on the Aeolian islands – also known as the Lipari islands – located just northeast of Sicily. Two varieties are used in the wine's production; Malvasia being the dominant grape (98% maximum) and Corinto Nero (5% to 8% maximum). The Florio version of this wine is from the island of Salina, directly north of Lipari; soils here are volca-nic and the climate is quite hot in the summer. Grapes are generally harvested by the third week of September; they are then placed on mats and left out in the sun for about three weeks. As they grapes dry naturally, they lose a great amount of their natural water content, shrivel in size and become quite intense; this is a *passito* wine.

Medium-full, this has a burnt orange/amber color, classic apricot and honey aromas and a lush feel on the palate with a moderately sweet finish; the beautiful cleansing acidity maintains admirable balance and makes this wine seem less sweet. The alcohol is a natural 14%; this is not a fortified wine. I love the freshness of this wine, one that is very appealing upon release; this can age quite well and can be enjoyed up to twelve to fifteen years of age. It is distinct and quite remarkable and would be wonderful on its own as a *vino da meditazi-one* or paired with blue cheeses or with a sweet pastry or cake with almond or hazelnut; the sleek packaging adds to the wine's appeal. **BRV**: 2009, 2008, 2007.

Sardegna
Principal Varieties

White:
Vermentino, Granazza,
Vernaccia, Torbato, Nardo, Moscato

Red:
Cannonau, Carignano, Monica, Cagnulari, Bovale

———

VIGNE SURRAU VERMENTINO DI GALLURA SUPERIORE "SCIALA"
I just love Vermentino, especially the examples of Vermentino di Gallura from a zone in the far north of the island, not far from the famed
Costa Smerelda. The vineyards here, situated some 200 to 500 feeet
above sea level, are comprised of granitic soils that bestow a distinct
minerality to the whites. The Superiore version of this wine from
Vigne Surrau, a relatively new producer, is a beautifully made version,
one with lovely aromas of honeydew melon, pear and jasmine. There
is lively acidity and a distinct note of saltiness in the finish, typical for
this wine type. Styled for drinking by its second or third birthday, this
is especially nice with just about any type of shellfish.

JANKARA VERMENTINO DI GALLURA SUPERIORE
Renato and Angela Spanu purchased an estate near Sant'Antonio
di Gallura in 2006; two years later they planted 27 acres of Vermentino at this site, situated almost 1000 feet above sea level. So far
the owners are off to an impressive start; hiring Genotti Menotti
as winemaker (he is best known for his superb wines at Villa Russiz

in Fiuli) was an inspired choice. The 2010 was a nicely balanced, very typical Vermentino, but the 2011 is a superior wine in almost every way, as it offers much greater depth of fruit and complexity. The 2011 features lovely green apple, grapefruit and jasmine aromas, marvelous texture and a lengthy finish with a light saltiness, a direct by-product of the vineyards' proximity to the sea. Aged solely in steel tanks, this is a delicious wine with great varietal purity; enjoy within two to three years of the vintage with most shellfish.

FEUDI DELLA MEDUSA VERMENTINO DI SARDEGNA "ALBITHIA"
While Vermentino di Gallura is regulated to a small district in northeastern Sardegna, Vermentino di Sardegna can be produced from grapes grown anywhere on the island. This version is from vineyards near Usini in the province of Sassari in the northwestern reaches of the island. Although there are fragrant aromas of mango and orange blossom, the nose is a bit shy; however there is notable depth of fruit which lasts on the finish. The acidity is lively and the wine has the usual touch of minerality associated with this type. This should be enjoyed between three and five years, preferably with crustaceans.

CANTINA MESA VERMENTINO DI SARDINIA "GIUNCO"
Cantina Mesa, located in far southwestern Sardegna, produces several versions of Vermentino, my favorite being the steel tank-aged "Guinco" bottling. Light yellow with a golden tint, this has beautiful aromas of melon, lime and basil and has impressive persistence; there is textbook lively acidity and there are well-defined notes of minerality and a subtle saltiness in the finish. This has excellent complexity as well as varietal character and I love the edginess of this wine; enjoy from two to five years of age.

ARGIOLAS "ISELIS" BIANCO
While Vermentino is the most famous white variety of Sardegna, there are a few indigenous whites that also yield first-class wines.

One of the most intriguing is Nardo, a grape used most frequently for dessert wines; however is it vinified dry in this marvelous white from Argiolas, one of the island's most respected producers. Nardo represents 85% of this white, with Vermentino comprising the remainder of the blend; offering fragrant perfumes of banana, apricot and jasmine, this has lovely harmony and texture. Aged solely in steel tanks and given as much as two months of lees contact, this has a distinct minerality in the finish along with notes of dried yellow fruit and excellent persistence. The structure and acidity are such that this wine retains its freshness even after being open for five to seven days. Enjoy this from two to five years of age. **BRV**: 2010, 2009.

SELLA & MOSCA TORBATO "TERRE BIANCHE"
Torbato is an ancient Sardegnan variety that has largely been abandoned by the island's producers; indeed Sella & Mosca is believed to be the only estate working with this grape. Sourced from the plantings near Alghero in the northwest reaches of the island – the "Terre Bianche" estate is named for the local white soils - the wine is largely aged in steel with about 30% being matured in older oak barrels. The aromas are quite distinct with notes of banana peel and apricot pit being evident immediately upon opening; after ten minutes or so, there are perfumes of mango and chamomile. Medium-full, this has lively acidity and a rich, nicely structured finish, so what starts out as an aromatic white ends up as a more classically structured wine. This is a delightful, delicious white to be enjoyed with ligher seafood over its first three to five years.

FEUDI DELLA MEDUSA CANNONAU DI SARDEGNA
Cannonau is for more or less, the same as Garnacha from Spain; indeed the variety may have come to this island from that country. There are excellent versions of this charming red produced from many zones of Sardegna; one of my favorites – and most distinctive – comes from Feudi della Medusa. Founded in 2000, this winery produces wines from vineyards in the far southern reaches of Sardegna, in Santa Margherita di Pula, very close to the Tyrhennian Sea. The Cannonau is sourced from sandy vineyards that contain a bit of limestone; situated some

1300-1500 feet above sea level, these are *albarello* vines. Displaying a deep garnet color and appealing aromas of dried plum, raspberry and cedar, this is medium-full with tart, almost zesty acidity, very light tannins and beautiful varietal character. This is simply delicious and is at is best from five to seven years of age. **BRV**: 2009, 2008, 2007, 2006.

GIUSEPPE GABBAS CANNONAU DI SARDEGNA "LILLOVE'"
Giusepe Gabbas established his winery near Supramonte, a mountainous area in central eastern Sardegna, near the town of Nuoro, in 1974. His 50 acres of vineyards sit 800 to 1000 feet above sea level; sea breezes help moderate temperatures. He produces two versions of Cannonau di Sardegna, a *riserva* called "Dule" and a regular bottling, "Lillové". While the former is a richer, riper wine, I prefer the delicacy and purity of the latter. Aged only in steel, this displays the herbal, slightly wild side of this wine, with aromas of tobacco, oregano, currant and sage along with tangy cherry notes. Medium-bodied, the tannins are moderate and there is a light rustic edge in the finish. This is best enjoyed from three to seven years of age. **BRV**: 2009, 2008, 2007.

TENUTE DETTORI ROSSO / "TENORES"
"Sono ciò che sono e non ciò che vuoi che siano." – "They are what they are and not what you want them to be."

This quote from the back label of the wines of Tenute Dettori, a small estate in Sennori in far northwestern Sardegna, is a mission statement about the company's wines and the individualistic nature of these products. The viticultural approach of Alessandro Dettori is one of simplicity and respecting the earth, as he uses biodynamic methods, such as cover crop mulching along with manure and silica in cow horns buried in his vineyards. His wines are natural – he mentions on the back label that the only ingredients used are grapes and sulphur.

Tasting the red wines here is a fascinating challenge, as these are offerings that truly represent a specific sense of place as well as offering subtle complexities that emerge from the overall minimalistic approach. I have selected two reds from Dettori, both made exclusively from the Cannonau grape. The Rosso is handled gently in the cellar and matured in cement vats in order to heighten the varietal purity. Deep garnet with enticing aromas of currant, wild strawberry and dried rose petals, this is quite ripe and at the same time, very sensual in its presentation; the acidity is very good and there are wonderful flavors of strawberry on the palate. The tannins are modest and the finish is quite long, with distinct notes of nutmeg and morel cherry. This is a marvelously complex wine, one that takes Cannonau in a different direction. This should be consumed from three to seven years of age. **BRV**: 2009, 2007, 2005, 2004.

The "Tenores," also aged in cement vats, is an equally fascinating wine with slight variations. Displaying a deep garnet appearance with aromas of currant, Queen Anne cherry, carnation and strawberry preserves, this is medium-bodied with very good acidity and persistence, moderate tannins and lovely varietal purity. Tasting the 2009 version of this wine as compared to the 2009 Rosso, I found I preferred the latter, as it had greater persistence, yet each wine has similar flavors and outstanding finesse and complexity. Enjoy the "Tenores" from three to five years of age. **BRV**: 2009, 2006.

CANTINA SANTADI CARIGNANO DEL SULCIS "GROTTA ROSA" / "ROCCA RUBIA" / TERRE BRUNE"
Established in 1960, Cantina Santadi is a specialist in Cariganano del Sulcis from southwestern Sardinia, producing as many as three versions per year (as well as a rosé). The entry level offering, "Grotta Rossa" is a delightful wine, aged in cement vats that is at its best from two to three years of age. The "Rocca Rubia" *riserva* is a beautifully crafted wine from ungrafted rootstock *albarello* vines; medium-full, this has appealing orange marmalade and strawberry jam aromas with a distinct note of tobacco in the finish. The acidity is very good as is the overall harmony; this is a stylish wine of lovely typicity. The "Terre Brune" is a richer, riper

style, matured in barriques with aromas of black cherry, menthol and coffee; medium-full, this has a long finish with light black spice notes. This needs a bit of time to settle down; consume with rich red meats from seven to ten years of age. **BRV** (Rocca Rubia): 2008, 2007, 2006, 2005, 2004. (Terre Brune): 2007, 2006, 2005, 2004.

CANTINA MESA "BUIO BUIO"

This large, modern winery is located in the Carignano del Sulcis wine zone; they produce various examples of red wines made from the Carignan variety they label as Isola dei Nuraghi IGT. There is a "Buio" bottling that is Cargnan *in purezza* that is matured in cement vats along with this 100% Carignan from *albarello* vines that age in used barriques for about ten months. This is an appealing release with strawberry jam and currant aromas along with a hint of coffee; medium-bodied, this has very good acidity, a hint of wood and beautiful harmony. This is a charming red wine with notable typicity and lovely drinkablity; enjoy from two to five years of age. **BRV**: 2009, 2008. 2007.

AGRICOLA PUNICA "BARRUA"

Established in 2002, Agricola Punica is a joint venture between Sardinian producer Cantina Santadi and the renowned Tuscan estate Tenuta San Guido, producers of the world famous Sassicaia. The estate vineyards are situated in southwestern Sardegna near the areas of Barrua and Narcao; this territory is the home of the Carignano del Sulcis wines. First produced from the 2002 vintage, Barrua is primarily Carignano (about 85%) with the remainder of the blend Cabernet Sauvignon and Merlot; it is matured in barriques (80% new) for approximately eighteen months. Displaying a beautiful deep garnet/ light ruby red color, the aromas are delightful, highlighted by the initial perfume of strawberry jam (just lovely!), there are also notes of maraschino cherry and sweet tobacco. Medium-full, there are modest tannins that are very supple, very good acidity and a nicely rounded finish of impressive length and persistence. This is a deeply endowed version of Carignano with wonderful varietal purity, ideal harmony as well as grace and charm. Enjoy this from three to seven years of age. **BRV**: 2009, 2008, 2006.

ARGIOLAS "TURRIGA"

This is one of the more unusual wines in this book, not because of the varieties used in the blend, but because of the style. A blend of Cannonau, Bovale and Malvasia Nera, this is a ripe, at times, showy red with a touch too much oak; this is definitely a modern red. Yet there is also a slight wild, rustic edge to this, as befits a Sardegnan *rosso*, so while I normally prefer a more-toned down red, I do admire the overall approach and complexity of this wine. The 2005, tasted in mid- 2012 still had a very deep color and good freshness. This is best enjoyed from five to twelve years of age. **BRV**: 2007, 2006, 2005, 2004.

SELLA & MOSCA "MARCHESE DI VILLAMARINA"

Given that there are so many intriguing indigenous varieties planted throughout Sardegna, traditionalists may wonder about the inclusion of a Cabernet Sauvignon in this section, but when a wine is this special, I have to call attention to it! 100% Cabernet Sauvignon from the winery's massive estate plantings near Alghero in northwestern Sardgena, this is a sumptuous red with a lengthy finish with excellent persistence, very subtle wood notes along with very good acidity that cleanses the palate and rounds out the tannins. Such beautiful complexity and varietal character, this is a sublime example of Cabernet Sauvignon, one of my favorite from anywhere in Italy; the primary reason being its sense of harmony and finesse. Structured for at least twelve to fifteen years of aging, this can be enjoyed at a relatively young age, given its roundness. **BRV**: 2006, 2005, 2004, 2001 (all outstanding).

Glossary

Albarello – Also known as bush vines, albarello (literally "small tree") vines stand only a few feet tall and are usually planted on their own rootstock. This is a head pruned vine that is found primarily in Sardegna, Sicilia and Pulgia, as this type of vine affords more protection from the heat and abundant sunshine typical for these regions.

Appassimento – A production system, most famously used to make Amarone, in which grapes are dried on mats or in plastic boxes in a temperature and humidity-controlled room. This air drying takes place for several months; the grapes lose much of their water and shrivel in size, intensifying flavors.

Barrique – A small oak barrel, often made from wood from French forests, although there are barriques from the United States, Hungary and Austria also in use some Italian cellars. The standard size for a barrique is 225 liters, although there are some specialty sizes, such as 300 liter bariques, in use.

Botte – A large wooden cask for aging wine. *Botti* (plural, also referred to often in this book as *botti grandi*) are the traditional vessels found in many wine zones in Italy; these traditionally have been made from Slavonian oak. These large casks vary in size; most wineries use *botti* ranging from 20 to 60 hectoliters (2000 to 6000 liters), although some are even larger.

DOC, DOCG, IGT – These terms refer to specific designations for Italian wines. DOC means *Denominazione di Origine Controllata*, a set of rules first created in 1963 to regulate production methods for certain wines; this included which grapes could be used in what percentage, how long the wine needed to be aged before release, minimum alcohol, etc. DOCG – the "g" meaning *garantita* – followed in 1980 for such wines as Barolo and Brunello di Montalcino. These wines would have stricter regulations and would be considered the "best" Italian wines. This was largely true for many years, but now a DOCG classification is too often nothing more than the result of aggressive marketing on the part of producers in certain areas to upgrade their wines.

With the EU regulations, DOC and DOCG are now being lumped into one large classification, DOP or *Denominazione di Origine Protetta*, a protected designation. As for IGT, these are wines in Italy that do not conveniently fall into a DOC or DOCG classification; the so-called Super Tuscans are examples of IGT wines.

Frutti di bosco – An Italian term meaning "fruits of the forest." This term is used to describe the aromas of certain red wines that offer perfumes such as berry fruits.

Millesimato – A term used with sparkling wines denoting that the wine in the bottle is from a specific vintage.

Passito – A wine (typically white, but also a few reds) made from grapes that are naturally dried for several weeks or months before fermentation. Vin Santo is a famous example.

Tonneau (tonneaux, plural) – An oak barrel that is 500 liters in size, or slightly more than twice the size of a barrique.

Vecchia vigna (*vecchie vigne*, plural) – Old vines.

Vino da meditazione – Literally a wine for meditation, this refers to a powerful table wine, such as Amarone or various sweet wines (Vin Santo, Recioto della Valpolicella) that are often best consumed on their own; the thinking here is that one can better enjoy and contemplate these wines without food.

Acknowledgments

Writing this book is the result of the friendship and assistance of hundreds of people. First and foremost, I want to thank the vintners of Italy who were gracious enough to welcome me into their cellars, walk with me through their vineyards, let me sample their wines and join me for lunch or dinner where I could learn about pairing their wines with wonderful local foods. These experiences were of immeasurable value, not only for academic reasons, but also for sensual and emotional ones.

I want to especially thank Annalisa Chiavazza from Piemonte and Stefania Tacconi from Toscana for their help over the years regarding organizing my visits in their specific locales.

A special thank you to three chefs in Italy: Antonella Iandolo, Maria Cristina Rinaudi and Roberto Rossi for their contributions on pairing food and wine.

Thank you also to Marina Nedic in Italy and Paul Wagner in the United States for their guidance and support over many years.

I also need to point out certain individuals such as Alyson Caraega, Paolo Domeneghetti, Jane Kettlewell, Lars Leicht and Deena Miskiel who have believed in me and encouraged me in my work for more than a decade.

Marina Thompson in Italy has also supported and encouraged my work for many years. She was also of invaluable assistance to me regarding this book.

Over the past several years, the staff at the Italian Trade Commission in New York City under the leadership of Augusto Marchini and Aniello Musella has been extraordinarily helpful to me regarding information I needed for my research. They have also aided me in my work as an educator in Italian wines.

Also, there are dozens of people in public relations, importing and distribution that assisted me with visits to Italy or helped me locate a specific wine. There are just too many of these special people to mention – basically, I don't want to leave anyone out – so thank you to all of them.

Finally, thank you to Stan Malinowski and Mick Rock for making me a better photographer.

Index of Producers

Made in the USA
Charleston, SC
13 October 2013